C++
FOR
DUMMIES®

Stephen R. Davis

IDG Books Worldwide, Inc.
An International Data Group Company

Foster City, CA ♦ Chicago, IL ♦ Indianapolis, IN ♦ Braintree, MA ♦ Dallas, TX

C++ For Dummies®

Published by
IDG Books Worldwide, Inc.
An International Data Group Company
919 E. Hillsdale Blvd.
Suite 400
Foster City, CA 94404

Library of Congress Catalog Card No.: 94-76647

ISBN: 1-56884-163-9

Printed in the United States of America

10 9 8 7 6 5

1B/RU/RS/ZV

Distributed in the United States by IDG Books Worldwide, Inc.

Distributed by Macmillan Canada for Canada; by Computer and Technical Books for the Caribbean Basin; by Contemporanea de Ediciones for Venezuela; by Distribuidora Cuspide for Argentina; by CITEC for Brazil; by Ediciones ZETA S.C.R. Ltda. for Peru; by Editorial Limusa SA for Mexico; by Transworld Publishers Limited in the United Kingdom and Europe; by Al-Maiman Publishers & Distributors for Saudi Arabia; by Simron Pty. Ltd. for South Africa; by IDG Communications (HK) Ltd. for Hong Kong; by Toppan Company Ltd. for Japan; by Addison Wesley Publishing Company for Korea; by Longman Singapore Publishers Ltd. for Singapore, Malaysia, Thailand, and Indonesia; by Unalis Corporation for Taiwan; by WS Computer Publishing Company, Inc. for the Philippines; by WoodsLane Pty. Ltd. for Australia; by WoodsLane Enterprises Ltd. for New Zealand.

For general information on IDG Books Worldwide's books in the U.S., please call our Consumer Customer Service department at 800-762-2974. For reseller information, including discounts and premium sales, please call our Reseller Customer Service department at 800-434-3422.

For information on where to purchase IDG Books Worldwide's books outside the U.S., contact IDG Books Worldwide at 415-655-3021 or fax 415-655-3295.

For information on translations, contact Marc Jeffrey Mikulich, Director, Foreign & Subsidiary Rights, at IDG Books Worldwide, 415-655-3018 or fax 415-655-3295.

For sales inquiries and special prices for bulk quantities, write to the address above or call IDG Books Worldwide at 415-655-3200.

For information on using IDG Books Worldwide's books in the classroom, or ordering examination copies, contact Jim Kelly at 800-434-2086.

For authorization to photocopy items for corporate, personal, or educational use, please contact Copyright Clearance Center, 222 Rosewood Drive, Danvers, MA 01923, or fax 508-750-4470.

is a trademark under exclusive license to IDG Books Worldwide, Inc., from International Data Group, Inc.

Welcome to the world of IDG Books Worldwide.

IDG Books Worldwide, Inc., is a subsidiary of International Data Group, the world's largest publisher of computer-related information and the leading global provider of information services on information technology. IDG was founded more than 25 years ago and now employs more than 7,700 people worldwide. IDG publishes more than 250 computer publications in 67 countries (see listing below). More than 70 million people read one or more IDG publications each month.

Launched in 1990, IDG Books Worldwide is today the #1 publisher of best-selling computer books in the United States. We are proud to have received 8 awards from the Computer Press Association in recognition of editorial excellence and three from Computer Currents' First Annual Readers' Choice Awards, and our best-selling ...For Dummies® series has more than 19 million copies in print with translations in 28 languages. IDG Books Worldwide, through a joint venture with IDG's Hi-Tech Beijing, became the first U.S. publisher to publish a computer book in the People's Republic of China. In record time, IDG Books Worldwide has become the first choice for millions of readers around the world who want to learn how to better manage their businesses.

Our mission is simple: Every one of our books is designed to bring extra value and skill-building instructions to the reader. Our books are written by experts who understand and care about our readers. The knowledge base of our editorial staff comes from years of experience in publishing, education, and journalism — experience which we use to produce books for the '90s. In short, we care about books, so we attract the best people. We devote special attention to details such as audience, interior design, use of icons, and illustrations. And because we use an efficient process of authoring, editing, and desktop publishing our books electronically, we can spend more time ensuring superior content and spend less time on the technicalities of making books.

You can count on our commitment to deliver high-quality books at competitive prices on topics you want to read about. At IDG Books Worldwide, we continue in the IDG tradition of delivering quality for more than 25 years. You'll find no better book on a subject than one from IDG Books Worldwide.

John Kilcullen
President and CEO
IDG Books Worldwide, Inc.

IDG Books Worldwide, Inc., is a subsidiary of International Data Group, the world's largest publisher of computer-related information and the leading global provider of information services on information technology. International Data Group publishes over 250 computer publications in 67 countries. Seventy million people read one or more International Data Group publications each month. International Data Group's publications include: **ARGENTINA:** Computerworld Argentina, GamePro, Infoworld, PC World Argentina; **AUSTRALIA:** Australian Macworld, Client/Server Journal, Computer Living, Computerworld, Digital News, Network World, PC World, Publishing Essentials, Reseller; **AUSTRIA:** Computerwelt, PC TEST; **BELARUS:** PC World Belarus; **BELGIUM:** Data News; **BRAZIL:** Annuário de Informática, Computerworld Brazil, Connections, Super Game Power, Macworld, PC World Brazil, Publish Brazil, SUPERGAME; **BULGARIA:** Computerworld Bulgaria, Networkworld/Bulgaria, PC & MacWorld Bulgaria; **CANADA:** CIO Canada, ComputerWorld Canada, InfoCanada, Network World Canada, Reseller World; **CHILE:** Computerworld Chile, GamePro, PC World Chile; **COLUMBIA:** Computerworld Colombia, GamePro, PC World Colombia; **COSTA RICA:** PC World Costa Rica/Nicaragua; **THE CZECH AND SLOVAK REPUBLICS:** Computerworld Czechoslovakia, Elektronika Czechoslovakia, PC World Czechoslovakia; **DENMARK:** Communications World, Computerworld Danmark, Macworld Danmark, PC World Danmark, PC World Danmark Supplements, TECH World; **DOMINICAN REPUBLIC:** PC World Republica Dominicana; **ECUADOR:** PC World Ecuador, GamePro; **EGYPT:** Computerworld Middle East, PC World Middle East; **EL SALVADOR:** PC World Centro America; **FINLAND:** MikroPC, Tietoverkko, Tietoviikko; **FRANCE:** Distributique, Golden, Info PC, Le Guide du Monde Informatique, Le Monde Informatique, Reseaux & Telecoms; **GERMANY:** Computer Business, Computerwoche, Computerwoche Extra, Computerwoche Focus, Electronic Entertainment, GamePro, I/M Information Management, Macwelt, PC Welt; **GREECE:** GamePro, Macworld & Publish; **GUATEMALA:** PC World Centro America; **HONDURAS:** PC World Centro America; **HONG KONG:** Computerworld Hong Kong, PCWorld Hong Kong, Publish in Asia; **HUNGARY:** ABCD CD-ROM, Computerworld Szamitastechnika, PC & Mac World Hungary, PC-X Magazine; **INDIA:** Computerworld India, PC World India, Publish in Asia; **INDONESIA:** InfoKomputer PC World, Komputek Computerworld, Publish in Asia; **IRELAND:** ComputerScope, PC Live!; **ISRAEL:** PC World 32 BIT, People & Computers; **ITALY:** Computerworld Italia, Computerworld Italia Special Editions, Lotus Italia, Macworld Italia, Networking Italia, PC Shopping, PC World Italia, PC World/Walt Disney; **JAPAN:** Macworld Japan, Nikkei Personal Computing, SunWorld Japan, Windows World Japan; **KENYA:** East African Computer News; **KOREA:** Hi-Tech Information/Computerworld, Macworld Korea, PC World Korea; **MACEDONIA:** PC World Macedonia; **MALAYSIA:** Computerworld Malaysia, PC World Malaysia, Publish in Asia; **MEXICO:** Computerworld Mexico, GamePro, Macworld, PC World Mexico; **MYANMAR:** PC World Myanmar; **NETHERLANDS:** Computable, Computer! Totaal, LAN Magazine, Macworld, Net Magazine; **NEW ZEALAND:** Computer Buyer, Computerworld New Zealand, MTB, Network World, PC World New Zealand; **NICARAGUA:** PC World Costa Rica/Nicaragua; **NIGERIA:** PC World Africa; **NORWAY:** Computerworld Norge, Computerworld Privat, CW Rapport Klient/Tjener, CW Rapport Nettverk & Telecom, CW Rapport Offentlig Sektor, IDG's KURSGUIDE, Macworld Norge, Multimedia World, PC World Ekspress, PC World Nettverk, PC World Norge, PC World's Produktguide, Windows Spesial; **PAKISTAN:** Computerworld Pakistan, PC World Pakistan; **PANAMA:** GamePro, PC World Panama; **PARAGUAY:** PC World Paraguay; **P. R. OF CHINA:** China Computerworld, China Infoworld, Computer & Communication, Electronic Product World, Electronics Today, Game Camp, PC World China, Popular Computer Week, Software World, Telecom Product World; **PERU:** Computerworld Peru, GamePro, PC World Profesional Peru, PC World Peru; **POLAND:** Computerworld Poland, Computerworld Special Report, Macworld, Networld, PC World Komputer; **PHILIPPINES:** Computerworld Philippines, PC Digest, Publish in Asia; **PORTUGAL:** Cerebro/PC World, Correio Informático/Computerworld, Mac•In/PC•In Portugal; **PUERTO RICO:** PC World Puerto Rico; **ROMANIA:** Computerworld Romania, PC World Romania, Telecom Romania; **RUSSIA:** Computerworld Rossiya, Network World Russia, PC World Russia; **SINGAPORE:** Computerworld Singapore, PC World Singapore, Publish in Asia; **SLOVENIA:** MONITOR; **SOUTH AFRICA:** Computing S.A., Network World S.A., Software World; **SPAIN:** Computerworld España, COMUNICACIONES WORLD, Dealer World, Macworld España, PC World España; **SWEDEN:** CAP&Design, Computer Sweden, Corporate Computing, MacWorld, Maxi Data, MikroDatorn, Nätverk & Kommunikation, PC/Aktiv, PC World, Windows World; **SWITZERLAND:** Computerworld Schweiz, Macworld Schweiz, PCtip; **TAIWAN:** Computerworld Taiwan, Macworld Taiwan, PC World Taiwan, Publish Taiwan, Windows World; **THAILAND:** Thai Computerworld, Publish in Asia; **TURKEY:** Computerworld Monitor, MACWORLD Turkiye, PC WORLD Turkiye; **UKRAINE:** Computerworld Kiev, Computers & Software Magazine, PC World Ukraine; **UNITED KINGDOM:** Acorn User, Amiga Action, Amiga Computing, Amiga, Appletalk, CD Powerplay, CD-ROM Now, Computing, Connexion, GamePro, Lotus Magazine, Macaction, Macworld, Open Computing, Parents and Computers, PC Home, PC Works, The WEB; **UNITED STATES:** Cable in the Classroom, CD Review, CIO Magazine, Computerworld, Computerworld Client/Server Journal, Digital Video Magazine, DOS World, Electronic, InfoWorld, I-Way, Macworld, Maximize, MULTIMEDIA WORLD, Network World, PC World, PUBLISH, SWATPro Magazine, Video Event, WebMaster; **URUGUAY:** PC World Uruguay; **VENEZUELA:** Computerworld Venezuela, GamePro, PC World Venezuela; and **VIETNAM:** PC World Vietnam   10/17/95

About the Author

Stephen R. Davis, who goes by the name of Randy, has been a programmer and author at E-Systems in Greenville, Texas, for fifteen years. He currently specializes in object-oriented programming and software engineering issues. Randy fights for computer time with his wife, Jenny, and son, Kinsey.

Randy can be reached for compliments at *srdavis@ACM.org*. Send all complaints to device NUL:.

Credits

Dedication

I would like to dedicate this book to my grandparents, John and Winnie Davis and J.C. and Gladys Blackwell, and to my wife's grandmother, Ethel Wilcoxson. Their loving support gave me the confidence to be the best Dummy I could be.

Acknowledgments

Any book, even a ...*For Dummies* book, requires the contributions of many individuals. Of course, I have to start with Dennis Ritchie, the originator of C, and Bjarne Stroustrup, the father of C++, for without them I would have nothing to write about (besides, it's required).

More recently, I would like to thank Phil Kelso, Dianne Neel, and my wife, who reviewed early versions of the manuscript and managed to laugh at the right places and not to laugh at the wrong places. I would also like to thank the many students who have suffered through my C and C++ courses, for these courses provide the raw material for books such as this.

Special thanks go to Bob Bourbonnais; his suggestions resulted in an improved book. I would also like to thank the rest of the gang at IDG books — you're a great bunch. (Maybe this will help me land another contract.) Thanks also go to Claudette Moore, my agent, who continues to look out for me.

My biggest thanks go to Susan Pink (a.k.a. spink), who spent tireless hours going over paragraph after paragraph, line after line until I was ready to store her number into my call blocking list.

Since no one but the author ever gets this far into something as boring as the acknowledgments, I would also like to thank my dogs, Trudie and Scooter. (See guys, told ya' I'd work your name in here somehow.)

Contents at a Glance

Introduction 1

Part I Charting a Course: A Review of C 7
Chapter 1 C, C Dick, C Jane 9
Chapter 2 C Pointers 23
Chapter 3 User-Defined Types: The C Structure 33
The C Version of Our Budget Program: BUDGET1.C 39
25-Minute Workout 47

Part II Getting Your Feet Wet: The Non-Object-Oriented
         Features of C++ 51
Chapter 4 Getting to C++ 53
Chapter 5 Some Simple Stuff 57
Chapter 6 Functions, I Declare! 69
Chapter 7 Stream Input and Output 87
Rewriting BUDGET as a C++ Program: BUDGET2.CPP 93
25-Minute Workout 99

Part III Wading In: Introduction to Classes 105
Chapter 8 Object-Oriented Programming 107
Chapter 9 Adding Class to C++ 115
Chapter 10 Do Not Disturb: Protected Members 127
Chapter 11 Getting an Object Off to a Good Start: The Constructor .. 139
Chapter 12 Finding the Classes 151
A Budget with Class: BUDGET3.CPP 159
25-Minute Workout 167

Part VI Warming to the Water: Getting Comfortable
         with Classes 175
Chapter 13 Making Constructive Arguments 177
Chapter 14 More New and Improved Keywords 197
Chapter 15 The Copy Copy Copy Constructor 203
Chapter 16 Changing an Object's Type 213
Chapter 17 Static Members: Can Fabric Softener Help? 219
Maintaining a More Reasonable Budget: BUDGET4.CPP 229
25-Minute Workout 237

Part V Plunging In: Inheritance 243

Chapter 18 Inheritance (How Do I Get Mine?) 245
Chapter 19 Virtual Member Functions: Are They for Real? 253
Chapter 20 Class Factoring and Abstract Classes 267
Using Inheritance to Rationalize the Budget: BUDGET5.CPP 283
25-Minute Workout 291

Part VI Advanced Strokes: Optional Features 303

Chapter 21 Multiple Inheritance 305
Chapter 22 Access Control Specifiers 315
Chapter 23 Overloading Operators 323
Chapter 24 The Assignment Operator 337
Chapter 25 Stream I/O 343
Chapter 26 Object Validation and Signature Fields 359

Part VII The Part of Tens 367

Chapter 27 Ten Ways to Avoid Adding Bugs to Your Program 369
Chapter 28 Almost Ten C++ Features Not Covered in This Book 377
Chapter 29 The Ten Most Important Compiler Switches (Plus Two More) 383

Appendix How Do Virtual Functions Work, Anyway? 391

Glossary 397

Index 401

Reader Response Card .... Back of Book

Cartoons at a Glance

by Rich Tennant

page 391

page 149

page 1

page 175

page 7

page 105

page 367

page 303

page 243

page 51

Table of Contents

· ·

Introduction *1*

Part 1 Charting a Course: A Review of C *7*

Chapter 1 C, C Dick, C Jane **9**
Declaring Simple Variables 10
Storage Classes 11
    Global variables 11
    Local variables 12
Declaring Functions 13
The Ins and Outs of C Expressions 14
    Smooth operators 15
    Mathematical operators 16
    Bitwise operators 17
    Logical operators 18
    Assignment operators 19
    Miscellaneous operators 19
    Special operator considerations 20
Conclusion 21

Chapter 2 C Pointers **23**
Declaring and Using Simple Pointers 23
Operations on Pointers 25
    Incrementing pointers 26
    Other operations on pointers 27
Arrays and Pointers: Can We Ever Get Them Together? 27
Passing Pointers to Functions 28
Pointers to Functions 30
Heap Memory 30
Conclusion 32

Chapter 3 User-Defined Types: The C Structure **33**
C Structures 101 33
Pointers to C Structures 35
    Operations on pointers to structures 35
    Using pointers to structures 36
Structures and Functions 37
Allocating Structures from the Heap 38
Conclusion 38

The C Version of Our Budget Program: BUDGET1.C **39**

25-Minute Workout **47**

Part II Getting Your Feet Wet: The Non-Object-Oriented Features of C++ 51

Chapter 4 Getting to C++ 53
How Did We Get Here? 53
    The early years (1950 –1960) 53
    The functional years (1960 –1975) 54
    The structured years (1975 –1990) 54
    The object-oriented years (1990 – present) 55
Why C++? 55
Conclusion 56

Chapter 5 Some Simple Stuff 57
A New Comment Style 57
    Why do I need it? 57
    How does it work? 57
Variable Declarations Anywhere You Want 58
    Why do I need them? 58
    How do they work? 59
Constant Variables 60
    Why do I need them? 61
    How do they work? 61
Volatile Variables 63
    Why do I need them? 64
    How do they work? 64
The Referential Type Specifier 65
    Why do I need it? 66
    How does it work? 66
Conclusion 68

Chapter 6 Functions, I Declare! 69
Function Prototypes 69
    Why do I need them? 70
    Why do I want my compiler bitching at me? 70
    How do they work? 72
Inline Functions 74
    Why do I need them? 74
    Can't I do that in C? 75
    How do they work? 76
    How much faster is faster? 77
Function Overloading 79
    Why do I need it? 79
    How does it work? 80
    What constitutes "sufficiently different"? 81
    So what's not different enough? 81
    Print what you want about me but don't mangle the name 82

Default Arguments to Functions 83
    Why do I need them? 84
    How do they work? 84
    Being overloadingly argumentative 85
Conclusion 86

Chapter 7 Stream Input and Output **87**
Why Do I Need Streams after the Rivers of printf( )s I'm Used To? 87
    The case for stream I/O: part 1 87
    The case for stream I/O: part 2 88
How Does Stream I/O Work? 89
Conclusion 91

Rewriting BUDGET as a C++ Program: BUDGET2.CPP **93**

25-Minute Workout **99**

Part III Wading In: Introduction to Classes *105*

Chapter 8 Object-Oriented Programming **107**
Abstraction and Microwaves 107
    Functional nachos 108
    Object-oriented nachos 109
Classification and Microwave Ovens 109
    Functional classification 110
    Object-oriented classification 110
    Why classify? 110
Object-Oriented Programming and Efficiency 112
Conclusion 113

Chapter 9 Adding Class to C++ **115**
Why Add Classes to C++? 116
How Do I Add Classes to C++? 116
    Naming member functions 117
Defining a Member Function in the Class 119
Keeping a Member Function after Class 119
Calling a Member Function 121
    Calling a member function with a pointer? 121
    Accessing members from a member function 122
Overloading Member Functions 124
Conclusion 125

Chapter 10 Do Not Disturb: Protected Members **127**
Protected Members 127
    Why do I need them? 127
    How do they work? 129
Tell Me Again Why I Should Use Protected Members 130
    The class can protect its internal state 130

It's easier to use a class with a limited interface 131
It's easier to support a class with a limited interface 131
What Are Friends for Anyway? 135
Why do I need friends?(I am a rock, I am an island) 136
How do they work? 136
Conclusion 138

Chapter 11   Getting an Object Off to a Good Start: The Constructor **139**
Creating Objects 139
Constructors 141
Why do I need them? 141
How do they work? 143
The Destructor 146
Why do I need it? 146
How does it work? 147
Conclusion 149

Chapter 12   Finding the Classes **151**
Object-Oriented Analysis and Design 151
An Example Analysis and Design Problem 152
Quick analysis and design: a structured approach 152
Quick analysis and design: an object-oriented approach 154
An OO solution to our problem 156
Conclusion 157

A Budget with Class: BUDGET3.CPP **159**

25-Minute Workout **167**

**Part IV Warming to the Water: Getting Comfortable
with Classes** *175*

Chapter 13   Making Constructive Arguments **177**
Constructors Outfitted with Arguments 177
Why do I need them? 178
How do they work? 178
Placing Too Many Demands on the Carpenter, or Overloading
the Constructor 181
Default Default Constructors 183
Constructing Class Members 185
Order of Construction 190
Local objects are constructed in order 191
Static objects are constructed only once 191
All global objects are constructed before main( ) 192
Global objects are constructed in no particular order 193
Members are constructed in the order in which they are declared 194
Destructors are invoked in the reverse order of the constructors 195
Conclusion 195

Chapter 14 More New and Improved Keywords 197

The *new* Keywords: Now You're *free( )* to delete *malloc( )*............................ 197

Why do I need them? 197

How do they work? 198

Allocating Arrays 199

Conclusion 200

Chapter 15 The Copy Copy Copy Constructor 203

The Copy Constructor 203

Why do I need it? 203

How does it work? 204

The Automatic Copy Constructor 205

Shallow Copies versus Deep Copies 208

It's a Long Way to Temporaries 211

Conclusion 212

Chapter 16 Changing an Object's Type 213

Nameless Objects 213

Why do I need them? 213

How do they work? 214

Type Conversion Using Constructors 215

Conclusion 218

Chapter 17 Static Members: Can Fabric Softener Help? 219

Static Data Members 219

Why do I need them? 219

How do they work? 220

Referencing static data members 221

Uses for static data members 222

Static Member Functions 224

Conclusion 227

Maintaining a More Reasonable Budget: BUDGET4.CPP 229

25-Minute Workout 237

Part V Plunging In: Inheritance *243*

Chapter 18 Inheritance (How Do I Get Mine?) 245

Why Do I Need Inheritance? 246

How Does Inheritance Work? 247

Constructing a Subclass 249

The HAS_A Relationship 250

Conclusion 251

Chapter 19 Virtual Member Functions: Are They for Real? 253

Why Do I Need Polymorphism? 255

How Does Polymorphism Work? 257

Making Nachos the Polymorphic Way 259

When Is a Virtual Function Not? 261
Virtual Considerations 263
Conclusion 265

Chapter 20 Class Factoring and Abstract Classes **267**
Factoring 267
Abstract Classes 273
How do they work? 274
Making an honest class out of an abstract class 276
Passing abstract classes 277
Why do I need pure virtual functions? 278
Determining the Run-Time Type 279
Conclusion 282

Using Inheritance to Rationalize the Budget: BUDGET5.CPP **283**

25-Minute Workout **291**

Part VI Advanced Strokes: Optional Features **303**

Chapter 21 Multiple Inheritance **305**
How Does Multiple Inheritance Work? 305
Inheritance Ambiguities 307
Virtual Inheritance 307
Constructing the Objects of Multiple Inheritance 312
In Conclusion, a Contrary Opinion 313

Chapter 22 Access Control Specifiers **315**
Really Exclusive Club: Private Members 315
When should I use private and when can I stay with protected? 316
How do I use private? 316
Secret Wills, or Non-Public Inheritance 317
When is a subclass not? 320
Conclusion 321

Chapter 23 Overloading Operators **323**
Why Do I Need to Overload Operators? 323
How Does an Operator Function and a Function Operate? 324
What Does This Have to Do with Overloading Operators? 325
How Does Operator Overloading Work? 326
A More Detailed Look 328
Operators as Member Functions 329
Yet Another Overloading Irritation 331
Cast Operator 333
Conclusion 335

Chapter 24 The Assignment Operator **337**
Why Is Overloading the Assignment Operator So Critical? 337
How Do I Overload the Assignment Operator? 338
Conclusion 340

Chapter 25   Stream I/O 343
How Does Stream I/O Work? 343
The fstream Subclasses 345
The strstream Subclasses 348
Manipulators 349
Custom Inserters 351
Smart Inserters 354
Conclusion 357

Chapter 26   Object Validation and Signature Fields 359
Invoking Member Functions with Invalid Pointers 360
So What Are the Consequences? 360
So What Do We Do About Invalid Pointers? 362
What Else Can isLegal( ) Do? 364
Conclusion 365

Part VII   The Part of Tens 367

Chapter 27   Ten Ways to Avoid Adding Bugs to Your Program 369
Enable All Warnings and Error Messages 369
Use STRICT Compilation 370
Insist on Clean Compiles 371
Adopt a Clear and Consistent Coding Style 371
Limit the Visibility 372
Use a Signature Field 374
Comment Your Code While You Write It 374
Single Step Every Path at Least Once 374
Don't Overload Operators 375
Avoid Multiple Inheritance 375

Chapter 28   Almost Ten C++ Features Not Covered in This Book 377
Templates 377
Exceptions 378
Run-Time Type Identification 379
Name Spaces 379
Overloading new and delete 380
Class String 380
Pointer to Member Operators ->* and .* 380
Intel 16-Bit Pointers 380

Chapter 29   The Ten Most Important Compiler Switches
(Plus Two More) 383
Outline Inline Functions 384
Define Preprocessor Symbols 384
Include Debug Information in .objs 385
Check for Stack Overflow 385
Memory Model 386
Type of Floating-Point Support 386

Compiler Optimizations 388
Enable Exceptions/RTTI 388
Data Alignment 389
Processor Support 389
Standard Stack Frame 390
Precompiled Headers 390

Appendix   How Do Virtual Functions Work, Anyway? *391*
Sex, Lies, and v_tables 392
Conclusion 394

Glossary *397*

Index *401*

Reader Response Card ....*Back of Book*

Introduction

W elcome to *C++ For Dummies*. Think of this book as *C++: Reader's Digest Edition*, bringing you everything you need to know without the boring stuff.

About This Book

C++ For Dummies, like all *...For Dummies* books, concentrates on you and your needs. This book couldn't be more exciting if I mailed it to you wrapped in plain brown paper.

Like its C counterpart, this book is a tutorial. It is meant to be read from front to back (not in one sitting, of course — the family starts to get anxious waiting that long).

The 5th Wave   By Rich Tennant

"OH SURE, $1.8 MILLION SEEMS LIKE A LOT RIGHT NOW, BUT WHAT ABOUT RANDY? WHAT ABOUT HIS FUTURE? THINK WHAT A COMPUTER LIKE THIS WILL DO FOR HIS S.A.T. SCORE SOMEDAY."

This book will not turn you into a C++ "language lawyer." (That's a person who is really into the details of a computer language — a real language nerd — like me.) Although I do touch on just about every aspect of the language, I spend more time on features that are at the heart of the power of C++ and less time on the "power user" features you don't need yet. (Plus, you'll be able pick these up from the manual after you feel more comfortable with the language.)

Unlike other C++ programming books, *C++ For Dummies* considers the "why" just as important as the "how." The features of C++ are like pieces of a jigsaw puzzle. Rather than just present the features, I think it's important that you understand how they fit together.

If you don't understand why a particular feature is in the language, you won't truly understand how it works. When you finish this book, you'll be able to write a reasonable C++ program, and just as important, you'll understand why and how it works.

This book cannot teach you how to install your compiler — there are too many different compilers and they're changing all the time. In addition, I can't go into the details of entering the program, getting it compiled, and so on. As long as you can edit a file, and compile, link, and execute the resulting program, you know enough for this book. (I do, however, devote a chapter to compiler options.)

What Is C++?

C++, as the name implies, is the next generation of the C programming language: the result of adding new-age academic computer linguistic thinking to that old workhorse C.

C++ is at its core C. It's almost upwardly compatible. Anything C can do, C++ can do too. C++ can even do it the same way. But C++ is more than just C with a new coat of paint slapped on. The extensions to C++ are significant and require some thought and some getting used to, but the results are worth it. This book will help you get from C to C++ as painlessly as possible.

This book teaches you Standard C++, which is endorsed by the ANSI C++ Standards Committee and 9 out of 10 dentists. This is the version of C++ implemented in Borland C++, Turbo C++, Visual C++, Symantec C++, and C++ from most other companies.

Vendors stick as close as possible to this standard, so everything in this book should apply to any other version of C++ as well. When I do come across something unique to the Borland or Microsoft variants, I flag it with a "nonstandard" icon (more on that in a minute).

Who Are You?

This book assumes that you already know at least some C. If you don't know C at all, stop now, casually slip this book back on the shelf (without attracting undue attention), and look right next to it for *C For Dummies*. (Remember where you put this book, though, because you'll want to come back.)

If your knowledge of C is a bit rusty, but you basically know it or at least knew it at one time, keep fumbling for your credit card. Part I reviews the most important aspects of C and lets you polish your skills quickly.

How This Book Is Organized

Each new feature is introduced by answering the following three questions:

- ✔ *What* is this new feature?
- ✔ *Why* was it introduced into the language?
- ✔ *How* does it work?

Small pieces of code are sprinkled liberally throughout the chapters. Each demonstrates some newly introduced feature or highlights some brilliant point I'm making. These snippets may not be complete and certainly don't do anything meaningful.

At the End of Each Part...

To help retain the material presented, I have included two aids at the end of each of the first five parts: an example program and an exercise section.

I think it's important to see the features of C++ working together in a complete program. However, I get distracted when I am forced to wade through many different example programs. I spend more time figuring out what each program does than understanding the language features it contains. In addition, I have difficulty comparing them because they don't do the same thing.

To avoid this, I use one simple example program, BUDGET. This program starts life at the end of Part I as a functionally oriented C program. Then I rewrite BUDGET to incorporate the features presented in each new part.

By the time we reach the end of Part V, BUDGET has blossomed into a completely object-oriented C++ debutante ready for the object-oriented cotillion. Some may find this a ghastly waste of time. (If so, just skip it and keep it to yourself — I convinced my editor that it was a really neat idea.) However, I hope that as you see BUDGET evolve, you will see how the features of C++ work together.

The second aid is the workout (exercise) section. Give the questions a try. (I present hints and warnings to steer you in the right direction.) When you finish your solutions, compare them to mine, which are provided along with an explanation.

Part I Charting a Course: A Review of C

In Part I, we make sure everybody is on the same sheet of music. If you already feel comfortable with your knowledge of C, you can breeze through this part. If you're really feeling confident, you might skip it altogether, but be sure to scan the BUDGET program and test your knowledge by answering the questions at the end of Part I.

Part II Getting Your Feet Wet: The Non-Object-Oriented Features of C++

In Part II, you are introduced to the non-object-oriented features of C++, including a new comment style, inline functions, and stream I/O. These are the features that make C++ a better C without making it a new language in any significant way. These features can be mastered fairly quickly because they don't require you to change your functional ways.

Part III Wading In: Introduction to Classes

In Part III, you venture far enough into C++ that you start to see the differences between it and C. I introduce the concept of object-oriented programming and discuss classes. Both of these make C++ a truly different language from C.

Part IV Warming to the Water: Getting Comfortable with Classes

The introduction to object-oriented programming with classes is a big step. This requires you to reexamine your functional programming ways and rethink problems that you thought you had solved a long time ago. Part IV gives you more time to let object-oriented programming sink in.

Part V Plunging In: Inheritance

Inheritance is what separates the object-oriented wheat from the procedural chaff. Understanding this most important of concepts is the key to effective C++ programming and the goal of Part V. There's no going back now — after you've completed this part, you can call yourself an Object-Oriented Programmer, First Class.

Part VI Advanced Strokes: Optional Features

By the time you get to Part VI, you know all you need to program effectively in C++. I touch on remaining, optional issues. You can read the chapters in this part in any order you like, using them as you would a reference.

Part VII The Part of Tens

What ...*For Dummies* book would be complete without the lists of ten? In the first chapter in Part VII, you find out the best ways to avoid introducing bugs into your programs. Then, in the interest of public disclosure, I touch on features not covered in this book. (Most of these features have only recently been adopted by the ANSI C++ standards committee and are not available in compilers yet.)

Have you noticed how many different compiler options there are these days? How do I know whether I want my vtable pointer to follow my member pointer? And what's the alternative to fast floating point? Slow floating point? In Part VII, I guide you through these options, pointing out those that are important and those that are better left alone.

What You Don't Need to Read

C++ is a big pill to swallow. There are easy parts and not-so-easy parts. To keep from swamping you with information that you may not be interested in at the moment, technical stuff is flagged with a special icon (see the next section).

In addition, certain background information is stuck into sidebars. If you feel the onset of information overload, feel free to skip these sections during the first reading. (Remember to read them sometime, though. In C++, what you don't know will hurt you — eventually.)

Icons Used in This Book

This is technical stuff you can skip on the first reading. ■

Tips highlight a point that can save you a lot of time and effort. ■

Remember this. It's important. ■

Remember this too. This one can sneak up on you when you least expect it and generate one of those really hard-to-find bugs. ■

This reminds you about some C feature you may have forgotten. ■

This indicates a nonstandard feature specific to compilers from Borland or Microsoft. ■

And when you reach the end of the text that goes with the icon, you'll see a little gray square, like this. ■

Now What?

Learning a programming language is not a spectator sport. I'll try to make it as painless as possible, but you have to power up the ol' PC and get down to some serious programming. Limber up the fingers, break the spine on the book so it lays flat next to the keyboard (and so you can't take it back to the bookstore), and let's dive in.

Part I
Charting a Course:
A Review of C

The 5th Wave — By Rich Tennant

"IT'S CHAOS — BUT IT'S CHAOS THAT WORKS."

In This Part...

Part I is a quick review of the C language. It is not intended as an introduction for those who are unfamiliar
with C (except as something to keep *B* and *D* from bumping
into each other). It is not even a complete review of C. Instead, Part I reviews the concepts critical to learning C++
that can cause problems.

C is an apparently simple but often subtle language. Because
C++ builds and expands on features in C, grasping these
subtleties is important to the understanding of C++.

Chapter 1
C, C Dick, C Jane

In This Chapter
▶ The history of C
▶ Declarations 101—the simple stuff
▶ Storage class, or "Where did I put that variable?"
▶ Function declarations
▶ Actually doing something: C expressions

*T*he C language was born at AT&T's Bell Labs in 1972. C was the proud progeny of Dennis Ritchie, who then used C to port the UNIX operating system to the early DEC PDP-11s.

AT&T bundled a C compiler called K&R C with the UNIX operating system when they began shipping UNIX to universities. (K&R C was named after Brian Kernighan and Dennis Ritchie, who wrote the first book describing the C language. Today K&R C is also known as Classic C.) Everyone who bought a copy of UNIX received a C compiler for free. Most liked C. Besides, UNIX was written in C, so if you wanted to understand UNIX you had to learn C. The fact that C was free didn't hurt either. The result was an instant standard.

As C became more popular, companies began introducing their own C compilers, including compilers that ran under operating systems other than UNIX. Each of these compilers introduced enhancements designed to address some perceived limitation of the original language. But enhancements that everyone does not agree with mean incompatibilities, so demand increased for a national standard. The American National Standards Institute (ANSI) version of C appeared in 1987. This version, variously known as ANSI C or Standard C, incorporated many significant improvements over Classic C.

Over the years, Classic C has fallen into almost total disuse outside the UNIX community. Even there, Standard C is the preferred lingua franca. When I refer to C in this book, I refer exclusively to the ANSI standard C. C++ is based on and is most compatible with ANSI C.

Declaring Simple Variables

Let's begin with one of the first topics that causes confusion to beginning C programmers: the declaration of different types of objects.

Declaring variables starts out simply. All variables must be declared before they are used in order to establish their type. A *type* may be user defined or one of the built-in intrinsic types. The intrinsic variable types are listed in Table 1-1.

Table 1-1:   Built-In Variable Types

Type	Meaning
char	Character
int	Integer
float	Single-precision floating point
double	Double-precision floating point

The *char* and *int* types can be adorned with the descriptors *unsigned* or *signed* and *long* or *short*. The default for *int* is *signed*. The default for *char* is usually *signed* as well, but many compilers let you change the default. Both *float* and *double* types are always *signed*.

The following are all legal declarations:

```
int i;              /*default is signed                  */
char c;             /*default for char is usually signed*/
unsigned char uc;
long int li;
unsigned short int si;
signed long sl;     /*int is assumed                     */
```

In addition to the variable types in Table 1-1, most PC-based compilers allow the declaration of a *long double,* which is 80 bits wide. This corresponds to the width of the internal registers in the Intel floating point units (FPUs). On the 80386 and earlier processors, the FPU is a separate chip bearing the designation 80x87. On the 80486DX, the FPU is built in. Motorola has a similar FPU called the 68881, which uses the same 80-bit format internally. ■

The size of each built-in variable type is not specified in the ANSI standard and therefore can vary according to the CPU and compiler. Most compilers running on a standard PC have the data allocation sizes shown on Table 1-2. The include file *limits.h* gives the ranges for each built-in variable type for the current compiler and can be used to write machine-independent programs.

Table 1-2: Typical Size of Simple Types on the PC

Type	Size
char	8 bits
short int	8 bits
int	16 bits
long int	32 bits
float	32 bits
double	64 bits
long double	80 bits

Storage Classes

In addition to type, each variable is declared local to a function or global. Local variables may also be declared *auto*, *static*, or *register*.

Global variables

Variables declared outside any function are called *global variables*. Global variables are created when the program starts and stay around until the program ends.

Global variables are accessible to any function declared in the same C file. Global variables declared in one C file can be made accessible to a second C file by including an *extern* declaration in the second C file.

You can specifically limit the scope of a global variable to the *.C* file in which it was created by declaring it static. Static variables are not accessible by other modules, even those with an *extern* declaration.

The following demonstrates the accessibility of global variables:

```
FILEA.C:
        int x;      /*potentially visible everywhere  */
static int y;       /*visible only inside FILEA.C     */

FILEB.C:
extern int x;       /*gives FILEB access to FILEA's x */
extern int y;       /*this doesn't work               */
```

Global variables reside in an area called the *data segment.* Because the number and size of all global variables is known before the program starts, the global segment is preallocated as part of the executable program. ∎

Local variables

A variable declared in a function is called a *local variable.* A local variable is visible only to the function in which it is declared. That is, one function cannot access another function's local variables by name. There is no *extern* for local variables.

Local variables may be declared *auto, static,* or *register.* Because the default is *auto,* you'll almost never actually see the keyword *auto* (*auto* is short for automatic, I guess).

An auto variable is created when the program enters the function containing the auto declaration, and is destroyed when the program exits the function.

A static local variable is created the first time the function is called but continues to exist and retains its value through subsequent returns and calls. For example:

```
void fn(void)
{
    int autoVar;                /*autoVar starts life here*/
    static int staticVar = 0;   /*value first time fn() is called*/
    autoVar = 10;
    staticVar = 20;
}                               /*autoVar ends life here*/
int main()
{
    fn();
    fn();
    return 0;
}
```

The first time *fn()* is called, the variable *staticVar* is initialized to 0. Unless specifically initialized, local variables contain an unknown and unpredictable value when they are created. The second time *fn()* is called, *staticVar* starts out life with the value it had when the program last exited *fn()*.

Static local variables are kept in the data segment along with global variables. Auto variables are stored on the function's stack. ∎

A register variable is like an auto variable in that it is created at the beginning and destroyed at the end of the function. However, a register variable is not stored in memory but cached in a register of the processor. Because register variables are not in memory, they have no address.

An interesting note: When I declare a variable *register*, it is only a request. The compiler (like my wife) is free to ignore me.

In the old days, when compiler optimizers weren't very good, a programmer could significantly improve the performance of a program by declaring the proper variables *register*. As optimizers got better, compilers were able to cache variables into registers in such a way as to optimize performance. Experience showed that a good optimizing compiler could do a better job than a person. Programmers usually just screwed things up by using up registers with the wrong variables. So don't use the *register* keyword. (Most modern compilers ignore the *register* keyword anyway because they know they can do better.) ∎

Declaring Functions

A *function declaration* establishes the number and type of arguments to the function as well as the type of the returned value, if any. A function declaration with no code is called a *function prototype*.

It is good programming style to always declare a function before using it. This allows the compiler to compare the way the function is called with the way it is declared. If the function is called improperly, the compiler can flag the call with a compiler error, saving you the trouble of finding the error yourself.

Function prototype declarations are often made in a *.h* include file to allow their easy inclusion in multiple *.c* files. Here's a function prototype in *multiply.h*:

```
/*the following is a prototype declaration*/
int multiply(int firstArg, int secondArg);
```

And here's *multiply.c*, which defines *multiply()*:

```
#include "multiply.h"
/*this is the actual definition of the function*/
int multiply(int firstArg, int secondArg)
{
    int result;

    result = firstArg * secondArg;
    return result;
}
```

Other *.c* files that include functions that call *multiply()* appear as follows:

```
#include "multiply.h"
/*some other functions...*/
int someOtherFn(int a, int b)
{
```

continued

```
        /*...other code...*/
        return multiply(a, b);   /*compiler compares this call...*/
}                               /*...to the prototype*/
```

Here the *multiply( )* function takes two integer arguments, multiplies them, and returns the integer result. Because function *someOtherFn( )* uses *multiply( )*, the module that contains it includes the *.h* file *multiply.h*. The prototype for *multiply( )* contained in *multiply.h* ensures that the function is used properly.

If a function does not return a value, its return type is *void*. If it takes no arguments, its argument type is *void*. For example:

```
void noReturn(int x, int y);
int  noArguments(void);
void neither(void);
```

If no return type is specified, C assumes type *int*. If you leave the argument list empty, C does not to check the number and type of arguments when the function is called. This can be specified explicitly using ellipses, as follows:

```
returnsAnInt(void);
void unspecifiedArguments();
void alsoUnspecifiedArguments(...);
```

If a function is not prototyped, C attempts to infer a prototype from the way the function is first used. This is called the Miranda prototype. ("If you cannot afford a prototype, one will be provided for you.")

The prototyping rules for C and C++ are different. The C rules are described here, in Part I. The C++ rules are presented and contrasted with the C rules in Part II. ■

Always provide prototypes for all of your functions. In addition, inform your compiler that you want it to generate a warning if it encounters a function that is used without a prototype. This may seem like a hassle, but it will save you time debugging problems that the compiler could have found for you. ■

The Ins and Outs of C Expressions

An *expression* is a C statement that has a value. Most executable C statements are expressions of one type or another. Expressions consist of smaller expressions, which I will call *subexpressions,* linked by operators. Consider the following example:

```
void fn(void)
{
    int x;
```

```
    int y = 2;
    x = 5 + 2 * y;        /*expression in question*/
}
```

You will quickly recognize *2 * y* in this code snippet as a subexpression whose value is 4. You may not recognize, however, that within this subexpression is another subexpression, *y,* which evaluates to 2. The constant 5 is yet another subexpression whose value is 5.

Besides a value, every expression also has a type. The type of the subexpression *y* is *int*. Likewise, the type of the subexpression *2 * y* is *int*.

In the example snippet, the complete expression, including the assignment operator, is

```
    x = 5 + 2 * y
```

In C, unlike most other languages, assignment is just another operator. The assignment operator says "take the value on the right and stuff it into the variable on the left *and return the resulting value and type of the thing on the left.*" I stress the end of the sentence because it highlights the fact that assignment is an operator.

Smooth operators

Given that expressions consist of subexpressions linked together by operators, it's important to know what the operators are.

Table 1-3 is a complete list of the operators in C. Every operator has a syntax, a precedence, and an associativity. Higher precedence operators are evaluated before lower precedence operators. In our earlier example expression:

```
    x = 5 + 2 * y
```

the multiplication was performed before the addition because the multiplication operator has a higher precedence than the addition operator.

Some operators, such as the – operator, seem to appear twice in Table 1-3. These operators have two forms: a one-argument, or unary, form and a two-argument, or binary, form. The unary form always has higher precedence than the binary form.

Operators fall into several broad categories: mathematical, bitwise, logical, assignment, and miscellaneous. The following sections present tables that identify these various operators along with notes on operators that may be confusing or may cause trouble.

Table 1-3: Operator Precedence

	Operator	*Associativity*
Highest precedence	() [] -> .	left to right
	! ~ + - ++ -- & * (cast) sizeof	right to left
	* / %	left to right
	+ -	left to right
	<< >>	left to right
	< <= > >=	left to right
	== !=	left to right
	&	left to right
	^	left to right
	|	left to right
	&&	left to right
	||	left to right
	?:	right to left
	= *= /= %= += -= &= ^= |= <<= >>=	right to left
Lowest precedence	,	left to right

Mathematical operators

Table 1-4 shows the mathematical operators. These operators are designed to work on whole numbers, such as *int*s, *float*s, and *double*s.

The increment and decrement operators come in both a prefix and postfix version. The value of the variable is the same with either version, but the value of the expression itself is different. Consider the following:

```
void fn()
{
   int z;
   int x = 5;
   int y = 5;
   z = ++x;          /*value of z is 6*/
   z = y++;          /*value of z is 5*/
}
```

Both *x* and *y* end up with the value 6. But ++*x* is the value of *x* after the increment, whereas y++ is the value of *y* before the increment.

Table 1-4: Mathematical Operators

Operator	Meaning
+ (unary)	Effectively does nothing
- (unary)	Reverse the sign of the argument
+ (binary)	Addition
- (binary)	Subtraction
* (binary)	Multiplication
/	Division
%	Modulo (returns the remainder after division)
++	Increment
--	Decrement

Bitwise operators

The bitwise operators are shown in Table 1-5. These operators allow the programmer to set, test, and clear individual bits in integer variables.

Table 1-5: Bitwise Operators

Operator	Meaning
~	Bitwise inverse
& (binary)	Bitwise AND
|	Bitwise OR
^	Bitwise eXclusive OR
<<	Left shift
>>	Right shift

When left shifting, a zero is always shifted into the least significant bit. When right shifting an unsigned integer, a zero is shifted into the most significant bit. When right shifting a signed integer, however, the compiler is free to copy the sign bit. There is no rotate operator in C.

Logical operators

Logical operators take the place of Boolean operators used in other languages. Logical operators work with integers. (Their counterparts in other languages work on Boolean values.) See Table 1-6.

Table 1-6: Logical Operators

Operator	Meaning
!	Logical inverse
&&	Logical AND
||	Logical OR
==	Equality (1 if left and right arguments are equal; 0 otherwise)
!=	Inequality (logical inverse of ==)

All logical operators use the rule that 0 is false and all other numbers are true. These operators generate either a 0 (false) or a 1 (true). The result of any of these operators can be stored in a variable or used in a larger expression.

The *&&* and *||* operators practice short-circuit evaluation. Consider the following example:

```
if ((x == y) && (y == z))
```

If *x* is not equal to *y*, the overall condition is false whether or not *y* is equal to *z*. There is no need to evaluate the second subexpression if the first subexpression fails. This is called *short-circuit evaluation*.

A similar short circuit is performed on *||*. If the first subexpression in a logical OR is true, the overall condition is true and the compiler skips the evaluation of the second subexpression.

Normally this is good because it results in a slightly faster program. Sometimes, however, it can cause unexpected results.

Consider the following:

```
if (g() && f())
```

The *g()* function is called first. If it returns a zero, the *f()* function is not called. Now if *f()* should do more than just perform this test, you may not see the results that you expect. ∎

Assignment operators

The assignment operators are shown in Table 1-7.

Table 1-7: Assignment Operators

Operator	*Meaning*
=	Assignment
*=	Multiply by
/=	Divide by
%=	Modulo by
+=	Add to
-=	Subtract from
&=	AND with
^=	eXclusive OR with
|=	OR with
<<=	Left shift by
>>=	Right shift by

The assignment operator (=) takes the value on the right and stores it in the variable on the left. The value and type of the expression correspond to the resulting value and type of the lefthand variable.

The other assignment operators are merely shorthand. In every case, the following equivalence is true:

z #= x is the same as $z = z$ # x

where # is a valid binary mathematical or bitwise operator.

Miscellaneous operators

Table 1-8 shows the remaining, miscellaneous operators.

The ternary operator is often confused with a control structure. It works as follows:

```
a ? b : c;
```

Table 1-8: Miscellaneous Operators

Operator	Meaning
()	Function call
[]	Array index
.	Member of the structure
->	Member of the structure pointed to
?:	Ternary operator
,	Comma operator

If *a* is true, the result of the operator is the value of *b*; otherwise, the result is the value of *c*. The ternary operator uses short-circuit evaluation too. If *a* is true, *c* is not evaluated; if *a* is not true, *b* is not evaluated.

The comma operator is really useful. It means: Evaluate the subexpression on the left of the operator and then evaluate the subexpression on the right. The value and type of the expression correspond to the subexpression on the right. Now how about that for an operator? It's a "get out of the way" operator, that is, it basically does nothing.

Actually, the comma has a few obscure uses. One of the uses of the comma operator is to cram extra stuff into the clauses of a *for* loop. For example:

```
for(x=0,  y = 100; x < y; x+=10, y-=10)
```

This initializes two loop counters and causes one to count up while the other counts down.

Special operator considerations

You can override the precedence of the operators by using parentheses. Consider the following example:

```
void fn(void)
{
    int a = 2;
    int b = 3;
    int c;

    c = 2 + a * b;      /*multiplication first; c = 8*/
    c = (2 + a) * b;    /*addition first; c = 12*/
}
```

Without parentheses in the first expression, *a* is multiplied by *b* and the result is added to 2 because multiplication has a higher precedence than addition. In the second expression, 2 is added to *a* and the result is multiplied by *b* because of the parentheses.

Except for the three short-circuit cases noted previously, the order of evaluation of subexpressions at the same precedence level is not known. Consider the following example:

```
z = f() * g();        /*don't know order functions are called*/
```

Because *()* has a higher precedence than *, both functions are called before the multiplication is performed. Fine. The problem is that the programmer does not know which function is called first. The compiler is well within its rights to call *f()* first and then *g()* or to change its mind and call *g()* first.

Parentheses have no effect on this particular property. The only way to affect the order is to break the expression into two statements, as follows:

```
z = f();              /*now f() is called first... */
z *= g();             /*...followed by g()          */
```

Conclusion

Beyond the basic expressions that make up C, the areas of greatest concern to C programmers are pointers and C structures. We examine these in further detail in the next two chapters.

Chapter 2
C Pointers

In This Chapter

▶ Declaring pointers to simple variables

▶ Using pointers

▶ Operations on pointers

▶ Passing pointers to functions

▶ Allocating and using memory off the heap

*T*his chapter covers that most dreaded of topics — pointers. The mere mention of the word sends otherwise battle-hardened programmers shrieking to the vending machine for more Jolt cola to calm their nerves. But it needn't be that way. Pointers are a powerful arrow in every C programmer's quiver, and it behooves us all to master them.

Declaring and Using Simple Pointers

A *pointer variable* is a variable that contains an address, usually the address of another variable. Consider the following example:

```
void fn()
{
   int i;
   int *pI;

   pI = &i;          /*pI now points to i*/
   *pI = 10;         /*stores 10 in i  */
}
```

Pointer variables are declared like normal variables except for the addition of the unary * character. In an expression, the unary & means "the address of" and the unary * means "pointed at by." Thus, we would read the first assignment as "store the address of *i* in *pI*." The second assignment is "store 10 in the location pointed at by *pI*."

To make this more concrete, let's assume that this function's memory starts at location 0x100. In addition, *i* is at address 0x102 and *pl* is at 0x106. The first assignment is shown in Figure 2-1. Here you can see that the value of *&i* (0x102) is stored in *pl*.

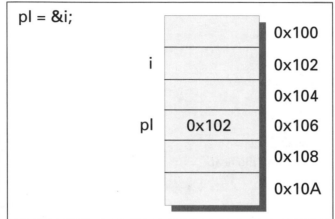

Figure 2-1:
Storing the
address of i
in pl.

The next assignment is demonstrated in Figure 2-2. The value 10 is stored in the address contained in *pl*, which is 0x102 (the address of *i*). That is, **pl* is the location pointed at by *pl*.

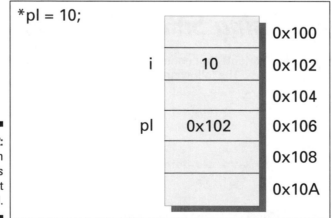

Figure 2-2:
Storing 10 in
the address
pointed at
by pl.

Remember that every expression has a type as well as a value. The type of the *&i* expression is pointer to an integer, written as *int** in C-ese. Comparing this to the declaration of *pl,* you see that the types match exactly.

Similarly, because *pI* is of type *int**, the type of **pI* is *int*. Expressed in plain English, the type of the thing pointed to by *pI* is *int*.

The pointer type *char** serves the role of a separate string type. Any string of characters in quotation marks is assumed to be of type *char**. In addition to the characters you code, C adds a trailing 0, which is used as a string terminator. This string terminator is convenient because it's easy to test for a 0 in loops. (Remember that 0 is the only value that is considered false.)

For example, consider the following function, which makes all the characters in a string passed to the function uppercase:

```
#include <ctype.h>
void upperCase(char *pS)
{
    while (*pS)
    {
        if (islower(*pS))
        {
            *pS = toupper(*pS);
        }
        pS++;
    }
}

void fn()
{
    char *pString;
    pString = "Davis";
    upperCase(pString);
}
```

In function *fn()*, the assignment to *pString* is allowed because both *pString* and *"Davis"* are of type *char**. The value of the subexpression *"Davis"* is the address of a string consisting of *'D'*, *'a'*, *'v'*, *'i'*, *'s'*, and a terminating *'\0'* added by C.

The call to *upperCase()* passes the address of this string. In the *while* condition in *fn()*, **pS* is true for every character in the string except the terminating *'\0'*, which C tacked on the end of the string for us. Encountering this character terminates the loop, which causes the program to exit the function.

Operations on Pointers

In the code snippet in the preceding section, notice the *pS++* in the function *fn()*. From this we can infer that some of the operators we saw in Chapter 1 are defined on pointer types as well. By "defined on pointer types," I do not mean defined on the object pointed at by a pointer, as in the following example:

```
void fn(void)
{
    int i = 5;
    int *pI = &i;
    int b;
    b = 2 * *pI;
}
```

pI is an integer. (It is the integer pointed at by *pI*.) Like any other integer, *pI* is subject to all the operations defined for other integers. Well then, what operations other than * are defined for *pI* itself?

Incrementing pointers

We already know that the ++ operator is defined for pointers. To see the results of incrementing a pointer variable, let's return to the graphical computer, shown in Figure 2-3. Let's assume that the string *"Davis"* is stored beginning at location 0x100, one character per byte, and that *pS* points to the beginning of that string.

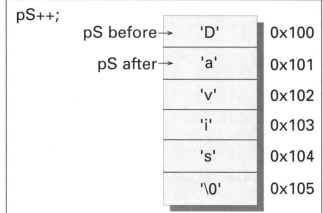

Figure 2-3:
Incrementing
a character
pointer.

If *pS* started out pointing at the 'D' with a value of 0x100, it makes sense that adding 1 to *pS* results in a value of 0x101, which happens to be the address of *'a'*, the next character in the string. Repeating the process moves the pointer to *'v'*, then to *'i'*, then to *'s'*. Finally, *pS* points to the trailing *'\0'*.

The designers of C thought this was really neat, and so do most C programmers. But what if a character required more than one byte? Or what if *pS* pointed not to a string of characters but to an array of integers, each of which take two bytes on the PC? Then the addition wouldn't work as well because 0x101 would not correspond to an even address.

The inventors of C made up a rule to retain the neat addition trick for all storage types, even those that take more than a byte: Pointer variable addition is always defined in terms of the size of the thing pointed at. ■

For example, if *pS* points to 2-byte integers, *pS*++ adds 2 to *pS* instead of 1. If *pS* points to some complex structure, *pS*++ might add 50 to the value of *pS*. Stated another way, if *pS* is the address of a house, *pS*++ moves *pS* to the next house down the block, irrespective of the size of the house.

Other operations on pointers

What other operators besides ++ are defined for pointers? Well, ++ moves the pointer one house up the block, and -- moves it one house down the block. In fact, any variation of integer addition or subtraction is defined. The result is always a pointer. For example:

```
void fn(void)
{
    int i;
    X *pX;

    pX + i;
}
```

Thus, if *i* is an integer and *pX* is a pointer to type *X*, *pX* + *i* is a pointer to *X*, *i* elements away from *pX*. That is, *pX* + *i* points to the *i*th house down the block.

The only other operation defined for pointers is the subtraction of two pointers of the same type. This results in an integer that is the number of elements between the two pointers. In other words, subtracting the address of one house from that of another results in a count of the number of houses between the two addresses.

Arrays and Pointers: Can We Ever Get Them Together?

There is a direct relationship between adding to a pointer and indexing an array. Consider what it means to index into an array of integers.

```
void fn(int i)
{
    int array[10];
    int *pI;
    array[i] = 0;        /*store 0 into the i'th element*/
```

continued

```
    pI = &array[0];
    *(pI + i) = 0;      /*has the same effect as previous*/
}
```

array[i] refers to the *i*th element in *array*. This is similar to the effect of adding to a pointer. If *pI* points to the *0*th element of the array, *pI* + *i* points to the *i*th element. Thus, storing a value at *pI* + *i* has the same effect as storing a value at *array[i]*.

In fact, C interprets the index operator, *[]*, in the following way:

   array[x] is interpreted as **(array + x)*

To highlight this relationship, C has a rule that if you give the name of an array without an index, you mean the address of the first element. Thus, *array* and *pI* are both of type *int**. In fact, all of the following statements are legal:

```
void fn(int i)
{
    int array[10];
    int *pI;

    pI = array;        /*both are of type int* so types match*/
    pI[i] = 0;         /*this is now same as array[i] = 0  */
    *(array + i) = 0;  /*this is also same as array[i] = 0 */
}
```

Compare the declaration of a pointer to that of an array:

```
int *pPointer;
int array[10];
```

The pointer declaration allocates space for an address but does not allocate space for the integer(s) to which the pointer points. The array declaration allocates space for the integers but does not allocate space for a pointer; instead, it treats the address of the array like a constant.

Keeping this relationship between arrays and pointers in mind can often help make sense out of the pointer ravings you find in many C programs.

Passing Pointers to Functions

Arguments to C functions are always passed by value. That is, when the call is made, only the value of the variable is passed. A function cannot change that value in the calling function. Consider the following example:

```
void fn(int i)
{
    i = 10;         /*this is legal and the...*/
                    /*...value is now 10 in fn()*/
}


int main()
{
    int i = 0;

    fn(i);          /*only the value 0 is passed to fn()*/
    return 0;       /*i is still 0 upon returning*/
}
```

If you want to change the value of a variable in the calling function, you must explicitly pass the address of the variable, as the following example demonstrates:

```
void fn(int *pI)
{
    *pI = 10;
}


int main()
{
    int i = 0;

    fn(&i);     /*this passes the address of i*/
    return 0;   /*now the value of i is 10    */
}
```

In this case, the address of *i* is passed to the function *fn()*. When *fn()* stores 10 in the integer pointed to by *pI*, it overwrites the old value of *i*.

Because the name of an array without a subscript is equal to the address of the array, calling a function with a simple array name passes the address of the array. The following snippet demonstrates this:

```
void zero(int i, int *pArray)
{
    pArray[i] = 0;
}


int main()
{
    int array[100];

    zero(10, array);
    return 0;
}
```

Pointers to Functions

It is also possible to store and manipulate the address of a function. However, the following does *not* declare a pointer to a function:

```
int *pFn();
```

Instead, this declares a function that returns a pointer to an integer. The *()* takes effect first because it has a higher precedence than *. To get the desired effect, parentheses are required:

```
int (*pFn)(float);
```

Now the * takes effect first. This is read as "*pFn* is a pointer to a function that takes a *float* argument and returns an *int.*" In use, its semantics are similar to those of an array:

```
int anotherFn(float f);   /*some function, somewhere*/
void myFunc(float x)
{
    int (*pFn)(float);    /*declare a pointer to a function*/

    pFn = anotherFn; /*function name alone refers to its address*/
    (*pFn)(x);       /*call the function pointed at by pFn*/
}
```

The extra parentheses are necessary when calling **pFn* (again) because the precedence of *()* is higher than that of *. ■

Heap Memory

The *heap* is an amorphous blob of memory from which your program can allocate chunks through a group of Standard C library calls, the most common of which is *void* malloc(size_t size)*. *malloc()* accepts as its argument either an *int* or a *long* (depending on your compiler), which represents the number of bytes of memory to allocate. *malloc()* returns a pointer to the memory allocated or a zero if it couldn't fulfill the request, usually because there isn't as much contiguous heap memory on hand as you asked for.

You can do whatever you want with the memory block returned from *malloc()*. When you're finished, however, you must remember to replace the memory block by calling *free()*, passing it the same pointer returned to you by *malloc()*. If you do not, your program will slowly starve itself by running out of heap memory (unless, of course, it ends soon enough). When your program terminates, any memory you have checked out of the heap is automatically returned for you.

So, what good are pointers to functions?

I have a lot of mottoes to get me through life. One of them is: "Not everything in the world that can be done is worth doing." Take bungy jumping, for example. Pointers to functions can be very useful in some unusual cases. One of these is the callback function.

The *callback function* works like a return address on a registration form. When a program executes under a graphical operating system, such as Windows or UNIX X-Windows, it can register itself to be alerted when certain events occur (for example, when the operator clicks the mouse in a window).

As part of the registration, the program provides the address of the function to be called. When the event occurs, the operating system calls that address, passing a structure containing a description of what happened. The following pseudo-code will give you a feel for how a callback function works:

```
/*callbackFunction - is called when EVENT_NAME occurs;
                     pPacketOfData points to a structure
                     that describes what just happened*/

void callbackFunction(struct Packet *pPacketOfData);

int main()
{
   /*other stuff and then...*/

   /*here, register callbackFunction as a function to be
     called when event EVENT_NAME occurs*/
   register(EVENT_NAME, callbackFunction);

   /*...life goes on*/
}
```

Somewhere deep in the bowels of the operating system, the address of *callbackFunction* is stored in a pointer to a function, like *pFn* declared earlier, and called indirectly when the event is detected.

Heap memory is nice because it's dynamically allocated. That is, heap memory is allocated at run time. This is great if you don't know how much memory you'll actually need until run time. In addition, heap memory allows you to use all available memory in the machine without the need to know how much that is at compile time.

Conclusion

So far, we have seen several important C concepts applied to the intrinsic variable types. However, C does allow programmers to define their own types as well. In the next chapter, we will see how these concepts can be applied to user-defined types.

Chapter 3

User-Defined Types: The C Structure

In This Chapter

▶ Declaring and initializing structures

▶ Declaring and using pointers to structures

▶ Structures and functions

▶ Retrieving structures off the heap

*I*n addition to the intrinsic types, programmers may define their own types using the C keyword *struct*. A complete understanding of the C structure is necessary to learning C++.

C Structures 101

A structure is defined and accessed as follows:

```
struct MyStruct
{
   int   firstElement;
   float secondElement;
};

void fn()
{
   struct MyStruct ms;
   ms.firstElement = 0;   /*refers to the integer member*/
   ms.secondElement = 1.0;/*refers to the float member  */
}
```

Structures differ from arrays in that elements in an array must each be of the same type but elements in a structure can be of different types. Because a structure's elements can be of different types, however, they must be declared and referenced by name rather than by subscript. Thus we see the names *firstElement* and *secondElement* assigned to the two members of *MyStruct*.

You need to differentiate between a structure and an instance of a structure (an instance of a structure is also known as an *object*). In the preceding snippet, the structure is *MyStruct*; the object is *ms*. To use an example closer to home: *Reader* is a class of people who read books, and you are an instance of class *Reader*.

Arrays and structures, can be mixed and matched. You can have an array of structures, as demonstrated by *ms* in the following, or a structure containing an array, as does *MyStruct*.

```
struct MyStruct
{
    float anElement;
    int   anArray[10];
};

void fn()
{
    struct MyStruct ms[20];

    ms[10].anElement = 10.0;
    ms[10].anArray[5] = 5;
}
```

Structures can be initialized when declared, as the following example demonstrates:

```
struct MyStruct
{
    int   firstElement;
    float secondElement;
};

void fn()
{
    struct MyStruct simple = {1, 2.0};
    struct MyStruct array[2] = {{1, 2.0}, /*array[0]*/
                               {1, 2.0}};/*array[1]*/
}
```

The only mathematical operator that is defined for structures is the assignment operator. Assignments such as the following are allowed if the source and destination types match:

```
void fn(MyStruct source)
{
    struct MyStruct target;

    target = source;      /*copy the source into the target*/
}
```

Such an assignment performs a binary copy of the source to the target.

Pointers to C Structures

The following example shows how to declare and use a pointer to a structure object:

```
struct MyStruct
{
   int firstElement;
   float secondElement;
};

void fn()
{
   struct MyStruct mc;
   struct MyStruct *pMC;

   pMC = &mc;              /*point pMC to the object mc    */
   pMC->firstElement = 1;/*reference the first element...*/
                          /*...of the object pointed...   */
                          /*...to by pMC                  */
   pMC->secondElement= 2.0; /*you get the idea            */
}
```

The type of *pMC* is *struct MyStruct* *, which you read as "*pMC* is a pointer to a *MyStruct* object." The -> operator is used to access members of structures pointed to by a pointer type.

Just as *array[i]* was really a shorthand for *(array + i)*, so *pMC->firstElement* is also a shorthand. Consider the following: If *pMC* is a pointer to an object of structure *MyClass*, *(*pMC)* must be the object pointed to by *pMC*. Thus, we could have written *(*pMC).firstElement*. (The parentheses are necessary because . has higher precedence than *. See Table 1-3.) Thus, the following equivalence holds true:

pMC->firstElement is equivalent to *(*pMC).firstElement*

Operations on pointers to structures

The same operations that are defined for pointers to intrinsic types are defined for pointers to user-defined types and with the same effect. For example, the following function initializes the *pName* field in an array of structures:

```
struct MyStruct
{
   char *pName;
   /*...other stuff...*/
};

void fn(int number, struct MyStruct *pMS)
```

continued

```
    {
        while (number > 0) /*loop until count exhausted*/
        {
            pMS->pName = (char*)0;
            number--;      /*decrement the count*/
            pMS++;         /*go to next element in array*/
        }
    }
```

Because addition is defined on pointers to structures, the index operator *[]* is also defined. Thus, this example function could have been written as follows:

```
void fn(int number, struct MyStruct *pArray)
{
    int i;

    for (i = 0; i < number; i++)
    {
        pArray[i].pName = (char*)0;
    }
}
```

Notice that the *pArray[i]* is not a pointer to an object but an object. Hence, it requires the . operator, not the -> operator.

Using pointers to structures

Pointers to structures are used in many of the same ways as pointers to intrinsics. However, pointers to structures are used also in one way that is unique to structures: with linked lists.

Intrinsic objects such as *int*s and *float*s have no way of "pointing to" each other. The only practical way that multiple intrinsic objects can be grouped is the array. However, the array is inconvenient for many applications. In particular, it is difficult to insert or remove an element from the middle of an array.

Structure objects can include pointers to other objects. This allows the objects to be connected in many ways that are more convenient to handle. For example, the following structure allows for the implementation of a linked list.

```
struct LList
{
    /*include whatever data you like*/
    int whatEverData;

    struct LList *pNext;      /*ptr to next object in list*/
};
struct LList *pFirst;         /*ptr to first object in list*/
```

The pointer *pFirst* is intended to point to the first element in the list. In each element of the list, *pNext* points to the next element. In the last element, *pNext* contains 0.

A singly-linked list is traversed easily. For example, the following function traverses a linked list of *LList* structures looking for an element with *whatEverData* set to 0:

```
void fn()
{
   struct Llist *pLL;

   /*start with the first; continue until pLL is 0;
     link from one element to the next each time*/
   for (pLL = pFirst; pLL; pLL = pLL->pNext)
   {
      if (pLL->whatEverData == 0)
      {
         /*...whatever processing you want here...*/
      }
   }
}
```

We will see linked lists in use in a working program in BUDGET4 at the end of Part IV.

Structures and Functions

When a structure object is passed to a function, a copy of the object must be made and given to the function. (Remember that C always passes by value.) Changes made to the structure object by the function do not affect the object's value in the calling function. For small objects, this may be what is desired. Copying large objects, however, can result in considerable overhead in both time and memory.

It is generally more efficient to pass the address of a structure object, as demonstrated in the following snippet:

```
struct MyStruct
{
   int lotsOfData[10000];
};

void fn1(MyStruct ms);
void fn2(MyStruct *pMS);

void fn()
{
   struct MyStruct ms;
   fn1(ms);   /*this passes some 10,000 integers to fn1()*/
   fn2(&ms);  /*this passes a single pointer*/
}
```

Here the call to *fn1()* results in an entire *ms*, some 10,000 integers, being copied onto the stack and passed to *fn1()*. The call to *fn2()*, however, copies only the address of the existing *ms* object onto the stack.

Allocating Structures from the Heap

Structure objects can be allocated from the heap, as the following code snippet shows:

```
#include <malloc.h>
struct MyStruct
{
    int data;
    /*...whatever other data you want...*/
};

struct MyStruct *getNewMS(int someData)
{
    struct MyStruct *pMS;
    pMS = (struct MyStruct*)malloc(sizeof struct MyStruct);
    if (pMS)
    {
        pMS->data = someData;
    }
    return pMS;
}
```

The *sizeof MyStruct* returns the number of bytes in a *MyStruct* object. This number is passed to *malloc()*, which attempts to allocate that much memory off the heap. If the request is successful, *malloc()* returns a nonzero pointer. This pointer must be recast into the proper type before being assigned to *pMS*. The function *fn()* stores whatever data it wants into this new object. Finally, *fn()* returns this pointer to the calling function.

fn() can continue to allocate *MyStruct* objects until heap memory is exhausted.

Conclusion

This concludes our review of critical but sometimes tricky C concepts. This has not been a full discussion of C or even a complete review. I have touched on only those features that we will need in the remainder of the book.

Next, we see a small C program, BUDGET.C. This program starts life here as a conventional functional program. We will watch this program grow throughout the book, as it takes on more and more properties of an object-oriented C++ program.

The C Version of Our Budget Program: BUDGET1.C

*A*s I mentioned in the Introduction, Parts I through V end with an example program. In Part I, the program starts life as a straight C program. In Parts II through V, I add to the program the features you just learned about. This lets you see how C++ programs differ from C programs. By comparing the new features with the old, you can come to appreciate their beauty. (Okay, maybe that word's a little strong, but a good program does get me choked up sometimes.)

Before you look at the first version of the example program, you should know something about my coding style. I more or less use the Borland naming conventions, as follows:

- Types, such as structures, start with an uppercase letter
- Variables start with a lowercase letter
- Pointers start with the letter *p*
- Each word (except the first) in a multiword variable name starts with an uppercase letter
- Macros and #defined constants appear in all uppercase

In addition, I try to be consistent about where I place open and closed braces and how far I indent.

The BUDGET program is a simple checkbook and savings register program. Here's what it does:

1. Allocates a savings account entry, allocates a checking account entry, or exits.

2. Assigns an account number.

3. Begins accepting transactions, consisting of deposits and withdrawals. A transaction of zero signals the end of this entry.

4. After the user chooses to exit, the program displays the ending balance of all accounts, the subtotals of all checking and savings accounts, and the total of all accounts.

Avoiding needless coding errors

We humans have a limited amount of CPU power between our ears. We need to direct our CPU power toward getting our programs working, not toward figuring out simple stuff (like indentation).

Be consistent with how you name variables, where you place opening and closing braces, and so on. This is called your coding style. Once you have developed a style, it's just as important that you stick to that style. After a while, your coding style will become second nature. You'll find that you can code your programs with less time and read your programs with less effort.

When working on a project with several programmers, it's important that you all use the same style to avoid a Tower of Babel effect with conflicting and confusing styles. In addition, I strongly suggest that you enable every error and warning message your compiler can produce. Even if you decide that a particular warning is not a problem, why would you want it suppressed? You can always ignore it. More often than not, even a warning represents a problem that needs to be corrected.

Some people don't like the compiler finding their slip-ups because they think it's embarrassing and because they think correcting things to get rid of the warnings wastes time. Just think how embarrassing and time consuming it is to painstakingly search for a bug only to find that it's a problem your compiler could have told you about hours ago.

Our program must mimic a few bank rules concerning transactions:

- ✔ Never let the balance become negative (banks may be friendly, but they're not that friendly).
- ✔ Never charge for making a deposit.
- ✔ Charge $.20 per check if the balance is less than $500.00; otherwise, checks are free.
- ✔ Charge $5.00 for each withdrawal from a savings account after the first withdrawal, which is free.

The following program should be straight ANSI C; no tricks. Feel free to compile this with your C++ compiler. If you want to make sure I'm not slipping in any C++, be sure the name of the program ends in .C and that the "C++ always" compiler option isn't set.

```
/*BUDGET1.C - calculates your bank account balances.
            There are two types of accounts:
                  Checking - $.20 per check if
                             balance < 500
                  Savings  - $5.00 per withdrawal
                             (first is free)
```

```c
*/
#include <stdio.h>

/*the maximum number of accounts you can have*/
#define MAXACCOUNTS 10

/*Checking - this describes checking accounts*/
struct Checking
{
    unsigned accountNumber;
    float    balance;
} chkAcnts[MAXACCOUNTS];

/*Savings - you can probably figure this one out*/
struct Savings
{
    unsigned accountNumber;
    float    balance;
    int      noWithdrawals;
} svgAcnts[MAXACCOUNTS];

/*prototype declarations, just to keep us honest*/
void initChecking(struct Checking *pCO);
void processChecking(struct Checking*);

void initSavings (struct Savings  *pSO);
void processSavings (struct Savings*);
int main();

/*main - accumulate the initial input and output totals*/
int main()
{
    char     accountType;      /*S or C*/
    unsigned keepLooping;      /*0 -> get out of loop*/
    float    chkTotal;         /*total in checking accounts*/
    float    svgTotal;         /*total in savings accounts*/
    float    total;            /*total of all accounts*/
    int      i;
    int      noChkAccounts;    /*no. of checking accounts*/
    int      noSvgAccounts;    /*no. of savings accounts*/

    /*loop until someone enters X or x*/
    noChkAccounts = 0;
    noSvgAccounts = 0;
    keepLooping = 1;
    while (keepLooping)         /*Note 1*/
    {
        printf("Enter S for Savings,"
               " C for Checking,"
               " X for exit\n");
        scanf("\n%c", &accountType);

        switch (accountType)
        {
            case 'c':
            case 'C':                 /*Note 2*/
                if (noChkAccounts < MAXACCOUNTS)
```

continued

```
                    {
                        initChecking(&chkAcnts[noChkAccounts]);
                        processChecking(&chkAcnts[noChkAccounts]);
                        noChkAccounts++;
                    }
                    else
                    {
                        printf("No more room for checking accounts\n");
                    }
                    break;

                case 's':
                case 'S':
                    if (noSvgAccounts < MAXACCOUNTS)
                    {
                        initSavings(&svgAcnts[noSvgAccounts]);
                        processSavings(&svgAcnts[noSvgAccounts]);
                        noSvgAccounts++;
                    }
                    else
                    {
                        printf("No more room for savings accounts\n");
                    }
                    break;

                case 'x':
                case 'X':
                    keepLooping = 0;
                    break;

                default:
                    printf("I didn't get that.\n");
            }
        }

        /*now present totals*/
        chkTotal = 0;                   /*Note 3*/
        printf("Checking accounts:\n");
        for (i = 0; i < noChkAccounts; i++)
        {
            printf("Account %6d = %8.2f\n",
                    chkAcnts[i].accountNumber,
                    chkAcnts[i].balance);
            chkTotal += chkAcnts[i].balance;
        }
        svgTotal = 0;
        printf("Savings accounts:\n");
        for (i = 0; i < noSvgAccounts; i++)
        {
            printf("Account %6d = %8.2f (no. withdrawals = %d)\n",
                    svgAcnts[i].accountNumber,
                    svgAcnts[i].balance,
                    svgAcnts[i].noWithdrawals);
            svgTotal += svgAcnts[i].balance;
        }
        total = chkTotal + svgTotal;
        printf("Total for checking account = %8.2f\n", chkTotal);
        printf("Total for savings account  = %8.2f\n", svgTotal);
```

```
    printf("Total worth              = %8.2f\n", total);
    return 0;
}

/*initChecking - initialize a checking account*/
void initChecking(struct Checking *pChecking)
{
    printf("Enter account number:");
    scanf("%d", &pChecking->accountNumber);
    pChecking->balance = 0.0;
}

/*processChecking - input the data for a checking account*/
void processChecking(struct Checking *pChecking)
{
    float transaction;

    printf("Enter positive number for deposit,\n"
           "negative for check, 0 to terminate");
    do
    {
        printf(":");
        scanf("%f", &transaction);

        /*is this a deposit?*/
        if (transaction > 0)
        {
            pChecking->balance += transaction;
        }

        /*how about a withdrawal?*/
        if (transaction < 0)
        {
            transaction = -transaction;
            if (pChecking->balance < transaction)
            {
                printf("Insufficient funds: "
                       "balance %f, check %f\n",
                       pChecking->balance, transaction);
            }
            else
            {
                pChecking->balance -= transaction;

                /*if balance falls too low, charge service fee*/
                if (pChecking->balance < 500.00)
                {
                    pChecking->balance -= 0.20;
                }
            }
        }
    } while (transaction != 0);
}

/*initSavings - initialize a savings account*/
void initSavings (struct Savings  *pSavings)
```

continued

```
{
    printf("Enter account number:");
    scanf("%d", &pSavings->accountNumber);
    pSavings->balance = 0.0;
    pSavings->noWithdrawals = 0;
}

/*processSavings - input the data for a savings
account*/
void processSavings(struct Savings *pSavings)
{
    float transaction;

    printf("Enter positive number for deposit,\n"
           "negative for withdrawal, 0 to terminate");
    do
    {
        printf(":");
        scanf("%f", &transaction);

        /*is this a deposit?*/
        if (transaction > 0)
        {
            pSavings->balance += transaction;
        }

        /*how about a withdrawal?*/
        if (transaction < 0)
        {
            transaction = -transaction;
            if (pSavings->balance < transaction)
            {
                printf("Insufficient funds: "
                       "balance %f, check %f\n",
                       pSavings->balance, -transaction);
            }
            else
            {
                if (++pSavings->noWithdrawals > 1)
                {
                    pSavings->balance -= 5.00;
                }
                pSavings->balance -= transaction;
            }
        }
    } while (transaction != 0);
}
```

A sample run of this program follows (just enough to give you an idea of how it works):

```
Enter S for Savings, C for Checking, X for exit
S
Enter account number:123
Enter positive number for deposit,
negative for withdrawal, 0 to terminate:500
```

```
:-50
:-50
:0
Enter S for Savings, C for Checking, X for exit
C
Enter account number:234
Enter positive number for deposit,
negative for check, 0 to terminate:200
:-25
:-20
:0
Enter S for Savings, C for Checking, X for exit
X
Checking accounts:
Account     234 =     154.60
Savings accounts:
Account     123 =      95.00 (no. withdrawals = 2)
Total for checking account =    154.60
Total for savings account  =     95.00
Total worth                =    249.60
```

Let's go over how the BUDGET1.C program works. Two *struct*s, *Checking* and *Savings*, contain the information needed for a checking and savings account. To keep the program as simple as possible, I allocated storage for these accounts from two arrays, *chkAcnts* and *svgsAcnts*.

The downside of the array approach as opposed to dynamic memory allocation is that there is a maximum number of accounts that can be accommodated (*MAXACCOUNTS*).

The main program is divided in two sections: the accumulation section, where the deposits and withdrawals are accumulated into accounts, and the display section. The accumulation section prompts the user for S, C, or X and then inputs a character (see the *Note 1* comment in the listing).

If the user enters *C*, control passes to the checking account case (*Note 2*). If the maximum number of checking accounts has not been reached, a new one is allocated, initialized (*initChecking()*), and processed (*processChecking ()*). When the maximum number of accounts is reached, further attempts to add accounts are rejected with an error message.

The *initChecking()* function merely asks for the account number and initializes the balance to 0. The program assumes that a deposit must precede any withdrawal.

The *processChecking()* function accepts transactions. Positive transactions are assumed to be deposits, negative transactions are withdrawals, and zero exits the function. (I know this is crude, but trees are a valuable national resource.) Deposits are accepted without comment, but withdrawals must go through a few hoops (such as ensuring that enough money is in the account) first.

Savings accounts are processed in a similar fashion to checking accounts by functions that are laid out the same but with slightly different names. However, the charging algorithm for savings account withdrawals is different than the one for checking account withdrawals.

When the user enters *X*, the *main()* function passes control to the display section of the program (*Note 3*). At that point, the program loops through all the accounts, spitting out the balances and adding them in the *chkTotal* and *svgTotal* variables.

There are a few general points to note about the program. First, information about checking and savings accounts is strewn throughout the program. Although I was careful to write *processChecking()* and *processSaving()* functions (which not all C programmers do), members of these structures are referenced in many other places. This can lead to side effect errors, in which changing a value in one place accidentally changes it somewhere else.

Also notice that despite the obvious similarities between savings and checking accounts, I was forced to write separate functions because it is impossible to relate two structures unless they are identical.

I could have written an *Account* structure that is either a savings account or a checking account depending on the value of some internal variable. This type of structure is called a *variant record*. C even encourages variant records by supplying the *union* keyword. However, using variant records can make the resulting code considerably more complicated. Whenever the accounts should be treated differently, the code must check the type of account and act accordingly. This has the effect of distributing even more information about the internals of an *Account* throughout the code. ■

Although there are other (maybe even better) ways to implement this program, it serves nicely as the basis for our investigations. As we progress in our knowledge of C++, we will see this pure C program morph into a full-blown, object-oriented C++ program.

25-Minute Workout

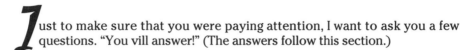

*J*ust to make sure that you were paying attention, I want to ask you a few
questions. "You vill answer!" (The answers follow this section.)

1 Declare the following. (In function declarations, assume that the functions take
no arguments.)

    a. An array of ten integers

    b. A pointer to an integer

    c. An array of ten pointers to integers

    d. A function returning a pointer to an integer

    e. A pointer to a function that takes an integer and returns nothing

2 Given the function:

```
int fn(int, float);
```

why will the following not work?

```
void anotherFn()
{
    int x;
    x = fn(1, 2);
}
```

What can you do to make it work? Hint: Don't change the call in this prototypical
problem.

3 What's wrong with the following *displayArray()* function?

```
#include <stdio.h>
void displayArray(int *pArray, int number)
{
    /*arrange in two columns*/
    int i;
    int noPairs = number / 2;
    int odd = number % 2;
    for (i = 0; i < (2 * noPairs);)
    {
        printf("array[%2d] = %d,  array[%2d] = %d\n",
               i, pArray[i++], i, pArray[i++]);
    }
```

continued

```
    if (odd)
    {
        printf("array[%2d] = %d\n", i, pArray[i]);
    }
}

int main()
{
    int array[] = {1, 2, 3, 4, 5};

    displayArray(array, 5);    /*may not generate proper output*/
    return 0;
}
```

4 Write and prototype a function that accepts from the keyboard two integer values, *x* and *y*, and returns their values in arguments passed from the calling function.

5 Assuming that you want to know the length in bytes of a particular structure, what's wrong with the following?

```
/*function to return size of a MyStruct*/
int sizeOfMyStruct()
{
    /*allocate an array of 2 MyStructs*/
    struct MyStruct ms[2];

    /*now return the difference of the address of
      the second element minus that of the first*/
    return &ms[1] - &ms[0];
}
```

Answers

Hey! Go back and try to answer the questions on your own first.

1

a. *int array[10];*

b. *int *pInt;*

c. *int *arrayPtrs[10];*

Note that *[ ]* has a higher precedence than ***, which is what keeps this from being a pointer to an array of ten integers.

d. *int *fn(void);*

e. *void (*pFn)(void);*

The parentheses around *pFn* are necessary to keep this from being a function that returns a pointer to an integer (like *2d*).

I gave you a big hint on this one (actually two hints).

Without a prototype, C passes both arguments as integers — what does it know? The first argument is fine, but *fn* expects a *float* for the second argument. The integer provided is interpreted as garbage.

The solution is to add a prototype:

```
int fn(int, float);

void anotherFn()
{
   int x;
   x = fn(1, 2);
}
```

Some of you might have said, "Ah well, let's just change the call."

```
void anotherFn()
{
   int x;
   x = fn(1, 2.0);
}
```

This doesn't work either. To maintain compatibility with the older K&R C, a *float* is passed as a *double* in the absence of a prototype. Thus, the second argument ends up at *fn()* as a *double* and not a *float*. As Homer Simpson would say, DOOO.

The answer is "maybe nothing," depending on your compiler. The potential problem is in the *printf()* statement:

```
printf("array[%2d] = %d,   array[%2d] = %d\n",
       i, pArray[i++], i, pArray[i++]);
```

Notice that this expression contains many subexpressions that have mutual side effects, namely *i*++. The programmer of this statement is assuming that the subexpressions are evaluated from left to right. They might well be, but ANSI C doesn't guarantee it. (Under Borland and Turbo C++, for example, subexpressions passed to a function are evaluated from right to left.)

Adding parentheses doesn't help. The only way to solve this problem is to break up the expression into several independent expressions, as follows:

```
printf("array[%2d] = %d,    ", i, pArray[i]);
i++;

printf("array[%2d] = %d\n"   , i, pArray[i]);
i++;
```

The following function does the trick:

```c
#include <stdio.h>

void fn(int *pX, int *pY)
{
    int localX, localY;

    /*first read value into local variables*/
    printf("Enter x & y:");
    scanf("%d%d", &localX, &localY);

    /*now copy into caller's arguments*/
    *pX = localX;
    *pY = localY;
}

int main()
{
    int x, y;

    fn(&x, &y);        /*have to pass the address here*/
    return 0;
}
```

This function first reads the data values into local variables, and then copies the variables to the caller's *x* and *y* variables.

Notice that the local variables are not necessary. The following works just fine:

```c
#include <stdio.h>

void fn(int *pX, int *pY)
{
    printf("Enter x & y:");
    scanf("%d%d", pX, pY);
}
```

The function *sizeOfMyStruct()* will always return a 1, irrespective of the actual size of a *MyStruct* structure. Remember that pointer addition and subtraction are always defined in terms of the sizes of the objects pointed to. Therefore, *&x[i]–&x[j]* is equal to *i–j* no matter what the type of *x*. Use the *sizeof* keyword to return the size of a structure or an object.

Part II

Getting Your Feet Wet: The Non-Object-Oriented Features of C++

The 5th Wave   By Rich Tennant

THE GREAT THING ABOUT OBJECT-ORIENTED PROGRAMMING IS, IT'S MADE SOFTWARE DEVELOPMENT AS EASY AS PUTTING ONE FOOT IN FRONT OF THE OTHER.

In This Part...

1n this part, we start by looking at how C++ came to be. We then look at the features that simply make C++ a better C. Eventually, we will have to discuss the feature that makes C++ a truly new language: OOP (as in "object-oriented programming" not as in "OOPs, I made a mistake trying to learn C++"). But let's start with the basics.

Chapter 4

Getting to C++

In This Chapter

▶ A quick history of C++

▶ A look at the evolution of programming languages (boy, doesn't that sound interesting!)

▶ Where does C++ fit in?

*I*n the early 80s, the good people at AT&T were trying to use C as a simulation language (simulating phone calls, I guess). One individual at AT&T, Bjarne Stroustrup, found C lacking for simulations and decided to extend the language by adding features from his favorite language, Simula67. Simula67 was one of the earliest object-oriented programming languages.

Bjarne was adamant that his new language remain upwardly compatible with C. He originally called it "C with Classes." When that proved too difficult to say, someone came up with a name that was even more difficult to pronounce: C++. I suppose everyone must have thought this use of C's increment operator was fiendishly clever because the new name caught on. (It was a bit shortsighted, though. What are we supposed to call the next version? C++++?)

How Did We Get Here?

Let's review the history of programming according to me. (Humor me here, I'm big on history.)

The early years (1950 – 1960)

First came what I prefer to call chaos programming. Programmers used no prescribed technique — data was stored anywhere, there was no such thing as a function call, and jumps abounded. As a result, programs were expensive and buggy, but that was okay because companies didn't rely on them yet. Important work was still accomplished by hand (fewer mistakes that way). Computers were locked away in big rooms with very big air conditioners and lots of guys in white coats attending to their every need.

Programmers were treated like prima donnas — companies would pay big bucks to get anything, whether or not it worked. The prototypical chaos languages were Micro BASIC and most assembly languages.

The functional years (1960–1975)

Then came the first functional languages. They allowed the programmer to define functions, but there was no concept of structured code and no user-defined data structures (like C's *struct*). *GOTO* statements were still the order of the day.

With functions, you could write bigger programs and you could write them faster, but the programs were still difficult to debug. The best example of a functional language is Fortran.

The structured years (1975–1990)

During the late 70s, programmers realized that they had to debug the code they wrote, and that jumping from one end of the program to the other didn't help the process. It was then that structured programming became the hot topic.

Professors wrote learned papers about how many control structures you must have (it was eventually decided three) and what they were (concatenation, selection, and repetition).[1] This was the software equivalent of the "how many angels can fit on the head of a pin" debate.

Structured programming did improve the state of the art in code writing, however. A well-structured function is easier to debug and maintain than a poorly structured one, so both software quality and programmer productivity improved.

In addition, structured programming made it possible for the programmer to define compound data structures. (To do this in C, you used the keyword *struct*.) For example, a programmer could make up a structure called *Student* and store in it all the relevant data features of a student: name, age, sex, grade point average, and whatever else the program needed. This kept all student data in one place — sort of the data equivalent to functional programming. C is a prototypical structured language.

---

[1] If you're really interested, see "Notes on structured programming," *Structure Programming*, O.J. Dahl, E.W. Dijkstra, and A. Hoare, Eds., Academic Press, New York, 1972, p. 19.

The object-oriented years (1990 – present)

Object-oriented programming, or OOP, was the next step in this progression. OOP expanded the concept of a structure into something called a *class*. Whereas a C structure was limited to describing the data aspects of an object, such as the student's age and address, a C++ class could describe active aspects as well, such as how a student finds a class. A *Student* class can provide a more complete description. You learn the details of the C++ class in Part III.

Why C++?

"Why C++?" is actually a good question. Can't you do object-oriented programming in C? Like most of the truly epochal questions of our time, the answer is an unequivocal "yes and no."

C is a powerful but low-level language. Most of the capabilities for generating classes are present in C. The problem is that the programmer is responsible for doing everything — pretty soon it's just too much trouble. C++, however, takes over much of the extra work of object-oriented programming.

Are there any other object-oriented languages? Sure. Some might even be better, but C++ is the de facto standard object-oriented programming language for the 90s. Using anything else is swimming upstream. Besides, it looks great on your resume.

Pretenders to the throne

C++ was not the only result of adding object-oriented features to C. Another language, Objective C, looked like it might give C++ a run for its money. But Objective C has a fatal flaw: it isn't upwardly compatible.

Remaining compatible with C makes C++ a little kludgy in places (okay, a lot kludgy). The authors of Objective C decided to make a fresh start, which smoothed out some of the rough spots. It was still C, but it wasn't 100% compatible C — a C program could not compile under an Objective C compiler. As soon as programmers with large inventories of C programs stuffed away found that out, they weren't interested.

Although Objective C was a simpler and in some ways superior language, this lack of compatibility doomed it to the software trash heap of history (right next to the TI personal computer). With Objective C out of the race, the field was wide open for C++; no other object-oriented language could capitalize on the immense popularity of C in the way that C++ could.

Conclusion

We can see that C++ is just the latest in a series of improvements in the technology of programming languages. This talk about the history of C++ is all very interesting but fairly useless if we never get around to the actual job of learning the language, so let's unfurl our sail and head out to C++.

Chapter 5

Some Simple Stuff

In This Chapter

▶ Getting a new comment style

▶ Declaring variables anywhere

▶ Introduction to the reference type and two new type specifiers, *const* and *volatile*

*I*n this chapter, we start our journey through C++ by covering a few simple additions to the language. First, C++ adds a new comment style. Second, C++ lets you define your variables anywhere in a function instead of only at the beginning. Third, C++ defines some new type specifiers.

A New Comment Style

Besides the old C standby of /* */ comments, C++ defines a new kind of comment. Anything following // on the same line is considered a comment.

Why do I need it?

The C++ alternate form of comment closes itself automatically with the end of the line. With the old comments, if you forget to close the comment properly with a */, anything up to the next */ is treated as if it were a comment. This new style is self-closing, so the problem doesn't arise. This argument is pretty weak, but then such a simple addition doesn't need much justification. Maybe Stroustrup just got tired of typing */.

How does it work?

The following code uses the old style of comments:

```
area = PI * r * r; /*did you remember how to
                calculate the area of a circle?*/
```

Notice how tempting it might be to insert code into the blank space. If you did, however, whatever you added would be commented out. For example:

```
area = PI * r * r; /*did you remember how to
vol = height * area; calculate the area of a circle?*/
```

The assignment to *vol* is in the comment.

In the new style of comments, anything to the right of // up to the new-line character is considered a comment. However, because the new-line character terminates the comment, a new // is required if the comment is spread over more than one line. For example:

```
area = PI * r * r; //did you remember how to
                   //calculate the area of a circle?
```

Not only does this look slightly more balanced, it avoids the problem of unintentionally commenting out code. The following works as expected:

```
area = PI * r * r;  //did you remember how to
vol = height * area;//calculate the area of a circle?
```

Here, the assignment to *vol* is not part of the comment.

 Several compilers, including Borland C++, allow the // form of comment to be used even when compiling in C mode. Be careful, though; if you try to move C code with C++ comments to a different C compiler, you might have to do a lot of editing. ■

 The // comment feature is unusual in the world of C++ in that it treats a new-line differently than any other form of white space. (*White space* consists of characters such as spaces, tabs, and new-lines.) ■

Variable Declarations Anywhere You Want

In C, variables must be declared at the beginning of the function, before any executable statements. C++ drops this restriction. Well, okay, it relaxes this restriction a whole bunch.

Why do I need them?

To a certain extent, this is another case of "Why not?" If I wanted an index for a *for* loop, for example, I always found it inconvenient to have to search for the beginning of the function I was in so that I could declare the index. Because I always forgot to set an editor bookmark, I then had to search for my old location in the program after I declared the variable.

In C++, all this nuisance is unnecessary. I can declare the variable right where I need it. It makes the code slightly easier to read as well because the reader can see the type of the variable immediately.

Besides the convenience, being able to declare variables in the middle of a function allows you to initialize variables with values calculated previously in the function.

How do they work?

In C, global variables can be declared anywhere you like at the module level; however, local variables must be declared at the beginning of the function. In C++, you can declare a variable almost anywhere. Now I don't have to jump all over the place with the editor. I can simply write things like the following:

```
void makeCopy(char *pT, char *pS)
{
   //first check for zero pointer
   if (pS == 0)
   {
      *pT = '\0';
      return;
   }

   //copy the block
   int i;            //C wouldn't let us get away with this
   for (i = 0; pT[i] = pS[i]; i++)
   {
   }
}
```

A variable exists from the point it is declared to the end of the function. Thus, in the preceding example, it would be illegal to try to reference *i* before the declaration at the end of the function. Just as always, it's illegal to declare two variables with the same name.

You can't access a variable before it is declared. In addition, you have to be careful not to jump around a declaration. If you attempt to use a variable whose declaration has been avoided, the results are unpredictable. Even if you don't attempt to access the variable, the compiler may not like it. For example, the Borland C++ compiler complains about the following code snippet:

```
//absValue - this is a silly way to take
//            absolute value
int absValue(int i)
```

continued

```
{
    if (i > 0)        //if i <= 0 ...
    {
        int j = -i;  //...then the declaration of j is skipped
    }
    return max(i, j);
}
```

There are a few places where you can't declare a variable:

✔ *In a conditional.* For example, the following is not allowed:

```
if (int i = f())
```

✔ *In the second or third expressions of a for loop.* Neither of the following examples is allowed:

```
//example 1
int i;
for (i = 0; int j = array[i]; i++)

//example 2
MyClass *ptr;
for (ptr = first; ptr; MyClass *p = ptr++)
```

However, the following is allowed:

```
//example 3
for (MyClass *ptr = first; ptr; ptr++)
```

✔ *In the call to a function.* For example:

```
result = fn(int temp = a);
```

In general, declare a variable immediately before the separately identifiable block of code in which the variable is used. There's no point in declaring variables in the middle of complex constructs, except to show how clever you can be. Often, this kind of cleverness can backfire by generating bugs. ■

I mention the following only to keep some book reviewer off my case and to impress you with my knowledge of C. The rule for C requires only that variables be declared at the beginning of a block. A *block* is a section of code surrounded by braces. It is possible to define blocks anywhere in a function, but I don't think I've ever seen it done and I'm certainly not going to suggest you do it. ■

Constant Variables

It is possible to declare a variable constant using the *const* keyword. Once you've declared a constant variable, its value cannot be changed.

Why do I need them?

One reason for using a constant variable instead of a numeric constant is because it enables you to assign a meaningful name to the constant. Consider the following example:

```
double speedOfLight = 2.9979E08;      //[meters/s]
double avogadrosConstant = 6.023E23;  //[molecules/mole]
int    radiusOfEarth = 3959;          //[miles]
```

Now I know that all of you would instantly recognize 3959 as the mean radius of the earth in miles, but others might not. By declaring a variable *radiusOfEarth* and using it instead of this strange number, the meaning is clear to all.

Unfortunately, declaring a variable to hold a constant introduces a potential error: What if someone changes it? We will assume for a minute that the radius of the earth shouldn't change. (If the radius of the earth actually does change, whether or not your program works is of absolutely no concern.) We would like to be able to declare a variable so that we get to use its name, but flag it unchangeable so that the compiler won't let anyone muck with it. Ta da! That's what *const* does.

Some may note that the capability to give constants recognizable names already exists in C through the use of *#define*. This is partially true. However, *const* variables are more flexible, as you will see. (For example, a *const* can be a structure object; a *#define* can be only a simple number.) Besides, the general trend in C++ is away from using the preprocessor for everything except *#include*. ■

How do they work?

To declare a constant variable, just tack the keyword *const* on the front of the declaration. For example:

```
const int radiusOfEarth = 3959; //[miles]

void someFn()
{
    radiusOfEarth = 0;          //illegal
    int r = ++radiusOfEarth;    //also illegal
}
```

The first assignment is illegal. The declaration of *r* is also illegal because it has the side effect of changing the constant.

Because the value of a *const* variable can't be changed, if it is to have any value except zero it must be initialized when defined, as in the previous examples. For example, the following is not allowed:

```
const int radiusOfEarth;
radiusOfEarth = 3959;    //this is not allowed, remember?
```

const variables must be initialized when declared. (You'll never get another chance.) ∎

const variables don't have to be initialized with a constant. They can be initialized also with the results of an expression. For example:

```
const int radiusOfEarthInMiles = 3959;
void fn()
{
   //example 1
   const int radiusOfEarthInKM = 1.609 * radiusOfEarthInMiles;

   //example 2
   const double distanceFromSun = calcDistanceFromSun();
}
```

There is one difference between the two cases shown, however. The compiler knows everything it requires to calculate the value of *radiusOfEarthInKM* at compile time (that is, while generating the code). However, it cannot calculate the value of *distanceFromSun* without executing the function *calcDistanceFromSun()*, which won't happen until the program executes.

So? Well, *const* variables whose values are known at compile time can be used to allocate arrays and things like that, but *const* variables whose values are not known at compile time can't. It's easier to show you than to explain it:

```
const int maxNameLength = 20;
const int numberOfNames = 100;

void fn()
{
   //this is allowed because both values are known
   //at compile time
   char blockForNames[maxNameLength * numberOfNames];

   //the following is not allowed because longestName
   //is not known until the program executes
   const int longestName = calcLongestName();
   char anotherBlock[longestName * numberOfNames];
}
```

Like all variables, a *const* variable can be declared external, as in the following example:

```
extern const int radiusOfEarth; //defined somewhere else
```

In this case, the value of the variable is not known at compile time and so it cannot be used to declare the size of arrays. In addition, this declaration does not attempt to initialize the value of the variable — the module that allocates the space gets to do that. Aside from these facts, an *extern const* is no different than other *const* variables.

The *const* keyword is part of ANSI C as well (they borrowed it from C++). In C, however, *const* variables are more like regular variables and less like constants. For example, *const* variables in C cannot be used to initialize arrays. ■

Volatile Variables

There is yet another storage class called *volatile*. This storage class has the same syntax as *const*, but almost the opposite meaning. Tagging a variable *volatile* tells the compiler that the value of the variable might change at any time.

Applying *const* to pointers

The *const* keyword can be applied to pointers. However, this introduces an interesting ambiguity. Where does the *const* go? Before the type? After the type but before the variable name? The answer is "either," but the results are different. Consider the following examples:

```
int main()
{
    const char * pCC = "this is a constant string";
    char * const cpC = "this is also a string";

    *pCC = 'a';                //assignment #1 - illegal
    *cpC = 'b';                //assignment #2 - legal

    pCC = "another string";    //assignment #3 - legal
    cpC = "another string";    //assignment #4 - illegal
    return 0;
}
```

What is and isn't constant in the declaration of *pCC* and *cpC*? The rule is that the "*const* ness" applies to the thing immediately to the right of the *const* keyword.

The four assignments help sort it out. Compiling the preceding example generates an error message on assignments 1 and 4. Thus, *pCC* is a normal pointer to a constant character string. That is, while *pCC* can be changed (assignment 3), the character string to which it points cannot (assignment 1). By comparison, *cpC* is a constant pointer to a normal character string. Thus, the string pointed to by *cpC* can be changed (assignment 2), but the pointer itself cannot (assignment 4).

Why do I need them?

Compilers try to cache into registers the value of frequently used variables. This results in fewer memory accesses, making the program faster. However, if a memory location might change at any time, the compiler must reload the variable every time it's referred to. Declaring a variable *volatile* precludes the compiler from caching it.

What could possibly change the value of a variable without the program knowing about it? On some processors (such as the 680x0 line of processors, which drive the Macintosh), input devices look like memory locations whose value magically changes as data comes pouring in. In the IBM PC world, the main types of volatiles are variables that refer to locations the program shares with other programs that execute asynchronously. In the DOS world, this means interrupt handlers. For example, programs that read the time variable directly from lower memory should declare it *volatile*. In Windows NT and OS/2, shared memory locations should also be declared volatile. ■

How do they work?

The syntax of *volatile* is identical to that of *const*. Compare the following code snippets to *const* variables:

```
volatile int volatileGlobal;
volatile int *pPointerToVolatile;
int * volatile *pVolatilePointerToNormalInt;
```

Declaring a variable *volatile* keeps the optimizer from caching the variable's value in a register. Every time the program refers to the variable, it is reloaded from memory.

For example, suppose that on our 68000 processor we were expecting input from our 8-bit device at location 0xF8000000. We might try looking for it like this:

```
//pointer to the input port
char *pInputPort = (char*)0xF8000000;

//readPort - read an input port for nonzero data
char readPort()
{
    char c;
    //keep reading the port until we get a nonzero
    while ((c = *pInputPort) == 0)
    {
    }
    //return whatever we got
    return c;
}
```

Because the compiler doesn't know that the location pointed to by *pInputPort* can change, it will probably fetch the value located there once and never look at it again. When data does arrive, our program will never notice it.

Declaring the pointer *volatile* solves the problem, as follows:

```
//pointer to the input port
volatile char *pInputPort = (char*)0xF8000000;

//readPort - read an input port for nonzero data
char readPort()
{
    char c;
    //keep reading the port until we get a nonzero
    while ((c = *pInputPort) == 0)
    {
    }
    //return whatever we got
    return c;
}
```

Declaring a variable *volatile* when it doesn't need to be results in a slightly slower program. PC programmers almost never need to declare variables *volatile*.

The Referential Type Specifier

C++ retains the pointer types introduced by C. In addition, C++ introduces something called reference variables. *Reference variables* allow you to declare a variable that acts as an alias to some other base variable. Once you declare the reference variable, accessing it has the same effect as accessing the base variable.

For example, in the following code snippet, *i* is an *int*. Adding the ampersand squiggle to the declaration of *refI* makes it a reference, in this case to *i*.

```
int i;
int &refI = i;
```

Any subsequent reference to *refI* is the same as referring to *i* directly. Thus, the following statements have the same effect:

```
int i;
int &refI = i;          //declared refI as an alias for i
int *pI;

i = 2;                  //sets i to 2 (what else?)
refI = 3;               //sets i to 3
```

continued

```
pI = &i;              //&i return address of i
pI = &refI;           //&refi also returns address of i
```

Notice that even *&refI* returns the address of *i*.

Why do I need it?

At first blush, this looks just about worthless. If accessing *refI* has the same effect as accessing *i*, why not just access *i* itself and be finished with it?

Reference variables solve in a very convenient way a nuisance that has been confusing programmers almost from the day they first went to C. Consider the following simplistic code segment:

```
void changeArgument(int I)
{
    I = 10;
}
int main()
{
    int i = 5;
    changeArgument(i);
    //the value of i here is still 5

    return 0;
}
```

Here, it's pretty obvious that the programmer wants the function *changeArgument()* to change the value of *I* not only in *changeArgument()* but also in *main()*. Because C always passes function arguments by value, however, that's not what happens. When *changeArgument()* is called, the value 5 is passed (because that's what *i* contains when the call is made). By the time the value gets to *changeArgument()*, there is no connection between *I* and *i*.

Declaring *I* to be reference to *i* solves the problem. Now, *I* becomes an alias to *i*. Anything you might do to *I* also affects *i* — even setting its value to 10.

How does it work?

Let's see how the preceding function would look with *I* declared as a reference:

```
void changeArgument(int &refI)    //just add the squiggle
{
    refI = 10;                //looks like a normal assignment
}
int main()
{
```

```
int i = 5;
changeArgument(i);    //no change to the call
//the value of i is now 10

return 0;
}
```

Adding the & squiggle to the declaration of *ref1* makes it a reference variable. Now when *main()* calls *changeArgument()*, *ref1* becomes a reference to *i*. Any change to *ref1* now affects *i* directly.

C programmers handle this problem by passing the address of the variable to the function. The function can then dereference the pointer back to the original variable. It looks like this:

```
void changeArgument(int *pI)
{
   *pI = 10;
}
int main()
{
   int i = 5;
   changeArgument(&i);
   //the value of i here is now 10

   return 0;
}
```

You can see that what gets passed to *changeArguments()* this way is not 5 but the address of *i*. This lets the function "reach back" into *i* and change its value.

This works okay, but it confuses people who aren't used to C pointers. (Sometimes it even confuses those who are.)

C++ is doing the same thing. The variable *ref1* is like a pointer that C++ initializes with the address of *i*. Every time *ref1* is used, C++ applies the * automatically. Thus, at the machine language level, the C++ reference solution is doing the same thing as the C solution, only references let C++ worry about the grungy details of taking addresses and dereferencing pointers. (This is fine with me because computers are a lot better at handling grungy details than I am.) ■

After a reference variable has been declared, there is nothing you can do to access the reference variable itself. That's why a reference variable must be initialized when it is declared — there is no other time when you have the opportunity to grab the reference variable without slipping through to the base variable. Reference variables declared as arguments to functions get initialized when the function is called.

A reference variable must be initialized when declared. ■

Passing variables to functions by reference can also save a considerable amount of memory and time. Normally when an object is passed to a function by value, the entire object is copied to the stack for the function to use. This is not a problem for small objects like integers and floats, but it can add up to a large amount of memory and time for large structures. Passing the object by reference causes the address of the object to be passed to the function. This address is the same size, irrespective of the size of the object.

Consider the following example:

```
struct ReallyBigArrayType
{
    int reallyBigArray[10000];
} reallyBigObject;
void fn1(ReallyBigArrayType rbo);
void fn2(ReallyBigArrayType &refRBO);
```

To call *fn1( )* a 10,000 word object must be copied to the stack. To call *fn2( )*, however, only a single address must be copied. ∎

Conclusion

You're probably feeling pretty sure of yourself now. "That C++ is no big deal," you say. But we've only started. Now that we've tickled our syntactic fancy with a few isolated features, let's take a look at how C++ handles functions.

Chapter 6
Functions, I Declare!

· ·

In This Chapter

▶ Formulating function prototypes

▶ The joys of strong typing

▶ Defining and using inline functions

▶ Overloading function names

▶ Providing default arguments to functions

· ·

*I*n this chapter, we discuss function prototypes. You may remember from your C days that function prototypes are not exactly a new feature to C. Even old K&R C allowed the programmer to declare the return type of a function, although not the function argument types. Nobody did, of course, because it wasn't required unless the function returned something other than *int* or *void*. ANSI C expanded the concept of function prototypes by allowing function arguments to be prototyped as well. C++ expands on the concept even further. In addition, C++ makes such prototypes a requirement.

Function Prototypes

C++ wants to know the type of each function called. The function type includes the type of the value returned by the function and the number and type of each argument. The programmer provides this information by including a prototype declaration of the function before calling the function.

The prototype declaration looks just like a function definition except that it has no code. (In computerese we say the function has no body, like my hair.)

Here I am using the politically correct terms *declaration* and *definition* currently in style among language lawyers. A *declaration* introduces a name into the program. ("Good day Mr. Program. This is function *f()*. Function *f()*, this is Mr. Program.") A *definition* is a declaration that also tells the program all there is to know about the function. Thus, these are declarations:

```
struct MyStruct;
int max(int x, int y);
```

whereas these are definitions:

```
struct MyStruct
{
    int a;
    int b;
};

int max(int x, int y)

{   return (x > y) ? (x) : (y);
}
```

Notice that a definition is automatically also a declaration. ■

Why do I need them?

I have a central rule (actually, I have a lot of central rules, but this one is way up on the list): If a machine can do the work instead of me, let it. In K&R C, calling functions with the wrong arguments is probably the most common program-ming error. Strict function prototyping makes this error a thing of the past.

After a function prototype declaration has been made, the compiler can care-fully compare each use of the function with the prototype to determine whether the function is being called properly. Calling the function with the wrong argu-ments sets off more alarms than leaning on a parked Porsche. And correcting the problem is easy when you've got bird dog C++ pointing straight to it.

Why do I want my compiler bitching at me?

Now why is it that I want my compiler complaining about my code? Don't I get enough hassle from my boss? Besides, it's embarrassing to have a mere ma-chine complaining, especially if it's right. (I don't have to worry about that with my boss.)

Humans and computers don't communicate well. They don't think alike or talk alike. You need to tell the compiler all you can about what you want it to do. You also want to turn the compiler into a skeptical curmudgeon — and avoid miscommunication — by enabling all the warning messages possible.

People didn't always have this idea. The first computer languages (such as Fortran) took the opposite approach. The motto was: Less work for the pro-grammer. Someone says, "Hey, no sense forcing the programmer to declare variables. We'll just use the first letter to determine the type and go from there." Great idea. Not!

Now if you misspell a variable name in Fortran, does the compiler tell you about it? Heck no. It just makes up a new variable with a slightly different name and a random value, and then pushes on. When you finish coding and the program doesn't work, you can debug the program and eventually find the misspelling.

But that's the rub: you, the human, must find a problem that the computer can find automatically.

This concept of "make sense out of whatever the programmer throws at us" was taken to its illogical extreme by IBM in the language PL/1. This compiler had a special Check Out version that was undauntable — it would make some kind of sense out of absolutely anything you provided it.

When I was just a wag in college, I was always looking for a way to have fun and show my superior intelligence. I just loved to torture PL/1 with existential statements like *IF*. That's it, just *IF*, not followed by anything. Believe it or not, PL/1 would construct what it thought I meant. (It derived *IF (.TRUE.) CONTINUE;* through some entertaining but amazingly complex logic that I really don't want to go into.)

Of course, what it thought I meant was wrong. I know it was wrong because I didn't mean anything at all. I was just having fun and wasting valuable CPU cycles. (People worried about wasted CPU cycles back then.)

Any time you leave these types of decisions up to the computer, you are asking for trouble because the computer might be wrong. Even if the computer is right most of the time, it will be wrong when you can least afford it, and you will spend time trying to find the misunderstanding.

How much better your programming life — and your personal relationships — will be if you just get these issues on the table up front and don't leave anything open to possible misinterpretation.

The moral is:

- ✔ Be honest in your relationships
- ✔ Enable all warnings
- ✔ Leave nothing to the computer's deranged imaginations
- ✔ If you are ever on a computer language standards committee, remember PL/1

How do they work?

A prototype declaration looks just like a function definition without any code. Consider the following example:

```
int max(int a, int b);
```

This declares *max()* to be a function that takes an integer followed by another integer and returns an integer. The statement doesn't say anything about what *max()* does with the integers it receives or how *max()* generates the integer it returns. That's left to the definition. The prototype just allows the compiler to check subsequent attempts to call the function and flag any that are wrong.

Place your definitions in a .CPP file. Place the prototype declarations in a .H file of the same name. Include the .H file in the .CPP file. During compilation, the compiler will check the definitions against the prototype declarations and flag any differences. You can then include the .H file in any file that calls one of the functions. The compiler compares the use of the function to the prototype declaration for accuracy.

For example, if *max()*, *min()*, and other functions were defined in a MATH.CPP file, we might define MATH.HPP as follows:

```
//MATH.H
int max(int a, int b);
int min(int a, int b);
```

The application file then appears as follows:

```
#include "MATH.H"
void myFunc(int a)

{    a = max(a, -a);           //make sure a is positive
                               //...etc...
}
```

Borland used .HPP for include files. Microsoft used .CXX for C++ source files and .HXX for include files. UNIX C++ compilers sometimes use this latter standard. However, the more recent convention is .CPP for source files and .H for include files. ■

If a function returns nothing, it should be declared as returning *void*. As in C, *void* in C++ is the word for "nothing." If the function takes no arguments, it should be declared with *void* arguments or with an empty argument list, as in *example3()*:

```
void example1(int a, float b); //takes an int and a float
                               //and returns nothing
```

```
void example2(void);        //takes nothing and returns nothing
void example3();            //same as example3(void)
```

When C++ sees an empty argument list, it assumes the argument is *void*.

In C, a prototype declaration with no arguments means any number of arguments of any type. In this way, ANSI C maintains maximum compatibility with legacy K&R C code, which didn't prototype the function arguments. (Over the years, a company can develop a large amount of code. This code is called *legacy code*. It represents a considerable investment and must be rewritten, at amazing cost, if the company changes to computer systems or languages that are not upwardly compatible. For this reason, ANSI C stays as upwardly compatible as possible with the older K&R C, and C++ stays upwardly compatible with ANSI C.) ■

If the function takes a variable number of arguments or if you don't want to say what arguments it takes, you may declare a function with ellipses, as in the following example:

```
void example4(...);         //any number of any type of args
```

The ellipses mean any number of any type of arguments. Ellipses can also be mixed with known arguments. For example, *printf( )* is commonly declared as a function that takes a pointer to a character followed by an unknown number of unknown arguments:

```
int printf(char* pChar, ...);
```

In a prototype declaration, only the types of the arguments are necessary, not the names of the arguments. The argument names, if present, are ignored. What should the compiler do with them anyway? When the function is called, you can use any argument names you like.

Thus, a function that takes two character pointers, for example, can be declared as follows:

```
int copyString(char *, char *);
```

However, this is generally a bad idea because the name of the variable can tell the reader a lot more about the role of the argument than simply its type.

Compare the preceding prototype declaration with the following:

```
int copyString(char *pTarget, char *pSource);
```

Now, what do the left and right hand arguments do? ■

Strongly typed function pointers

Pointers to functions need to be strongly typed as well. Consider the following example:

```
void function1(int, char*, float);
void function2(int, int);
void fn()
{
    void (*pFn)(int, char*, float);
    pFn = function2;        //this is not allowed; types don't match
    pFn = function1;        //types match here
    (*pFn)(10, 10);         //error here too - wrong arguments
    (*pFn)(10, "ten", 10.0); //arguments match again
}
```

The pointer *pFn* is a fully typed function pointer. We read this as "*pFn* is a pointer to a function that takes an *int*, a *char**, and a *float* and returns a *void*" (or "returns nothing"). In techno shorthand its type is *void (*)(int, char*, float)*.

The first assignment to *pFn* generates a compiler error because the arguments to *function2* are not the same as those specified by *pFn*. In addition, the first attempt to call the function is in error because the use doesn't match the declaration.

Inline Functions

C++ allows functions to be defined with the new keyword *inline*. An *inline function* appears like a normal function in use, but it doesn't act the same. An inline function does not result in a call to a single function; rather, the code for the inline function expands in place wherever the function is used.

Why do I need them?

When a normal function is compiled, the code is put in one location. Every place where the function is called, the compiler sticks in code to jump to that one function. (The program stores the return address so that the function knows where to return when it's finished.) Because only one copy of the code is produced, the resulting executable (.EXE) file is smaller than if the code was duplicated in all the places it's needed. However, the program might be slightly slower because it takes time to make the call.

The overhead of making the call discourages extremely performance-minded programmers from writing small functions even when it might be desirable to do so. Inline functions allow programmers to retain a highly modular style without incurring any overhead.

Can't I do that in C?

C attempts to use *#define* macros, which are defined as follows, to do the same thing that inline functions do:

```
#define square(a)   a * a
```

Unfortunately, macros are tricky. They are processed by a separate preprocessor that has a slightly different syntax than "real" C. Further, because the C compiler sees the output of the preprocessor, which is different than the input you and I see, macros can generate errors that are difficult to track down.

The preceding macro can be easily confused. (Actually, the programmer who tries to use the macro will be confused.) Consider the following example:

```
int squareOfSum(int r1, int r2)
{
   return square(r1 + r2);
}
```

As simple as this function appears, it's not correct. (It's embarrassing when a function with one statement is wrong.) When the preprocessor expands *square()*, it does so directly, without frills. Thus, what the compiler sees is the following:

```
int squareOfSum(int r1, int r2)
{
   return r1 + r2 * r1 + r2;
}
```

Because multiplication is performed before addition, this gets intrepreted as follows. (Go and check the operator precedence rules in Part I if you don't believe me.)

```
int squareOfSum(int r1, int r2)
{
   return r1 + (r2 * r1) + r2;
}
```

Although this and most other problems with macros can be solved, macros are still undesirable because the problems are usually difficult to find.

Inline functions are part of the C++ language and are not processed by the pre-processor. Thus, inline functions do not share the problems of macros. So forget about macros and use inline functions instead. ∎

How do they work?

To inline a function, the programmer adds the keyword *inline* in front of the definition. For example:

```
inline int max(int a, int b)
{
    return (a > b) ? a : b;
}
```

Notice the verb usage in the first sentence. To "inline a function" is to make a function an inline function. A normal (that is, non-inline) function is known in C++ jargon as an *outline function*. This also has a verb form: to outline a function is to force an inline function outline. Also notice that *inline* is now a keyword. If you like to name your C variables "inline," you'll have to find another name now. Have you noticed how I can ramble on about the silliest things? ∎

An inline function is invoked just like any other function. However, rather than generating a single function that each invocation jumps to, the code for an inline function is expanded in place. Thus, the following does not generate a conventional function call:

```
int betterSalary, mySalary, urSalary;
betterSalary = max(mySalary, urSalary);
```

Because the code body is necessary to expand an inline function, you must define an inline function before it can be used — a prototype declaration is not enough. It is common to define inline functions in the same .H files in which you prototype your outline functions.

Inline functions are the only type of function that you should define in an include file. Conventional outline functions should not be defined in include files. ∎

Inline functions are useful only for small functions. There is little overhead when making a function call. If the function is more than a few lines, the time to make the call is swamped by the time required to execute the function. As the function's size increases, the disadvantage of expanding the function every time it's called also increases.

The break-even point for an inline function is about three executable lines. Thus, if a function contains three executable lines or less and is executed often (**in a time critical loop**, for example), consider making it an inline function. ∎

How much faster is faster?

To demonstrate the types of improvement you can expect using inline functions, I timed the following program:

```
//inline max function
inline int maxi(int x, int y)
{
    return (x > y) ? x : y;
}

//outline version of the same thing
int maxo(int x, int y)
{
    return (x > y) ? x : y;
}

int main()
{
    int i, j = 5000, k, loop;

    //first straight
    for (loop = 0; loop < 100; loop++)
    {
        for (i = 0; i < 10000; i++)
        {
            k = (i > j) ? i : j;
        }
    }

    //now as an inline function
    for (loop = 0; loop < 100; loop++)
    {
        for (i = 0; i < 10000; i++)
        {
            k = maxi(i, j);
        }
    }

    //now as an outline function
    for (loop = 0; loop < 100; loop++)
    {
        for (i = 0; i < 10000; i++)
        {
            k = maxo(i, j);
        }
    }
    return 0;
}
```

The straight and inline versions of the loop showed identical execution times (23 ticks). The outline version of the loop took over three times longer to execute (87 ticks). Advantage: inline.

I then repeated the experiment with a more complicated version of the *max()* function. (Okay, the additions are nonsensical, but that doesn't make any difference.)

```
inline int maxi(int x, int y)
{
   x = (x * 4) >> 2;          //this has no effect
   y = (y * 4) >> 2;          //but what does the compiler know?
   x = (x * 4) >> 2;
   y = (y * 4) >> 2;
   return (x > y) ? x : y;
}
int maxo(int x, int y)
{
   x = (x * 4) >> 2;
   y = (y * 4) >> 2;
   x = (x * 4) >> 2;
   y = (y * 4) >> 2;
   return (x > y) ? x : y;
}
```

The resulting *maxi()* function ran only 11% faster than the outline version (98 versus 110 clock ticks). Deuce.

Because an inline function is expanded as part of each line that calls it, you cannot single step an inline function with the debugger. The entire inline function executes as a single line no matter how many lines it contains and no matter how much havoc those lines might cause.

This is a problem during debugging. To debug an inline function, you should first change it to an outline function. To do this, you can just remove the *inline* keyword and recompile. Because this is a hassle, most compilers provide a compile-time switch that automatically outlines all inline functions. For the Borland C++, Turbo C++, and Microsoft Visual C++ compilers, this switch is under the C++ compiler options. When you have finished debugging, recompile without the compiler option switch to re-inline the inline functions. ■

Even if you declare a function to be inline, several things might force the function outline. For example, including any type of looping statement (such as a *for* loop) in a function usually forces it outline. You shouldn't declare a function like that inline anyway, because the time it takes to execute the loop overshadows any minor gain from declaring the function inline. Depending on the compiler, other things might force a function outline as well. (The draft standard for C++ allows for all sorts of things.) ■

Borland C++ is pretty good about keeping inline functions inline; loops are about the only thing it can't handle. In addition, Borland C++ generates a warning when it is forced to outline an inline function because of something you've done in the function.

Microsoft compilers before Visual C++ outlined an inline function if it had any control structures, such as *if*. Visual C++ has a compiler switch that allows the programmer to force the function outline, force the function outline if it has any "funny stuff" (such as *if*s), or keep the function inline unless absolutely forced out. ■

Function Overloading

Unlike most other languages, C++ allows functions to have the same name if it can tell the functions apart by the number and type of the arguments to the function during use. For example, the following two functions are not considered the same:

```
int date(int   year);
int date(char *pPerson);
```

That is, applying the function *date( )* to a *year* is different than applying *date( )* to *aPerson*.

This is known as *overloading* the function name.

Why do I need it?

Why not? I have two friends named David and I have no trouble telling them apart; their hair color is different and one has a broken arm. I have no trouble telling *date(1993)* and *date(someGuy)* apart, so why should the computer?

Function overloading is useful in avoiding an annoyance. In C, I am forced to use different names for similar functions. For example, consider the following set of C *square( )* functions. Each is designed to return the square of its argument:

```
int    squareInt(int);   //square for int
float  squareFlt(float); //square for float
double squareDbl(double);//square for double
```

If I had more functions, I would need a set of *...Int* functions, each with a corresponding *...Flt* and *...Dbl* function. With function overloading, this isn't necessary:

```
int    square(int    i);
float  square(float  f);
double square(double d);
```

You could argue, "Why have all those silly functions? Just define the *double* version and use it for *float*s and *int*s as well." This is not a convincing argument.

(If it were, I wouldn't have mentioned it.) Squaring a double-precision floating point number takes a lot more computing than squaring an integer. Besides, I could think of other examples (just give me a moment) where using a single function wouldn't work anyway.

How does it work?

There's not too much to declaring overloaded functions: declare them as you would any other function. Just make sure that the arguments are sufficiently different to allow the functions to be differentiated in use.

The technical term for differentiating two or more overloaded functions by the way they are used is *disambiguation*, believe it or not. ■

For example, I might implement the previously mentioned set of square functions as follows:

```
int square(int i)
{
    return i*i;
}
float square(float f)
{
    return f*f;
}
double square(double d)
{
    return d*d;
}

int main()
{
    int   i = 2;
    float f = 3.0;
    double d = 4.0;
    i = square(i);    //calls square for ints
    f = square(f);    //calls square for floats
    d = square(d);    //calls square for doubles
    return 0;
}
```

Compile and execute this program to convince yourself that this works. Single step through each function call. It's amazing the first time you do it. When I was learning C++ (many moons ago), executing this program was the first time I got the feeling that C++ was not just a jazzed up C. ■

The argument types are said to be part of the function's extended name (also called the *function signature*). Thus, the name of the function might be *square()* while the extended name is *square(int)* (pronounced "square int"). ■

What constitutes "sufficiently different"?

Okay, so we've said that C++ can tell two or more functions with the same name apart as long as the arguments are sufficiently different. The problem is: what constitutes "sufficiently different"?

Obviously the following functions are different:

```
int fn(int i);
int fn(char c);          //different argument type
int fn(int i, int j);    //different no. of arguments
int fn(int *pI);         //pointer to an int is not the
                         //same type as an int
```

Different pointer types are sufficiently different as well:

```
int fn(int  *pI);
int fn(char *pC);        //char* is not same as int*
```

Signed-ness (for example, *int* versus *unsigned int*) and *const*-ness are also sufficiently different to tell functions apart. But if you do something like the following, you're probably just trying to confuse yourself and anyone else who might come along and try to read your code:

```
int fn(int i);
int fn(unsigned i);      //this is a different function
```

So what's not different enough?

So what types of differences don't qualify as different enough? Functions cannot be differentiated by their return type. For example, the following functions are not sufficiently different.

```
int   fn(int i);
float fn(int i);         //must differ by more
                         //than return type
```

A simple type cannot be overloaded with a reference type:

```
int   fn(int  i);
int   fn(int &refI);     //not different enough
```

Functions with non-specific arguments cannot be overloaded for obvious reasons. Consider the following example:

```
int fn(int i, ...);      //int followed by anything
int fn(int i, float f);  //int followed by a float
int main()
```

```
{
    fn(1, 2.0);                //which one?
}
```

Finally, all C functions, including those that make up the Standard C Library, cannot be overloaded.

Print what you want about me but don't mangle the name

How does C++ keep functions with the same name straight during the link step? For example, suppose MOD_A.CPP has two functions, *f(int)* and *f(char)*. If a function in a separate module calls one of these functions, how does the linker keep them straight?

C++ uses a complex technique called *name mangling* to sort the versions of functions with the same name at link time. A complete discussion of name mangling is too complicated to go into here. The main point is that the types of the arguments become part of the function name that is passed to the linker. For example, the previous two functions might be called something like *f_i()* and *f_c()*. For the most part, you can ignore name mangling. However, you do need to be aware of two cases in which name mangling does cause a problem.

Case 1

C doesn't allow function overloading and therefore has no use for name mangling. Therefore, when declaring a C function you need to tell C++ not to mangle it. C++ extended the *extern* keyword to allow you to do this, as follows:

```
extern "C" int printf(char *, ...);
```

This declares *printf()* to be a C function. Because it isn't a C++ function, its name doesn't get mangled. If you have more than one C function to declare, you can combine them as follows:

```
extern "C"
{
    int firstCFunc();
    int secondCFunc();
    int thirdCFunc();
}
```

Such a block can also include an include file:

```
extern "C"
{
#include "myinclud.h"
}
```

In this construct, all the functions declared in the include file are declared as C functions.

Normally, you have to enclose an include file in an extern "C" block only if you have a library of C routines that you link with your programs and for which you don't have the source.

If you forget to declare a C function properly, you get an obscure link time error rather than a compile time error. Consider the following example:

```
int printf(char*,....);
int main()
{
    printf("Hello world\n");
    return 0;
}
```

C++ assumes from the prototype that *printf()* is a C++ function. It then mangles the name to add the *char** and ... signature to the extended name. When it then tries to link, the linker sees no connection between the C++ function *printf(char*, ...)* and the C function *printf()*. The result is the following:

```
Error: undefined external function printf(char*)
```

You can solve the problem by including the proper standard C library .H file, which declares functions correctly by using extern "C" blocks where necessary.

```
#include <stdio.h>
int main()
{
    printf("Hello world\n");
    return 0;
}
```

This works as expected. ■

Case 2

In general, you cannot link object files from two different C++ compilers. Name mangling is not standardized and functions won't link correctly. For example, if your friend compiles a file with the Microsoft compiler and gives you the .OBJ file to link with your Borland modules, it won't work. Just recompile your friend's source code and things should work out fine. ■

Default Arguments to Functions

C++ allows functions to be declared with default arguments. If a default argument is not provided in the call, the default value is provided automatically. In the following function, the second argument defaults to zero. Thus the calls on line 2 and line 3 are equivalent.

```
//the second argument defaults to zero if not present
int sampleFunc(int x, int y = 0);
int main()
{
    sampleFunc(1, 2);     //Line 1 - this is okay;
                          //         don't use the default
    sampleFunc(1, 0);     //Line 2
    sampleFunc(1);        //Line 3 - same as line 2
    return 0;
}
```

Because the call on line 3 provides only one argument, C++ provides the default second argument of 0 from the prototype declaration.

Why do I need them?

This is another cutesy feature. I can't think of any overpowering reason for it, but it can be sort of nice. For example:

```
int calculateWeeklyPay(int payRate, int hoursWorked = 40);
```

This function is designed to calculate the pay an employee will receive for one week's employment. Because the normal work week is 40 hours, I put that in as the default; however, if a particular employee works something other than 40 hours, that's allowed as well.

How do they work?

Default values can be provided for more than one argument, but they must be specified from right to left. For example, if you have a function that takes two arguments, you can't provide a default value for only the first (left) one.

Defaults are filled in by the compiler in a strictly right to left fashion as well, even if the types would seem to indicate that the programmer had some grander scheme in mind. Consider the following:

```
void fillInGrade(char *pLName, char *pMI = "NMI", int age = 0);
int main()
{
    fillInGrade("Davis", 37); //not legal
    return 0;
}
```

You and I can see that what's missing in the call is the middle initial argument, but C++ makes no attempt at this type of interpretation. If there are two arguments provided in the call, it must be the third argument that is defaulted, resulting in the following (mis)interpretation:

```
int main()
{
    fillInGrade("Davis", 37, 0); //interpretation of preceding
    return 0;
}
```

Because the integer 37 cannot be converted to a pointer to a character, an error is generated.

You can get the desired effect of a default middle argument using function overloading, as in the following example:

```
void fillInGrade(char *pName, char *pMI, int age = 0);
inline void fillInGrade(char *pName, int age = 0)
{
    fillInGrade(pName, "NMI", age);
}
```

Now a call such as *fillInGrade("Davis", 37)* invokes the inline function, which turns right around and calls the first function with the *pMI* argument filled in with the desired default. This is why default arguments are not really necessary — the clever use of function overloading can generate the same effect. ∎

Being overloadingly argumentative

Default arguments can sometimes confuse function overloading. Consider the example in the preceding section. Suppose we had the following (clever) function declarations:

```
void fillInGrade(char *pName, char *pMI = "NMI", int age = 0);
void fillInGrade(char *pLast, char *pFirst);
```

Now a call like the following is ambiguous:

```
int main()
{
    fillInGrade("Davis", "Stephen"); //which one?
    return 0;
}
```

You and I can see that this call is trying to access the second function. But the compiler, being stupid, doesn't know that you're not trying to call the first function with a default age of 0. Because the compiler can't decide which of the two functions you mean to call, it generates an error.

When both overloading and providing default arguments, make sure that all the possible ways that the functions can be called are unambiguous. When in doubt, don't use default arguments for overloaded functions. ■

Conclusion

The function declaration is optional in K&R C but a requirement in C++. Rather than being forced to eat in K&R's kitchen, function declaration can take its rightful place at the head of the table in C++. Function declarations not only allow the compiler to do a better job of error detection, they also allow the same function name to be overlaid with different meanings. This feature will prove to be very important in later chapters.

With all we've seen, C++ still looks like C with racing stripes. With the introduction of stream I/O in the next chapter, however, C++ begins to look like a truly new language.

Chapter 7
Stream Input and Output

· ·

In This Chapter

▶ Introduction to stream I/O

▶ What's wrong with *printf()*?

▶ Using stream I/O

▶ Drawing parallels between C I/O and stream I/O

· ·

C++ defines a new input/output mechanism in addition to *printf()*. This mechanism, called *stream I/O*, is based on redefining the << operator to perform output and the >> operator to perform input.

When redefined, << is known as the *insertion operator* and >> is called the *extraction operator* to differentiate them from the left-shift and right-shift operators.

Why Do I Need Streams after the Rivers of printf ()s I'm Used to?

The change to stream I/O is probably the most difficult adjustment for the beginning C++ programmer. "What? Take my *printf()*? You'll have to pry it from my cold, dead fingers." To me, *printf()* and *scanf()* are like my old, beat-up Honda. They work, I'm familiar with them, but if the truth be known they break down sometimes and they don't carry very much. To say the same thing in computerese, they're not type safe and they're not extensible.

The case for stream I/O: part 1

Ladies and gentlemen of the jury, let's consider the first charge first (that's logical): strong typing. Prototype declarations save us from ourselves in lots of different cases, but they aren't much help with *scanf()* and *printf()*. The number and type of function arguments that *printf()* and *scanf()* expect depends on information encoded in the first argument. This information isn't available to the compiler, so the compiler cannot check my calls to *printf()* and *scanf()* to see if they are proper.

If I call either function improperly, there's nothing that C or C++ can do to help me out. Usually, this is not a big problem with *printf()*; I get garbage for output and check what's wrong.

The situation with *scanf()* is much worse. Consider the following example:

```
int i = 10;
scanf("%d", i);
```

The call is in error because I should have passed the address of *i* instead of the value of *i*. However, without a descriptive prototype to tell it otherwise, the compiler does not complain. The compiler assumes that the value *scanf()* gets (10 in this example) is an address, and it stores the integer read into that address. In this case, the value that *scanf()* reads is stored in location 10.

We can only hope that this mistake is fatal so that we are alerted to the problem. (On UNIX systems it probably is fatal; on DOS or Mac systems, it probably isn't, at least not right away.) If it isn't, we've just overwritten some random location that will eventually come back to haunt us. These problems (and premature hair loss) are the kinds of problems that keep systems programmers like myself awake at night.

The case for stream I/O: part 2

Now, jury members, let us consider the second charge before us today, that of extensibility. But before we do that, what is extensibility anyway? *Extensibility* means that we can add to the definition of our I/O mechanism to handle any new structures that we might create.

printf() knows how to output strings, integers, and floating points. That's basically it. Sure, you can change the number of significant digits, change the base to 10 or 16, control whether the left or the right is padded with spaces or zeros, and control a host of other things, but these features are window dressing. You can't teach *printf()* to output a new structure of your own invention.

Stream I/O is extensible. For example, having defined a structure *MyStruct*, I can teach the insertion operator how to output one of those and I can teach the extraction operator how to read one. The details of how we do this are left to Chapter 25.

How Does Stream I/O Work?

Before you can use I/O streams in your program, you must include *iostreams.h*. This include file is one of the standard include files provided by C++.

Depending on the environment, *iostreams.h* is a very big include file. Therefore, you might want to enable the precompiled headers switch if your compiler supports that. Both Borland and Microsoft do. (Look in the compiler options menu under the C++ options). ■

Precompiled headers is a feature in which the compiler saves in a separate file the result of compiling the include files. The next time you compile your module, the compiler rereads that file rather than recompile the sometimes enormous include files. It does this as long as you don't edit one of the include files or change the order in which they're included in the module. This feature greatly increases the speed of compilations, except for the first one.

Note that precompiled headers also work for different source files if they include the same include files in the same order. The basic rule is: Include files in the same way and your compilations will be faster all day. (Check your compiler documentation for details.) ■

The *iostream.h* include file defines some default devices. These are shown in Table 7-1. Standard input is normally the keyboard. Standard output and standard error output are normally the screen.

Table 7-1: The Standard Stream Devices

C++ name	Device	C name	Default meaning
cin	keyboard	stdin	standard input
cout	screen	stdout	standard output
cerr	screen	stderr	standard error
cprn	printer	stdprn	printer

Table 7-1 also shows the corresponding default devices in C. Remember that *printf()* is just shorthand for *fprintf(stdout,...)* and *scanf()* is shorthand for *fscanf(stdin,...)*. ■

The object *cout* corresponds to the default input (usually the display) just like *stdout* does with *fprintf()*. Likewise, *cin* corresponds to the default input (usually the keyboard), just like *stdin* does with *fscanf()*.

The following function outputs to the display whatever name is passed it:

```
#include <iostream.h>
void outName(char *pName)
{
   cout << "My name is";
   cout << pName;
   cout << "\n";
}
```

Both insertion and extraction operations can be strung on a single line. Thus, the preceding function and the following one have the same effect:

```
#include <iostream.h>
void outName(char *pName)
{
   cout << "My name is "
        << pName
        << "\n";
}
```

The extra newlines in the previous code snippet are ignored. I could have written the following:

```
cout << "My name is " << pName << "\n";
```

but I thought the three separate lines looked nicer.

In the previous examples, all the objects being inserted are of the same type, *char**; however, different types can be strung together as well. This is shown in the following example:

```
void outSSNum(long ssNumber)
{
   cout << "Social Security Number ="
        << ssNumber
        << '\n';
}
```

Here we see the advantage of streams over *printf()*. Nothing about the output line, other than the object itself, tells the compiler the types of the objects to be printed. Compare this with the equivalent *printf()*-based function:

```
void outSSNum(long ssNumber)
{
   printf("Social Security Number = %ld\n",
          ssNumber);
}
```

The *%ld* tells *printf()* that *ssNumber* is a *long*. If this information is not correct, *printf()* will not generate the proper output. With the stream output solution, this type of error is not possible.

Conclusion

Stream I/O is one of those features that you can ignore for a while, if you absolutely insist. However, I think you should give it a try. You already bought the book.

In Chapter 25, when we know a lot more about C++, we will revisit stream I/O. Then you'll find there's a lot more that stream I/O can do for you, and you might be more tempted to try it.

After you've finished the book and done a little C++ programming using streams, feel free to return to your old *printf()* ways, if you really want to.

Rewriting BUDGET as a C++ Program: BUDGET2.CPP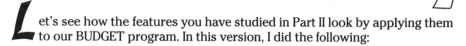

*L*et's see how the features you have studied in Part II look by applying them to our BUDGET program. In this version, I did the following:

- ✔ Changed comments to the new style
- ✔ Overloaded the functions *init()* and *process()* to highlight the similarities between the checking and savings account versions
- ✔ Used referential arguments to avoid pointer types
- ✔ Converted *init()* to an inline function because of its small size
- ✔ Declared variables near their point of use
- ✔ Converted my I/O to stream I/O
- ✔ Replaced *#defines* with *const* variables

Although this is a C++ program (if you don't believe it, just try compiling it with your old C compiler), not much has changed philosophically. This is not an object-oriented program in any sense of the word.

```
//BUDGET2.CPP - Budget program in the "C++ as a better C"
//              version.

#include <iostream.h>

//the maximum number of accounts you can have
const int maxAccounts = 10;

//Checking - this describes checking accounts
struct Checking
{
   unsigned accountNumber;
   float    balance;
} chkAcnts[maxAccounts];

//Savings - you can probably figure this one out
struct Savings
{
   unsigned accountNumber;
   float    balance;
```

continued

```
    int      noWithdrawals;
    } svgAcnts[maxAccounts];

//prototype declarations
void process(Checking &checking);        //Note 1
void process(Savings &savings);

//inline functions
//init(Checking) - initialize a checking account
inline void init(Checking &checking)    //Note 2
{
    cout << "Enter account number:";
    cin  >> checking.accountNumber;
    checking.balance = 0.0;
}

//init(Savings) - initialize a savings account
inline void init(Savings  &savings)
{
    cout << "Enter account number:";
    cin  >> savings.accountNumber;
    savings.balance = 0.0;
    savings.noWithdrawals = 0;
}

//main - accumulate the initial input and output totals
int main()
{
    /*loop until someone enters an 'X' or 'x'*/
    int noChkAccounts = 0;      //count the number of accounts
    int noSvgAccounts = 0;
    char     accountType;       //S or C

    unsigned keepLooping = 1;
    while (keepLooping)
    {
        cout << "Enter S for Savings, "
                "C for Checking, X for exit\n";
        cin  >> accountType;

        switch (accountType)
        {
            case 'c':
            case 'C':
                if (noChkAccounts < maxAccounts)
                {
                    init(chkAcnts[noChkAccounts]);
                    process(chkAcnts[noChkAccounts]);
                    noChkAccounts++;
                }
                else
                {
                    cout << "No more room for checking accounts\n";
                }
                break;
```

```
        case 's':
        case 'S':
            if (noSvgAccounts < maxAccounts)
            {
                init(svgAcnts[noSvgAccounts]);
                process(svgAcnts[noSvgAccounts]);
                noSvgAccounts++;
            }
            else
            {
                cout << "No more room for savings accounts\n";
            }
            break;

        case 'x':
        case 'X':
            keepLooping = 0;
            break;

        default:
            cout << "I didn't get that.\n";
    }
}

//now present totals
float chkTotal = 0;      //total of all checking accounts
cout << "Checking accounts:\n";
for (int i = 0; i < noChkAccounts; i++)  //Note 3
{
    cout << "Account " << chkAcnts[i].accountNumber
         << " = "        << chkAcnts[i].balance
         << "\n";
    chkTotal += chkAcnts[i].balance;
}
float svgTotal = 0;      //total of all savings accounts
cout << "Savings accounts:\n";
for (i = 0; i < noSvgAccounts; i++)       //Note 4
{
    cout << "Account "                << svgAcnts[i].accountNumber
         << " = "                     << svgAcnts[i].balance
         << " (no. withdrawals = " << svgAcnts[i].noWithdrawals
         << ")\n";
    svgTotal += svgAcnts[i].balance;
}

float total = chkTotal + svgTotal;
cout << "Total for checking accounts = " << chkTotal << "\n";
cout << "Total for savings accounts  = " << svgTotal << "\n";
cout << "Total worth                 = " << total << "\n";
return 0;
}

//process(Checking) - input the data for a checking account*/
void process(Checking &checking)
{
    cout << "Enter positive number for deposit,\n"
```

continued

```
                            "negative for check, 0 to terminate";

    float transaction;
    do
    {
        cout << ":";
        cin  >> transaction;

        //is it a deposit?
        if (transaction > 0)
        {
            checking.balance += transaction;
        }

        //how about withdrawal?
        if (transaction < 0)
        {
            //withdrawal
            transaction = -transaction;
            if (checking.balance < transaction)    //Note 5
            {
                cout << "Insufficient funds: balance "
                        << checking.balance
                        << ", check "
                        << transaction
                        << "\n";
            }
            else
            {
                checking.balance -= transaction;

                //if balance falls too low, charge service fee
                if (checking.balance < 500.00)
                {
                    checking.balance -= 0.20;
                }
            }
        }
    } while (transaction != 0);
}

//process(Savings) - input the data for a savings account
void process(Savings &savings)
{
    cout << "Enter positive number for deposit,\n"
            "negative for withdrawal, 0 to terminate";

    float transaction;
    do
    {
        cout << ":";
        cin  >> transaction;

        //is this a deposit?
        if (transaction > 0)
        {
            savings.balance += transaction;
        }
```

```
        //is it a withdrawal?
        if (transaction < 0)
        {
            transaction = -transaction;
            if (savings.balance < transaction)
            {
                cout << "Insufficient funds: balance "
                     << savings.balance
                     << ", withdrawal "
                     << transaction
                     << "\n";
            }
            else
            {
                if (++savings.noWithdrawals > 1)
                {
                    savings.balance -= 5.00;
                }
                savings.balance -= transaction;
            }
        }
    } while (transaction != 0);
}
```

If you give this program the same test data as you gave the C version in Part I,
the output appears almost the same:

```
Enter S for Savings, C for Checking, X for exit
S
Enter account number:123
Enter positive number for deposit,
negative for withdrawal, 0 to terminate:200
:-50
:-50
:0
Enter S for Savings, C for Checking, X for exit
C
Enter account number:234
Enter positive number for deposit,
negative for check, 0 to terminate:200
:-25
:-20
:0
Enter S for Savings, C for Checking, X for exit
X
Checking accounts:
Account 234 = 154.600006
Savings accounts:
Account 123 = 95 (no. withdrawals = 2)
Total for checking accounts = 154.600006
Total for savings accounts  = 95
Total worth                 = 249.600006
```

Notice first that all the comments have changed. (Whoopee. But really, the new
comment style grows on you.)

Also, the names of the functions *processSavings()* and *processChecking()* have been changed to simply *process()*, with the distinction made by the argument types. (See the *Note 1* comment in the code.) In addition, the argument is now a reference to the object rather than a pointer to the object.

The *init()* functions (*Note 2*) have been not only renamed, but also inlined. These are the nice short types of functions that bear inlining (even though there's no performance reason to do so).

The references to *printf()* and *scanf()* have been replaced by their iostream equivalents, which requires inclusion of the *iostream.h* include file instead of *stdio.h*. Notice that I had used fancy *printf()* controls to reduce the number of significant digits after the decimal point to two (for the cents). I didn't do that with iostreams, because we haven't yet seen how to format stream output. For now, we'll have to put up with all those extra digits.

Making declarations at the point of use makes it easier to associate a variable's type with its use. This is especially obvious in places such as the *for* loop (*Note 3*). Notice, however, that after *i* is declared in the first *for* loop, it is not necessary (nor even allowed) to be redeclared in the second *for* loop (*Note 4*).

The arguments to the two *process()* functions are now referential. This means that the . operator is used instead of the -> operator throughout the functions (*Note 5*). These functions could have been declared as follows:

```
void process(Checking checking);
```

This would have also allowed us to use the . notation. However, passing by value would have resulted in a common error that is difficult to find. When *checking* is passed by value, a copy of the original *Checking* object — not the original itself — is passed to the function. The function goes about merrily changing the copy, which is thrown away when the function returns, leaving the original unchanged. (Don't believe it? Just remove & in the argument *checking* in both the prototype and the function, and recompile the program.)

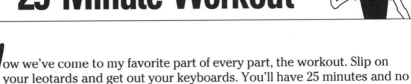

25-Minute Workout

*N*ow we've come to my favorite part of every part, the workout. Slip on your leotards and get out your keyboards. You'll have 25 minutes and no cheating.

1 a. Given the following macro, list any potential problems you can find with it:

```
//TWO_MIN - return 2 * minimum of two numbers
#define TWO_MAX (x, y) x > y ? (2 * x) : (2 * y)
```

b. How can these problems best be avoided?

2 C++ doesn't allow arguments other than the last to be given default values. Thus, the following is wrong:

```
void aFunc(int x, float y = 0.0, char z) {
   cout << "x = "    << x
        << ", y = " << y
        << ", z = " << z
        << "\n";
}
```

Is there some way we can achieve the result we want in this example? (Don't *overload* your brain thinking about this one.)

3 Which of the following overloaded functions are called in each of the calls in *main()*? If any of the calls are ambiguous (that is, they can't be resolved), list all candidates:

```
void fn(int x) {}           //1
void fn(char *x) {}         //2
void fn(void *x) {}         //3
void fn(int x, float y) {}  //4
void fn(int x, double y) {} //5
int main()
{
   fn(1);                   //a
   fn("1");                 //b
   int i;
   fn(&i);                  //c
   fn('1' );                //d
   fn(1, 2);                //e
   return 0;
}
```

4 The following program compiles but does not link properly. Why?

```
int printf(const char *, ...);
int main()
{
    printf("Hello world\n");
    return 0;
}
```

I mentioned the solution in the text, but don't go back and look until you've thought about it.

5 In Part I, you were asked to write and prototype a function that accepts two integer values, *x* and *y*, from the keyboard and returns them in arguments passed from the calling function. Do it again, but this time use referential arguments. Solve the problem twice, the first time using *scanf()* and the second time using stream input.

6 Let us assume the existence of a new mathematical class called *Davis*. (I'll be immortalized.) All the operations defined on real numbers are defined also on *Davis*. Write the prototypes for a set of overloaded functions called *multiply()* that perform multiplication between *Davis* numbers and *Davis* numbers and between *Davis* numbers and floating-point numbers. (Notice that a *Davis* times a *Davis* returns a *Davis* and a *Davis* times a *float* returns a *Davis*.)

7 The first program that anyone writes in C is the following "Hello world" program:

```
#include <stdio.h>
int main()
{
    printf("Hello, world\n");
    return 0;
}
```

Rewrite this program to use stream output.

Answers

1 a. This is the list that I came up with:

> ✔ If the argument is an expression with an operator of lower precedence than multiplication, the results will be wrong because *x* is not surrounded by parentheses. For example:

```
TWO_MAX(3 + a, b) ==> 3 + a > b ? (2 * 3 + a) : (2 * b)
```

which, given the precedence of the operators, is interpreted as:

```
TWO_MAX(3 + a, b) ==> ((3 + a) > b) ? ((2 * 3) + a) : (2 * b)
```

Notice the appearance of *(2*3)+a* instead of the intended *2*(3+a)*.

> ✔ If the macro is involved in an expression with operators of the same or higher precedence, the results will be wrong because the expression is not surrounded by parentheses. Consider the following example:

```
a = 2 * TWO_MAX(b, c); ==> a = 2 * b > c ? b : c;
```

> which is interpreted as

```
a = (2 * b) > c ? b : c;
```

> ✔ If the macro is invoked with an argument that has side effects, the side effects will "take effect" twice because *x* appears more than once. This is demonstrated in the following snippet

```
a = TWO_MAX(b++, c) ==> a = b++ > c ? b++ : c;
```

> If *b++* is greater than *c*, then *b* is actually incremented twice.

b. These problems can be corrected by making the macro an inline function:

```
//twoMax - implement as an inline function
inline twoMax(int x, int y)
{
    return x > y ? 2 * x; 2 * y;
}
```

This inline version does not suffer from any of the problems mentioned previously.

 As with most profound questions of our time, the answer is in the question. It is possible to overload the function with another function of the same name which can then turn around and call our function with the default value. You can even make this ersatz function inline if you're really worried about performance overhead:

```
#include <iostream.h>
void aFunc(int x, float y, char z)
{
    cout << "x = " << x << ", y = " << y << ", z = " << z << "\n";
}
inline void aFunc(int x, char z)
{
  aFunc(x, 0.0, z);
}
int main()
{
    aFunc(1, 2.0, '3' );   //calls the function
```

continued

```
    aFunc(4, '5' );          //calls the ersatz function
    return 0;
}
```

Executing the simple test program generates the following results:

```
x = 1, y = 2.0, z = 3
x = 4, y = 0.0, z = 5
```

Here are how the calls match up:

a. Calls 1; this is straightforward

b. Calls 2; a constant character string is of type *char**

c. Calls 3; any pointer type can be converted to *void**

d. Calls 1; a character can be promoted to an *int*

e. Ambiguous between 4 and 5; the *int* could be converted into either

Without a declaration to tell it otherwise, C++ would assume that *printf()* is a C++ function and attempt to mangle the name. The *stdio.h* include file includes *extern "C"* declarations to make sure that C++ knows that this is a C function.

My solution using *printf()* and *scanf()* I/O appears as follows:

```
#include <stdio.h>
void fn(int &x, int &y)
{
    printf("Enter x & y:");
    scanf("%d%d", &x, &y);
}
void main() {
    int i, j;
    fn(i, j);
    printf("i = %d, j = %d\n", i, j);
}
```

Notice that we still have to pass the address of *x* and *y* to *scanf()* because it knows nothing about referential arguments. However, the remainder of both the calling and called functions are simpler.

The stream I/O solution makes no direct reference to pointers:

```
#include <iostream.h>
void fn(int &x, int &y) {
    cout << "Enter x & y:";
    cin  >> x >> y;
}
void main() {
    int i, j;
    fn(i, j);
```

```
    cout << "i = " << I
         << ", j = " << j
         << "\n";
}
```

Here is my solution:

```
Davis multiply(Davis&, Davis &);
Davis multiply(Davis &, float);
Davis multiply(float, Davis &);
float  multiply(float, float);
```

Notice that *Davis, float* must be listed twice: the first time with *Davis* first and the second time with *float* first. There is no association between the two functions. (One of the functions can be an inline function that calls the other, so it's not a big deal.)

My solution is as follows:

```
#include <iostream.h>
int main()
{
    cout << "Hello, world\n";
    return 0;
}
```

Notice that *stdio.h* has been replaced by *iostream.h*. This is critically important. Without *iostream.h*, C++ will not recognize << as the insertion operator.

Part III

Wading In:
Introduction to Classes

The 5th Wave   By Rich Tennant

©RICHTENNANT

"OH YEAH, AND TRY NOT TO ENTER THE WRONG PASSWORD."

In This Part...

So far, C++ still looks basically like C — a slightly improved C maybe, but C nonetheless. If that were all there were to it, C++ certainly would not have generated as much interest as it has (and my editors probably would not have agreed to let me write this neat book).

The feature that differentiates C++ from C is C++'s support for object-oriented programming. Object-oriented is about the most hyped phrase in the computer world, next to Windows NT. Computer languages, editors, and databases all claim to be object-oriented, sometimes with justification, but most of the time without.

What is it about object-oriented that makes it so desired around the world? Let's find out.

Chapter 8
Object-Oriented Programming

● ●

In This Chapter
▶ Making nachos

▶ Quick overview of object-oriented programming

▶ Introduction to abstraction and classification

▶ Why is object-oriented programming important?

● ●

*O*kay, you've waited long enough. What, exactly, is object-oriented programming? *Object-oriented programming,* or OOP as we in the know prefer to call it, relies on two principles you learned before you ever got out of Pampers: abstraction and classification. To explain, let me tell you a little story.

Abstraction and Microwaves

Sometimes when my son and I are watching football, I use the microwave oven to whip up a terribly unhealthy batch of nachos. I dump some chips on a plate, throw on some beans, cheese, and lots of jalapeños, and nuke the whole mess in the microwave oven for 5 minutes.

To use my microwave, I open the door, throw the stuff in, and punch a few buttons on the front. After a few minutes, it's done. (I try not to stand in front of the microwave while it's working lest my eyes start glowing in the dark.)

Now think for a minute about all the things I don't do to use my microwave:

✔ I don't rewire or change anything inside the microwave to get it to work. The microwave has an interface — the front panel with all the buttons and the little time display — that lets me do everything I need.

✔ I don't have to reprogram the software used to drive the little processor inside my microwave, even if I cooked a different dish the last time I used the microwave.

> ✔ I don't look inside the case of my microwave. (I know there's a Klystron tube and a transformer inside there, but I don't have to think about that.)
>
> ✔ Even if I were a microwave designer and knew all about the inner workings of a microwave, including its software, I would still use it to heat my nachos without thinking about all that stuff.

These are not profound observations. We can think about only so much at one time. To reduce the number of things we must deal with, we work at a certain level of detail. In object-oriented (OO) computerese, the level of detail at which we are working is called the *level of abstraction*. To introduce another OO term while I have the chance, I *abstract away* the details of the microwave's internals. ■

When I'm working on nachos, I view my microwave oven as a box. (As I'm trying to knock out a snack, I can't worry about the innards of the microwave oven and still follow the Cowboys on the tube.) As long as I use the microwave only through its interface (the keypad), there should be nothing I can do to cause the microwave to enter an inconsistent state and crash or, worse, turn my nachos into a blackened, flaming mass.

This is serious stuff. If a sequence of keystrokes caused the microwave to burst into flames and it damaged my house, for example, I could sue the makers of the microwave and undoubtedly collect a large settlement. That's why the microwave has a box around it. I can't very well hold the manufacturer responsible if I reach into the microwave and change some wires around and it subsequently fries me or my nachos. The machine is responsible for its actions as long as input is through the approved interface (no matter how illogical that input may be). Go around that interface and all bets are off.

Functional nachos

Suppose I were to ask my son to write an algorithm for how Dad makes nachos. Once he understood what I wanted, he would probably write "open a can of beans, grate some cheese, cut the jalapeños," and so on. When it came to the part about microwaving the concoction, he would write something like "cook in the microwave for 5 minutes."

That description is straightforward and complete. But it's *not* the way a functional programmer would code a program to make nachos. Functional programmers live in a world devoid of objects such as microwave ovens and other appliances. They tend to worry about flow charts with their myriad functional paths. In a functional solution to the nachos problem, the flow of control would pass through my finger to the front panel and then to the internals of the microwave. Pretty soon, flow would be wiggling around through complex logic paths about how long to turn on the Klystron and whether to sound the "come and get it" tone.

In a world like this, it's difficult to think in terms of levels of abstraction. There are no objects, no abstractions behind which to hide inherent complexity.

Object-oriented nachos

In an object-oriented approach to making nachos, we would first identify the types of objects in the problem: chips, beans, cheese, and an oven. Then we would begin the task of modeling these objects in software, without regard to the details of how they will be used in the final program.

While we are doing this, we are said to be working (and thinking) at the level of the basic objects. We need to think about making a useful oven, but we don't have to think about the logical process of making nachos yet. After all, the microwave designers didn't think about the specific problem of my making a snack. Rather, they set about the problem of designing and building a useful microwave.

After the objects we need have been successfully coded and tested, we can ratchet up to the next level of abstraction. We can start thinking at the nacho-making level, rather than the microwave-making level. At this point, we can pretty much translate my son's instructions directly into C++ code.

Classification and Microwave Ovens

Critical to the concept of abstraction is that of classification. If I were to ask my son, "What's a microwave?" he would probably say, "It's an oven that..." If I then asked, "What's an oven?" he might reply, "It's a kitchen appliance that..." (If I then asked "What's a kitchen appliance?" he would probably say, "Why are you asking so many stupid questions?")

That's because he understands that our particular microwave is an example of the type of things called microwave ovens. In addition, my son sees microwave ovens as just a special type of oven, which is in turn a special type of kitchen appliance.

In object-oriented computerese, we say that my microwave is an *instance* of the *class* microwave. The class microwave is a subclass of the class oven, and the class oven is a subclass of the class kitchen appliances. ■

Humans classify. Everything about our world is ordered into taxonomies. We do this to reduce the number of things we have to remember. Take, for example, the first time you saw a Saturn. The advertisement called the Saturn "revolutionary, the likes of which have never been seen." But you and I know that that just isn't so. I like the looks of the Saturn, but hey, it's a car. As such, it shares all of (or at least most of) the properties of other cars. It has a steering wheel, seats, a motor, brakes, and so on. I bet I could even drive one without help.

I don't have to clutter my limited storage with all the things that a Saturn has in common with other cars. All I have to remember is "a Saturn is a car that..." and tack on those few things that are unique to a Saturn. It goes further. Cars are a subclass of wheeled vehicles, of which there are other members, like trucks and pickups. Maybe wheeled vehicles are a subclass of vehicles, which include boats and planes. And on and on and on.

To see categorization taken to the extreme, look at the biological sciences. In an attempt to make sense of the world around us, every living creature is classified according to kingdom, family, phylum, genus, and species.

Functional classification

Functional programming has no concept that is similar to classification. Because there are no objects in functional programming, there are no classes of objects. Every solution has to be solved on its own, without the possibility of generalizing from existing types.

Object-oriented classification

In object-oriented languages, such as C++, objects are grouped into classes. In addition, the classes are related in the same types of hierarchies we use to describe Saturns, cars, wheeled vehicles, and so on.

Why classify?

True to form, one of the important questions we ask in this book is "Why?" Why do we want to classify? It sounds like a lot of trouble. (Besides, I've been programming the functional way for so long. Why do I need to change now?)

It might seem easier to design and build a microwave oven specifically for our one problem, rather than build a separate, more generic oven object. Suppose, for example, that I wanted to build a microwave to cook nachos and nachos only. There would be no need to put a front panel on it, other than a START button. You always cook nachos the same amount of time. We could dispense with all that DEFROST and TEMP COOK nonsense. It would need to hold only one flat little plate. Three cubic feet of space would be wasted on nachos.

For that matter, let's just dispense with the concept of "microwave oven" altogether. All we really need is the guts of the oven. Then, in the recipe, we put the instructions to make it work: "Put nachos in the box. Connect the red wire to the black wire. Notice a slight hum. Try not to stand too close if you intend to have children..." Stuff like that.

But the functional approach has some problems:

- ✔ *Too complex.* We don't want the details of oven building mixed into the details of nacho building. If we can't define the objects and pull them out of the morass of details to deal with separately, we must deal with all the complexities of the problem all the time.

- ✔ *Not flexible.* If we need to replace the microwave oven with some other type of oven, we should be able to do so as long as its interface is the same. Without being clearly delineated and developed separately, it becomes impossible to cleanly remove an object type and replace it with another.

- ✔ *Not reusable.* Ovens are used to make lots of different dishes. We don't want to create a new oven every time we encounter a new recipe. Having solved a problem once, it would be nice to be able to reuse the solution in future programs.

Turning lead into gold and achieving software reuse

Software reuse has been the philosophers' stone of the software industry for the last twenty years. Any company that could achieve true reuse would rake in the bucks through reduced software production costs.

Functional software reuse is theoretically possible, but it hasn't worked very well in practice. The large amount of interaction between conventional functions and its surroundings makes reusing them difficult. An object, with its well-defined interface and "black box" approach, is a more likely candidate for software reuse.

Is making software objects like hardware objects important? Let's look at the progress made by our hardware brethren over the last few years and compare it with our own.

For the past decade or so, the component density and performance of computer ICs have been doubling roughly every two years. You might think that the time required to design and build these increasingly complex chips would be increasing also or at least remaining constant. This doesn't appear to be true. New processors are appearing at an ever increasing rate.

During this same period, software productivity has increased by maybe, and I say maybe, 50 percent. The functional approach to programming just isn't getting the job done.

We need the software equivalent of microwave ovens. We need to design and build a software solution, provide it with an interface to the outside world, test it, slap a box around it, and use it. Use it in this program and again in the next program. If it breaks, someone may need to take the top off and fix it or come out with a new model, but as long as it works, we use it without thinking about what's inside.

Object-Oriented Programming and Efficiency

It has been claimed that OOP does not produce the most efficient programs. True to my argumentative nature, let me respond to that criticism with a question: Does our modular approach to appliances generate the most efficient kitchen? Probably not.

Did you ever notice that your microwave has a transformer, as does your refrigerator and your dishwasher and even the phone? I've got a great idea, says the functional programmer. Let's combine all these transformers into one big transformer designed to run all these appliances. Fewer transformers. Less parts. Big savings. Wrong!

We can see how patently silly this approach is. Sure, you might end up with a slightly cheaper initial purchase price (although I doubt it after all the extra wiring is in place), and it might run just a skosh more efficiently with only one transformer. But this solution is a maintenance nightmare. I couldn't even replace the telephone without worrying about what impact this might have on the refrigerator!

This is exactly the way we write functional software. We make our data structures visible to the entire program and let functions from all over the program reach in and tap whatever information they like in the name of efficiency. The result: every time we change a structure, we have to worry about what impact that change might have on the entire system.

Experience has shown the opposite trend. When I was but a lad, quality stereos normally came as all-in-one console units; the receiver, turntable, amplifier, and speakers were all built into one box. Looking inside, we could see that all the different units shared components as well.

Over the years, however, stereos went modular. Now people buy high-quality audio components (*components* is just another word for *objects*) that they hook together into a system. The result is not necessarily better sounding, but it is:

- *More flexible to changing demands*. Need more power? No problem. Replace that tired 20-watt amplifier with a 100-watt unit.

- *Extensible*. Want to add digital audio tape? No problem. Buy a DAT player and plug it into the system. Notice this works even if DAT tapes didn't exist when you bought your stereo! (Think about that in software terms to see what a profound statement it is.)

> ✔ *Debuggable*. Suppose the system starts sounding awful (or quiet) all of a
> sudden. In a modular system, I can tap into the signal between the
> components to isolate the problem down to the component. I still need a
> component expert to fix the problem in the component, but the ability to
> not get the amplifier man involved when the problem is in the tape drive is
> significant.

Let me pose a second question: Does functional programming generate the
absolute greatest efficiency? What about after 5 years? Theoretically, the
answer to both questions is yes, but in fact the answer is no. The inherent
complexity of problems keeps us programmers from being able to grasp all the
logic paths through the forest of possibilities.

Even if we do a good job of the initial release, functional programs are difficult
to change. After several revisions, the kludges that programmers are forced to
put into such programs reduces their efficiency below that of the more flexible
object-oriented program.

Conclusion

This has been a high-level, somewhat theoretical discussion of object-oriented
programming. (You can tell by the absence of listings in this chapter.) In the
rest of Part III, we see how C++ brings some of the object-oriented features
we've been discussing to C. Then we revisit our Budget program in its first
object-oriented incarnation.

Chapter 9
Adding Class to C++

• •

In This Chapter

▶ Transforming a structure into a class

▶ Declaring and defining member functions

▶ Accessing member functions

▶ Overloading member functions

• •

C structures enable you to group related data elements into a single entity. For example, in the Budget program, we were able to create a structure *Savings* with the following information:

```
struct Savings
{
    unsigned accountNumber;
    float    balance;
};
```

Every instance of *Savings* contains the same two data elements:

```
void fn(void)
{
    Savings a;
    Savings b;
    a.accountNumber = 1;  /*this is not the same as...
    b.accountNumber = 2;  /*...this one*/
}
```

The two *accountNumber*s are different because they belong to different objects (*a* and *b*).

Note that the keyword *struct* is no longer necessary in declarations in C++ (it's allowed but nobody includes it). Thus, we say *Savings a* in C++, not *struct Savings a* as in C. ■

As nice as C structures may be, however, they are limited to data elements. The C++ *class* does not have this restriction. A class can have both data and function members:

```
class Savings
{
  public:
   unsigned accountNumber;
   float    balance;

   unsigned deposit(unsigned amount)
   {
      balance += amount;
      return balance;
   }
};
```

Here, the function *deposit()* is a member of the class *Savings* just like the two data members.

Why Add Classes to C++?

Remember that our goal is to create a software analog to real-world objects, such as microwaves and savings accounts. Real-world objects certainly have data-type properties, such as time, account numbers, and balances. This makes a C *struct* a good starting point. But real-world objects can also do things. Ovens cook. Savings accounts accumulate interest. CDs charge a substantial penalty for early withdrawal. However, a C *struct* does not have such active properties.

We could just associate conventional functions with our data structures and allow these functions to represent the active elements of the object. In fact, we did that in BUDGET.C and it's done in most other well-written C programs. But this association between functions (the active elements) and *struct*s (which contain the data elements) is strictly voluntary and not recognized by the language. Thus, what we need to do is allow *struct*s to have member functions as well as member data. That's called a *class*.

How Do I Add Classes to C++?

To demonstrate classes, let's start by defining a class *Student*. One possible representation of such a class follows:

```
class Student
{
  public:
   int    semesterHours;  //hours earned toward graduation
   float gpa;
   float addCourse(int hours, float grade); //add a completed...
                          //  course to the record
};
```

We can see that this class declaration looks very much like a structure declaration. In fact, this declaration looks exactly like the declaration of a *struct*, except that:

- ✔ It substitutes the keyword *class* for *struct*
- ✔ It adds the keyword *public*
- ✔ It declares a member function along with the data members

The *class* keyword is a new keyword in C++ used in place of *struct* to differentiate a class from a structure. Other than that, the syntax of *class* and *struct* are the same. (We'll skip the *public* keyword for now.)

The function *addCourse(int, float)* is called a member function of the class *Student*. In principle, it's a property of the class like the data members *semesterHours* and *gpa*.

Functions defined in a class are called *member functions*. Their data buddies are called data members. Together, they're both known as members of the class.

There isn't a name for functions or data that are not members of a class. I'll refer to them as *non-members*. All the functions you wrote in C were non-member functions because they didn't belong to any class. ■

For historical reasons, member functions are also called *methods*. This term has an obtuse meaning in other object- oriented languages, but none in C++. Nevertheless, it has gained some popularity in OO circles because it's easier to say than "member function." (The fact that it sounds more impressive probably didn't hurt either.) So, if your friends start spouting off at a dinner party about "methods of the class," just replace *methods* with *member functions* and reparse anything they say. Because the term *method* has little relevance to C++, I won't use it here. ■

Naming member functions

The full name of the function *addCourse(int, float)* is *Student::addCourse(int, float)*. The class name in front indicates that the function is a member of the class *Student*. (The class name is added to the extended name of the function like arguments are added to an overloaded function name.) We could have other functions called *addCourse()* that are members of other classes, such as *Teacher::addCourse(int, float)* or even *Golf::addCourse()*. A function *addCourse(int, float)* without any class name is a conventional non-member function.

Data members are not any different than member functions with respect to extended names. Outside a structure, it is not sufficient to refer to *semesterHours* by itself. The data member *semesterHours* makes sense only in the context of the class *Student*. The extended name for *semesterHours* is *Student::semesterHours*.

The *::* is called the *scope resolution operator* because it indicates to which class a function belongs. The *::* operator can be used with a non-member function as well by using a null structure name. The non-member function *addCourse* can be referred to as *::addCourse(int, float)*, if you prefer.

The operator is optional except when two functions of the same name exist. For example:

```
float addCourse(int hours, float grade)
{
   return hours * grade;
}

class Student
{
  public:
    int   semesterHours;  //hours earned toward graduation
    float gpa;

    //add a completed course to the record
    float addCourse(int hours, float grade)
    {
       //...whatever stuff...
       addCourse(hours, grade);//call global function(?)
       //...more stuff...
    }
};
```

We want the member function *Student::addCourse()* to call the non-member function *::addCourse()*. Without the *::* operator, however, a call to *addCourse()* from *Student* refers to *Student::addCourse()*. This results in the function calling itself. Adding the *::* operator to the front directs the call to the global version, as desired:

```
class Student
{
  public:
    int   semesterHours;  //hours earned toward graduation
    float gpa;

    //add a completed course to the record
    float addCourse(int hours, float grade)
    {
       //...whatever stuff...
       ::addCourse(hours, grade);//call global function
       //...more stuff...
    }
};
```

The extended name of a function includes not only the arguments, as we saw in Part II, but also the class name to which the function belongs. ∎

Defining a Member Function in the Class

A member function can be defined either in the class or separately. When defined in the class definition, the function looks like the following in *STUDENT.HPP*:

```
class Student
{
  public:
    int    semesterHours;   //hours earned toward graduation
    float gpa;

    //add a completed course to the record
    float addCourse(int hours, float grade)
    {
        float weightedGPA;

        weightedGPA = semesterHours * gpa;

        //now add in the new course
        semesterHours += hours;
        weightedGPA += grade * hours;
        gpa = weightedGPA / semesterHours;
        return gpa;
    }
};
```

Member functions defined in the class default to inline (unless they have been specifically outlined by containing a loop or by a compiler switch). Mostly, this is because a member function defined in the class is usually very small, and small functions are prime candidates for inlining. ■

There is another good, but more technical, reason to inline member functions defined within a class. Remember that C structures are normally defined in include files, which are then included in the *.C* source files that need them. Such include files should not contain data or functions, because these files are compiled multiple times. Including an inline function is okay, however, because it (like a macro) expands in place in the source file.

The same applies to C++ classes. By defaulting member functions defined in classes inline, the preceding problem is avoided. ■

Keeping a Member Function after Class

For larger functions, putting the code directly in the class definition can lead to some very large, unwieldy class definitions. To prevent this, C++ lets us define member functions somewhere else.

When written outside the class definition, our *Student* example looks like the following in *STUDENT.H*:

```
class Student
{
  public:
    int   semesterHours;  //hours earned toward graduation
    float gpa;

    //add a completed course to the record
    float addCourse(int hours, float grade);
};
```

The actual code appears in *STUDENT.CPP*:

```
#include "student.h"
float Student::addCourse(int hours, float grade)
{
    float weightedGPA;

    weightedGPA = semesterHours * gpa;

    //now add in the new course
    semesterHours += hours;
    weightedGPA += grade * hours;
    gpa = weightedGPA / semesterHours;
    return gpa;
}
```

Here we see that the class definition contains nothing more than a prototype declaration for the function *addCourse()*. The actual function definition appears separately.

The analogy with a prototype declaration is exact. The declaration in the structure *is* a prototype declaration and, like all prototype declarations, is required.

Notice that when the function was among its *Student* buddies in the class, it wasn't necessary to include the class name with the function name — the class name was assumed. When the function is by itself, the fully extended name is required. It's just like at my home. My wife calls me by only my first name (provided I'm not in the doghouse). Among the family, the last name is assumed. Outside the family (and my circle of acquaintances), others call me by my full name. ■

I have flagged the preceding structure and member function definitions as being in separate *.H* and *.CPP* files. They don't have to be, but it's a good idea. Other functions that want to use *Students* need to include the structure definitions but need to link with only the stuff in the *.CPP* file. ■

Calling a Member Function

Before we look at how to call a member function, let's refresh our memory as to how we reference a data member. Using an object of class *Student* defined earlier appears as follows:

```
#include "student.h"
Student s;
void fn(void)
{
   //access one of the data members of s
   s.semesterHours = 10;
   s.gpa          = 3.0;
}
```

We must specify an object along with the member name. In other words, the following makes no sense:

```
#include "student.h"
Student s;
void fn(void)
{
   //access one of the data members of s
   //neither of these is legal
   semesterHours = 10;      //member of what object of what class?
   Student::semesterHours = 10; //okay, I know the class but
                                //I still don't know the object
}
```

Member functions are invoked with an object just like data members, as follows:

```
Student s;
void fn()
{
   //all of the following reference an object
   s.semesterHours = 10;
   s.gpa          = 3.0;
   s.addCourse(3, 4.0);  //call the member function
}
```

Calling a member function without an object makes no more sense than referencing a data member without an object. The syntax for calling a member function looks like a cross between the syntax for accessing a data member and for calling a conventional function.

Calling a member function with a pointer?

The same parallel for the objects themselves can be drawn for pointers to objects. The following references a data member of an object with a pointer:

```
#include "student.h"

void someFn(Student *pS)
{
    pS->semesterHours = 10;
    pS->qpa           = 3.0;
    pS->addCourse(3, 4.0);  //call the member function
}

Student s;
int main()
{
    someFn(&s);
    return 0;
}
```

Calling a member function with a reference to an object appears identical to the simple case of using the object itself. Remember, when passing or returning a reference as an argument to a function, C++ passes only the address of the object. In using a reference, however, C++ dereferences the address automatically as the following example shows:

```
#include "Student.h"

//same as before, but this time using references
void someFn(Student &refS)
{
    refS.semesterHours = 10;
    refS.qpa           = 3.0;
    refS.addCourse(3, 4.0);  //call the member function
}

Student s;
int main()
{
    someFn(s);
    return 0;
}
```

Accessing members from a member function

I can see it clearly: you repeat to yourself, "Member functions must be invoked with an object. Referencing a data member without an object makes no sense." Just about the time you've accepted this, you look at the member function *Student::addCourse()* and BAMMO, it strikes you: This function is accessing class members without reference to an object!

Okay, which is it, can you or can't you? Believe me, you can't. When you reference a member of *Student* from *addCourse()*, that reference is against the *Student* object with which the call to *addCourse()* was made. Huh? Let's go back to our example.

```
#include "student.h"
float Student::addCourse(int hours, float grade)
{
    float weightedGPA;
    weightedGPA = semesterHours * gpa;

    //now add in the new course
    semesterHours += hours;
    weightedGPA += hours * grade;
    gpa = weightedGPA / semesterHours;
    return gpa;
}

Student s;
Student t;
int main()

{
    s.addCourse(3, 4.0);   //here's an A+
    t.addCourse(3, 2.5);   //give this guy a C
    return 0;
}
```

When *addCourse()* is invoked with the object *s*, all of the otherwise unqualified member references in *addCourse()* refer to *s*. Thus, *semesterHours* refers to *s.semesterHours*, *gpa* to *s.gpa*. But in the next line of *main()*, when *addCourse()* is invoked with the *Student t*, these same references refer to *t.semesterHours* and *t.gpa* instead.

The object with which the member function was invoked is the "current" object, and all unqualified references to class members refer to this object. Put another way, unqualified references to class members made from a member function are always against the current object. ∎

How does the member function know what the current object is? It's not magic — the address of the object is passed to the member function as an implicit and hidden first argument. In other words, the following conversion is taking place:

s.addCourse(3, 2.5) is like *Student::addCourse(&s, 3, 2.5)*

(Note that you can't actually use the syntax on the right; this line just shows you the way C++ interprets the call on the left.)

Inside the function, this implicit pointer to the current object has a name, in case you need to refer to it. It is called *this*, as in "Which object? *this* object." Get it? The type of *this* is always a pointer to an object of the appropriate class.

Anytime a member function refers to another member of the same class without providing an object explicitly, C++ assumes *this*. You also can refer to *this* explicitly, if you like. We could have written *Student::addCourse()* as follows:

```
#include "student.h"
float Student::addCourse(int hours, float grade)
{
    float weightedGPA;
    weightedGPA = this->semesterHours * this->gpa;

    //now add in the new course
    this->semesterHours += hours;
    weightedGPA += hours * grade;
    this->gpa = weightedGPA / this->semesterHours;
    return this->gpa;
}
```

Whether we explicitly include *this*, as in the preceding example, or leave it implicit, as we did before, the effect is the same. ▪

Overloading Member Functions

Member functions can be overloaded in the same way that conventional functions are overloaded. Remember, however, that the class name is part of the extended name. Thus, the following functions are all legal:

```
class Student
{
  public:
    //grade - return the current grade point average
    float grade();

    //grade - set the grade and return previous value
    float grade(float newGPA);

    //...data members and stuff...
};

class Slope
{
  public:
    //grade - return the percentage grade of the slope
    float grade();

    //...stuff goes here too...
};

//grade - return the letter equivalent of a numerical grade
char grade(float value);

int main()
{
    Student s;
    s.grade(3.5);            //Student::grade(float)
    float w = n.grade();     //Student::grade()
    char c = grade(v);       //::grade(float)
```

```
        Slope o;
        float m = o.grade();   //Slope::grade()
        return 0;
    }
```

Each call made from *main()* is noted in the comments with the extended name of the function called.

When calling overloaded functions, not only the arguments of the function but also the type of the object (if any) with which the function is invoked are used to disambiguate the call. (The term *disambiguate* is object-oriented talk for "decide at compile time which overloaded function to call.")

In the example, the first two calls to the member functions *Student::grade(float)* and *Student::grade()* are differentiated by their argument lists. The third call has no object, so it unambiguously denotes the non-member function *grade(float)*. Because the final call is made with an object of type *Slope*, it must refer to the member function *Slope::grade()*.

Conclusion

Well, we finally saw *class* peak its nose out of its hole — and we lived to tell about it (it wasn't even all that painful). Now that we've seen a class, let's learn more about it.

Chapter 10
Do Not Disturb: Protected Members

• •

In This Chapter

▶ Declaring members protected

▶ Accessing protected members from within the class

▶ Accessing protected members from outside the class

• •

*I*n the preceding chapter, I asked you to ignore the *public* keyword with a campaign promise that I would return to it real soon. Let me make good on that promise now.

Protected Members

The members of a class can be marked *protected,* which makes them inaccessible outside the class. The alternative is to make the members *public*. Public members are accessible to all.

Why do I need them?

To understand the role of *protected*, let's think about the goals of object-oriented programming:

- Protect the internals of the class from outside functions. Remember that we were going to build a software microwave (or whatever), provide it with a simple interface to the outside world, and then put a box around it to keep others from messing with the insides. The *protected* keyword is that box.

- Make the class responsible for maintaining its internal state. It's not fair to ask the class to be responsible if others can reach in and manipulate its internals (anymore than it was fair to ask that microwave designer to be responsible for the consequences of me mucking with the microwave's internal wiring).

✔ Limit the interface of the class to the outside world. It's easier to learn and use a class that has a limited interface (the public members). Protected members are hidden from the user and need not be learned. The interface becomes the class (abstraction, remember).

✔ Reduce the level of interconnection between the class and other code. By limiting interconnection, you can more easily replace one class with another, or use the class in other programs.

Now, I know what you functional types out there are saying: "You don't need some fancy feature to do all that. Just make a rule that says certain members are publicly accessible and others are not."

Although that is true in theory, it doesn't work. People start out with all kinds of good intentions, but as long as the language doesn't at least discourage direct access of protected members, these good intentions get crushed under the pressure to get the product out the door.

Let me borrow another analogy. (Oh, no, there he goes with another analogy.) Have you ever tried to read or change a record in the files in the personnel office? Go ahead, give it a shot. Security measures keep you at a distance — the personnel records are protected.

However, some people (trustworthy people, we hope) can change anything they want. These people are the members of the personnel department. You must ask one of them when you need access to certain information. They can give out only certain information; some data is so private that it can't go outside the personnel department.

In addition, the information you receive is just a copy of the information in the company database. You can mark up your copy all you want, but if you want your changes to become permanent you must give the information back to the personnel department. Your changes will be checked and entered into the company's permanent records only if the changes are consistent with the rules the department has established. In this way, the company ensures the integrity of its files.

Could we make up a rule and say only certain people are allowed access to the records without an enforcement mechanism? Sure we could. Would it work? No better than the structure access rules in C. When deadlines and tempers start getting short, rules like this are quickly forgotten.

Can someone defeat the protection against access to personnel records? Sure. Can programmers defeat C++'s protection? No problem. But they must go to a lot of trouble to do so, and what they've done will be obvious to anyone who looks.

How do they work?

Adding the keyword *public* to a class makes subsequent members public, which means they are accessible by non-member functions. Adding the keyword *protected* makes subsequent members of the class protected, which means they are not accessible by non-members of the class. You can switch between public and protected as often as you like.

Let's return to the class *Student*. Suppose that the following capabilities are all that a fully functional, upstanding *Student* needs (notice the absence of *spendMoney()* and *drinkBeer()* — this is a highly stylized student):

> *addCourse(int hours, float grade)* — add a course
>
> *grade()* — return the current grade point average
>
> *hours()* — return the number of hours earned toward graduation

The remaining members of *Student* can be declared *protected* to keep other functions' prying opcodes out of *Student*'s business.

```
class Student
{
  public:
    //grade - return the current grade point average
    float grade()
    {
       return gpa;
    }
    //hours - return the number of semester hours
    int hours()
    {
       return semesterHours;
    }
    //addCourse - add another course to the student's record
    float addCourse(int hours, float grade);

   //the following members are off-limits to others
   protected:
    int    semesterHours;  //hours earned towards graduation
    float gpa;
};
```

Now the members *semesterHours* and *gpa* are accessible only to other members of *Student*. Thus, the following doesn't work:

```
Student s;
int main()
{
   //raise my grade (don't make it too high; otherwise, no
   //one would believe it
   s.gpa = 3.5;     //<- generates compiler error
```

continued

```
float gpa = s.grade(); //<- this public function reads
                       //a copy of the value, but you can't
                       //change it from here
return 0;
}
```

The application's attempt to change the value of *gpa* is flagged with a compiler error.

It's considered good form to start a class with either the *public* or *protected* keyword. I use this style and I recommend that you use it too. ■

Class members can be protected from access by non-member functions also by declaring them *private*. In fact, *private* is the default for classes (that is, classes start out in *private* mode). The difference between *protected* and *private* first becomes apparent in the presence of inheritance, which we don't cover until Chapter 18. For a detailed discussion of *private*, see Chapter 22. ■

Tell Me Again Why I Should Use Protected Members

Now that you know a little more about how to use protected members in an actual class, let's replay the arguments for using protected members.

The class can protect its internal state

Making the *gpa* member protected precludes the application from setting the grade point average to some arbitrary value. The application can add courses, but it can't change the *gpa*.

If the application has a legitimate need to set the grade point average directly, the class can provide a member function for that purpose, as follows:

```
class Student
{
  public:
    //same as before
    float grade()
    {
        return gpa;
    }

    //here we allow the grade to be changed
    float grade(float newGPA)
    {
```

```
        float oldGPA = gpa;
        //only if the new value is valid
        if (newGPA > 0 && newGPA <= 4.0)

        {
            gpa - ncwGPA;
        }
        return oldGPA;
    }

    //...other stuff is the same including the data members:
    protected:
    int   semesterHours;   //hours earned toward graduation
    float gpa;
};
```

The addition of the member function *grade(float)* allows the application to set the *gpa*. Notice, however, that the class still hasn't given up control completely. The application can't set *gpa* to any old value; only a *gpa* in the legal range of values (from 0 through 4.0) is accepted.

Thus, *Student* has provided access to an internal data member without abdicating its responsibility to make sure that the internal state of the class is valid.

It's easier to use a class with a limited interface

Admittedly, the example class *Student* doesn't have many members, but that's mostly for publishing reasons. (I don't feel like typing in hundreds of lines of meaningless fields, and you wouldn't want to read them.) A real-world C *struct* can have a lot of data members and therefore a lot of different fields. To use the structure, the programmer (that's you) must understand all those fields.

A class provides a limited interface. To use a class, all you need (or want) to know are its public members, what they do, and what their arguments are. This can drastically reduce the number of things you need to learn — and remember — to use the class.

It's easier to support a class with a limited interface

As conditions change or as bugs are found, you want to be able to change the internal workings of a class. When you have hidden the internal workings of the class, changes to those details are less likely to require changes in the external application code.

Consider the following simple example program:

```
#include <math.h>
#include <iostream.h>
//Point - determine a point on a 2-D graph
class Point
{
  public:
   //set point location
   void set(double ix, double iy)
   {
      x = ix;
      y = iy;
   }
   //read point location
   double xOffset()
   {
      return x;
   }
   double yOffset()
   {
      return y;
   }
   double angle()
   {
      return (180./3.14159) * atan2(y, x);
   }
   double radius()
   {
      return sqrt(x*x + y*y);
   }

  protected:
   //x and y offsets from the origin
   double x;
   double y;
};

//main - exercise the Point class a little bit
int main()
{
    Point p;
    double x, y;

    for (;;)
    {
       cout << "Enter x and y:\n";
       cin  >> x >> y;
       if (x < 0)
       {
          break;
       }
       p.set(x, y);
       cout << "angle = "    << p.angle()
            << ", radius = " << p.radius()
            << ", x offset=" << p.xOffset()
```

```
                     << ", y offset=" << p.yOffset()
                     << "\n";
        }
        return 0;
    }
```

The class *Point* represents a point on a two-dimensional graph or screen. This implementation stores the location of each point object as x and y offsets, which are stored in the protected members *x* and *y*. These values are set using the *set()* member function. Non-member functions can read the x and y locations using the *xOffset()* and *yOffset()* functions. The member function *angle()* returns the angle (measured counter-clockwise from the x axis) of a line segment drawn from the origin to the point, and *radius()* returns the length of this line segment (see Figure 10-1).

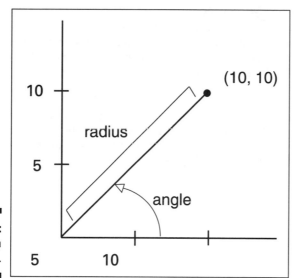

Figure 10-1:
Graphing a
point.

I have provided a simple *main()* to demonstrate the class. The results are as follows (my input is in boldface):

```
Enter x and y:
10 10
angle = 45.000038, radius = 14.142136, x offset=10, y offset=10
Enter x and y:
50  0
angle = 0, radius = 50, x offset=50, y offset=0
Enter x and y:
0  50
angle = 90.000076, radius = 50, x offset=0, y offset=50
Enter x and y:
```

continued

```
50  1
angle = 1.145764, radius = 50.009999, x offset=50, y offset=1
Enter x and y:
1  50
angle = 88.854312, radius = 50.009999, x offset=1, y offset=50
Enter x and y:
-1 -1
```

The program uses the x, y pairs I entered as the x and y arguments to *set()* and then spits back the results from each of the access member functions.

Now, let's assume that this class is finished and installed in an application. But for some reason our supervisor isn't satisfied. Instead of orthogonal (x and y) coordinates, our boss wants spherical coordinates (angle and radius) used internally.

This change would require lots of work in a structured C program. (I know it wouldn't mean lots of work for this silly little program, but remember that we're thinking about real-world applications with potentially thousands of lines of code.) Changing the internal members of *Point* would be easy, but finding and then changing all the places where the *Point* structure is referenced could be difficult.

For an object-oriented C++ program, however, the job is simple. We would change the internals of the class as with the C program, but if we don't change the external interface of the class, we don't have to change any non-member functions. Thus, the program would appear as follows:

```
#include <math.h>
#include <iostream.h>
class Point

{
  public:
   //set the point location
   void set(double ix, double iy)

   {
     a = atan2(iy, ix);              //convert to angle...
     r = sqrt(ix * ix + iy * iy); //...and radius
   }
   //read the values out
   double xOffset()
   {
      return r * sin(a);             //recreate x or...
   }
   double yOffset()
   {
      return r * cos(a);             //...y offset
   }
   double angle()
```

```
    {
        return (180./3.14159) * a;   //convert radian to degrees
    }
    double radius()
    {
        return r;
    }

  protected:
    double r;
    double a;
};

//main - exercise the Point class a little bit
int main()
{
    Point p;
    double x, y;

    for (;;)
    {
        cout << "Enter x and y:";
        cin  >> x >> y;
        if (x < 0)
        {
            break;
        }
        p.set(x, y);
        cout << "angle = "     << p.angle()
             << ", radius = " << p.radius()
             << ", x offset=" << p.xOffset()
             << ", y offset=" << p.yOffset()
             << "\n";
    }

    return 0;
}
```

The output of this program appears unchanged.

No changes to *main()* are required. Because the interface to class *Point* didn't change — that is, the same five public member functions generate the same results — I could pop the previous implementation of *Point* out, drop in the new one, and go. I have changed the internal wiring of the black box but the control panel remains the same.

What Are Friends for Anyway?

Occasionally, we want a non-member function to have access to the protected members of a class. We can do this by naming that function a friend of the class using the keyword *friend*.

Why do I need friends? (I am a rock, I am an island)

Sometimes an external function requires direct access to a data member. Without some type of friend mechanism, the programmer would be forced to declare the member public, thereby giving access to not only the one function but everyone else as well.

Let's return to our personnel department analogy. Are any members of the company who are not in the personnel department allowed access to protected data? Usually the answer is yes. Certain officers of the company or members of other departments need to access part of the personnel database. Although giving outsiders access to this information could be risky, it's better than making this information public to everyone. In the same way, granting access by declaring a non-member as a friend is better than granting access to all.

It's like having a neighbor check on your house during your vacation. Giving non-family members the key to your house is not normally a good idea, but it beats the alternative of leaving the house unlocked.

How do they work?

The friend declaration appears in the class that contains the protected member. The friend declaration is like a prototype declaration in that it includes the extended name and the return type. In the following example, the function *initialize()* can now access anything it wants in *Student*:

```
class Student
{
    friend void initialize(Student*);
  public:
    //same public members as before...

    protected:
    int    semesterHours;   //hours earned toward graduation
    float gpa;
};

//the following function is a friend of Student
//so it can access the protected members
void initialize(Student *pS)
{
    pS->gpa = 0;               //this is now legal...
    pS->semesterHours = 0;     //...when it wasn't before
}
```

A single function can be declared to be a friend of two classes at the same time. Although this can be convenient, it tends to bind the two classes together. This binding of classes is normally considered bad because it makes one class dependent on the other. If the two classes naturally belong together, however, it's not all bad. For example:

```
class Student;       //forward declaration
class Teacher
{
   friend void registration();
  protected:
   int        noStudents;
   Student *pList[100];
  public:
   void assignGrades();
};

class Student
{
   friend void registration();
  public:
   //same public members as before...

  protected:
   Teacher *pT;
   int    semesterHours;   //hours earned towards graduation
   float gpa;
};
```

In this example, the function *registration()* can reach into both the *Student* and *Teacher* classes to tie them together at registration time, without being a member function of either one.

Notice that the first line in the example declares the class *Student* but none of its members. Remember, this is called a forward declaration and just defines the name of the class so that other classes, such as *Teacher*, can refer to it. Forward references are necessary when two classes refer to each other. ■

A member function of one class may be declared a friend of another class. For example:

```
class Teacher
{
   //...other members as well...
  public:
   void assignGrades();
};

class Student
{
   friend void Teacher::assignGrades();
  public:
   //same public members as before...
  protected:
   int    semesterHours;   //hours earned towards graduation
```

continued

```
    float gpa;
};
void Teacher::assignGrades()
{
    //can access protected members of Teacher from here
}
```

Unlike in the non-member example, the member function *assignGrades()* must be declared before the class *Student* can declare it to be a friend.

An entire class can be named a friend of another. This has the effect of making every member function of the class a friend. For example:

```
class Student;        //forward declaration
class Teacher
{
  protected:
    int       noStudents;
    Student *pList[100];
  public:
    void assignGrades();
};

class Student
{
    friend class Teacher; //make entire class a friend
  public:
    //same public members as before...
  protected:
    int    semesterHours;  //hours earned toward graduation
    float gpa;
};
```

Now any member function of *Teacher* has access to the protected members of *Student*. Declaring one class a friend of the other inseparably binds the two classes together.

Conclusion

As prospective parents of objects, we can read all the child-rearing books we want about how to protect our little charges from outside, non-member functions. If we don't get them off to a good start, however, it won't do any good. In the next chapter, we look at how to start objects properly as upstanding members of their class.

Chapter 11

Getting an Object Off to a Good Start: The Constructor

In This Chapter

▶ Comparing objects and classes

▶ Creating and destroying objects

▶ Declaring constructors and destructors

▶ Invoking constructors and destructors

*L*ike objects in the real world, objects in our program are created and scrapped. If the class is to be responsible for its well-being, it must have some control over this process. As luck would have it (I suppose some preplanning was involved as well), C++ provides just the mechanism we need. But first, let's make sure we know what it means to create an object.

Creating Objects

So far we've been a little sloppy in our use of the terms *class* and *object*. What is the difference? What is the relationship?

I can create a class *Dog* that describes the relevant properties of man's best friend. At my house, we have two dogs. Thus, my class *Dog* has two instances, *Trudie* and *Scooter*. (They were so disappointed when they read my last book that I promised I would somehow work their names into this one.)

A class describes a type of thing. An object is an instance of a class. The class is *Dog*, and the objects are *Trudie* and *Scooter*. There is a separate object for each dog, but only one class *Dog* no matter how many dogs I might have. ■

Objects are created and destroyed, but classes simply exist. My pets *Trudie* and *Scooter* might come and go, but the class *Dog* (evolution aside) is perpetual.

Different types of objects are created at different times. Global objects are created when the program first begins execution. Local objects are created when the program encounters their declaration (see Chapter 5).

In the following example, *Princess* and *Dwarf* are classes, *snowWhite*, *sleepy*, and *dopey* are objects (*snowWhite* is an instance of *Princess* whereas *sleepy* and *dopey* are instances of the class *Dwarf*).

Remember that in the naming convention I use throughout the book, classes begin with an uppercase letter and objects begin with a lowercase one. ■

```
class Princess
{
   //...members of some kind here...
}
class Dwarf
{
   //...information here as well...
};
Princess snowWhite;        //snowWhite created globally
                           //before anybody else

void forest()
{
   Dwarf sleepy;           //sleepy created within the forest

   //...code goes here...
   Dwarf dopey;            //dopey gets created here
   //...snowWhite eats the apple...
   return;                 //bye bye sleepy and dopey
}
```

In this example, the global object *snowWhite* is created when the program first starts executing, even before control is passed to *main()*. The object *sleepy* is created when control passes through its declaration immediately after entering the *forest()*. The second object, *dopey*, is not created until later in the function *forest()*. That is, the object *dopey* is created when control passes through its declaration.

Both *sleepy* and *dopey* are destroyed when the program returns from *forest()*. The object *snowWhite* is not destroyed until the program is over.

An object doesn't have to have a name. In the following code snippet, all seven dwarfs are created at the same time.

```
void forest(Princess& snowWhite)
{
   Dwarf dwarf[7];
   //...don't eat the apple this time!...
}
```

dwarf[0] refers to the first object of class *Dwarf, dwarf[1]*, another, and so on to *dwarf[6]*.

But what are the initial values of *snowWhite* and the others? Under C rules, *snowWhite* would be initialized to all zeros because it's global. The dwarfs would have no particular initial value because they are declared local to a function. This is probably not acceptable to our classes. All zeros may not be the proper initial value for class *Princess*, and random values certainly are not correct for class *Dwarf*.

C++ allows the class to define a special member function that is invoked automatically when an object of that class is created. It is the job of this member function, called the *constructor,* to initialize the object to some valid initial state. In addition, the class may define a *destructor* to handle the destruction of the object. These two functions are the topic of the remainder of this chapter.

Constructors

The constructor is a member function that is called automatically with an object when an object of a certain class is created. Its primary job is to initialize the object to a legal initial value for the class.

Why do I need them?

For a C structure, we can initialize an object as part of the declaration. For example:

```
struct Student
{
    int   semesterHours;
    float gpa;
};

void fn()
{
    Student s = {0, 0};
    //...function continues...
}
```

But this doesn't work for a class because the application doesn't have access to the protected members of the class. The following snippet is invalid:

```
class Student
{
  public:
    //...public members...
```

continued

```
    protected:
      int    semesterHours;
      float gpa;
};

void fn()
{
    Student s = {0, 0};    //illegal; data members not accessible
    //...function continues...
}
```

In this example, the non-member *fn()* can't write to the protected members *semesterHours* and *gpa*.

We could outfit the class with an initialization function that the application calls as soon as the object is created. Because this initialization function is a member of the class, it would have access to the protected members. This solution appears as follows:

```
class Student
{
  public:
    void init()
    {
        semesterHours = 0;
        gpa = 0.0;
    }
    //...other public members...

  protected:
    int    semesterHours;
    float gpa;
};

void fn()
{
    Student s;         //create the object...
    s.init();           //...then initialize it
    //...function continues...
}
```

The only problem with this solution is that it abrogates the responsibility of the class to look after its own data members. In other words, if the application fails to call *init()*, the object is full of garbage and who knows what might happen.

Okay, so let's take the responsibility for calling the *init()* function away from the application code and give it to the compiler, because it knows when objects are created. Every time an object is created, the compiler can insert a call to the special *init* function to initialize it.

That's a constructor!

How do they work?

The constructor is a special member function that is called automatically when an object is created. It carries the same name as the class. That way, the compiler knows which member function is the constructor. (The designers of C++ could have made up a different rule, such as: "The constructor must be called *init().*" It wouldn't have made any difference, as long as the compiler could recognize the constructor.)

With a constructor, the class *Student* appears as follows:

```
class Student
{
  public:
    Student()
    {
        semesterHours = 0;
        gpa = 0.0;
    }
    //...other public members...

    protected:
      int    semesterHours;
      float gpa;
};

void fn()
{
    Student s;          //create the object and initialize it
    //...function continues...
}
```

At the point of the declaration of *s*, the compiler inserts a call to the constructor *Student::Student()*.

This simple constructor was written as an inline member function. Constructors can be written also as outline functions. For example:

```
class Student
{
  public:
    Student();
    //...other public members...

    protected:
      int    semesterHours;
      float gpa;
};
Student::Student()
{
    semesterHours = 0;
    gpa = 0.0;
}
```

continued

```
void fn()
{
    Student s;        //create the object and initialize it
    //...function continues...
}
int main()
{
    fn();
    return 0;
}
```

I added a small *main()* function here so that you can execute this program. You really should single step this simple program in your debugger before going any further. (The debuggers built into the Turbo C++, Borland C++, or Microsoft C++ packages will work just fine.)

As you single step through this example, control eventually comes to rest at the *Student s;* declaration. Select Step Into or Trace one more time and control magically jumps to *Student::Student()*. (If you are using the inline version, be sure to compile with the "Outline inline functions" compiler switch enabled; otherwise the entire constructor is executed as a single statement and you won't notice the call.) Continue single stepping through the constructor. When the function is completed, control returns to the statement after the declaration.

Multiple objects can be declared on a single line. Rerun the single step experiment with *fn()* declared as follows:

```
void fn()
{
    Student s[5];     //create an array of objects
    //...function continues...
}
```

You should see the constructor invoked five times, once for each element in the array.

For some compilers, such as Turbo C++, you may have to set a breakpoint in the constructor to see it execute during the initialization of an array of instances of a class. ■

If you can't get the debugger to work (or you just don't want to bother), add an output statement to the constructor so that you can see output to the screen whenever the constructor is invoked. The effect is not as dramatic, but it is convincing. ■

The constructor can be invoked only automatically. It cannot be called like a normal member function. That is, you cannot use something like the following to reinitialize a *Student* object.

```
void fn()
{
   Student s;          //initialize the object
   //...other stuff...
   s.Student();        //reinitilize it; this doesn't work
}
```

The constructor has no return type, not even *void*. (The reason for this is not clear. It's obvious that the constructor doesn't return anything because it's not called like a normal member function. But it seems that giving it a return type of *void* would have been more consistent.)

If a class contains a data member that is an object of another class, the constructor for that class is called automatically as well. Consider the following example. Output statements have been added so that you can see the order in which the objects are invoked.

```
#include <iostream.h>
class Student
{
  public:
   Student()
   {
      cout << "constructing student\n";
      semesterHours = 0;
      gpa = 0.0;
   }
   //...other public members...

  protected:
   int    semesterHours;
   float gpa;
};

class Teacher
{
  public:
   Teacher()
   {
      cout << "constructing teacher\n";
   }
};

class TutorPair
{
  public:
   TutorPair()
   {
      cout << "constructing tutor pair\n";
      noMeetings = 0;
   }

  protected:
   Student student;
```

continued

```
        Teacher teacher;
        int     noMeetings;
};

int main()
{
    TutorPair tp;
    cout << "back in main\n";
    return 0;
}
```

Executing this program generates the following output:

```
constructing student
constructing teacher
constructing tutor pair
back in main
```

Creating the object *tp* in *main* invokes the constructor for *TutorPair* automatically. Before control passes into the body of the *TutorPair* constructor, however, the constructors for the two member objects *student* and *teacher* are invoked.

The constructor for *Student* is called first because it is declared first. Then the constructor for *Teacher* is called. Once these objects have been constructed, control returns and the constructor for *TutorPair* is allowed to construct the remainder of the object.

It would not do for *TutorPair* to be responsible for initializing *student* and *teacher*. Each class is responsible for initializing its own objects. ∎

The Destructor

Just as objects are created, so are they destroyed (ashes to ashes, dust to dust). If a class can have a constructor to set things up, it should also have a special member function that's called to destruct, or take apart, the object. This member is called the *destructor*.

Why do I need it?

A class may allocate resources in the constructor; these resources need to be deallocated before the object ceases to exist. For example, if the constructor opens a file, the file needs to be closed. Or if the constructor allocates memory from the heap, this memory must be freed before the object goes away. The destructor allows the class to do these clean-up tasks automatically without relying on the application to call the proper member functions.

How does it work?

The destructor member has the same name as the class but with a tilde (~) added to the front. (C++ is being cute again — the tilde is the symbol for NOT in C. Get it? A destructor is a "not constructor.") Like a constructor, the destructor has no return type. For example, the class *Student* with a destructor added appears as follows:

```
class Student
{
  public:
   Student()
   {
      semesterHours = 0;
      gpa = 0.0;
   }
   ~Student()
   {
      //...whatever assets are returned here...
   }
   //...other public members...

  protected:
   int    semesterHours;
   float gpa;
};
```

The destructor is invoked automatically when an object is destroyed, or in C++ parlance, when an object is destructed. That sounds sort of circular ("the destructor is invoked when an object is destructed"), so I've avoided the term until now. You can also say, "when the object goes out of scope." A local object goes out of scope when the function returns. A global or static object goes out of scope when the program terminates.

If more than one object is being destructed, the destructors are invoked in the reverse order in which the constructors were called. This is also true when destructing objects that have class objects as data members. For example, here's the example tutor pair program from Chapter 11, with destructors added:

```
#include <iostream.h>
class Student
{
  public:
   Student()
   {
      cout << "constructing student\n";
      semesterHours = 0;
      gpa = 0.0;
   }
   ~Student()
   {
```

continued

```
            cout << "destructing student\n";
        }
        //...other public members...

    protected:
      int    semesterHours;
      float gpa;
};

class Teacher
{
    public:
      Teacher()
      {
          cout << "constructing teacher\n";
      }
      ~Teacher()
      {
          cout << "destructing teacher\n";
      }
};

class TutorPair
{
    public:
      TutorPair()
      {
          cout << "constructing tutor pair\n";
          noMeetings = 0;
      }
      ~TutorPair()
      {
          cout << "destructing tutor pair\n";
      }

    protected:
      Student s;
      Teacher t;
      int      noMeetings;
};

int main()
{
    TutorPair tp;
    cout << "back in main\n";
    return 0;
}
```

If we execute this program, it generates the following output:

```
constructing student
constructing teacher
constructing tutor pair
back in main
destructing tutor pair
destructing teacher
destructing student
```

The constructor for *TutorPair* is invoked at the declaration of *tp*. The destructor is invoked at the closing brace of *main( )*.

Conclusion

Now that we know how to declare a class and instance that class with a few objects in good standing, let's work through how we might solve a problem using classes and objects. In the next chapter, we'll see our BUDGET program with classes defined to describe the savings and checking account types. The definitions of deposit and withdrawal will be made part of the class, just like the account number and balance.

Chapter 12
Finding the Classes

● ●

In This Chapter

▶ The role of object-oriented design

▶ Finding the classes in all that detail

▶ Attributing properties to classes

▶ Describing the relationship between classes

● ●

*I*t's all very nice that we know how to build a class in C++, but that's not of much use if we don't know where classes fit into a real-world problem. So let's take a simple problem, solve it using an OO approach and contrast that with a conventional structured approach. (The structured approach is what you've been doing in C until now.)

Object-Oriented Analysis and Design

The process of writing a program can be divided into three distinct steps: analysis, design, and coding. Some people think programming involves only the last step — coding — but programming includes all three.

Problems start out in the real world, often called the *problem domain.* Solving a problem at this point is difficult because of all the confusing details of the problem. During the *analysis phase,* we extract the essential elements of the problem and abstract away the unimportant details. The result of this analysis is a model of the problem. This model is written by and for humans. (One type of model is a block diagram; boxes represent the agents and arrows connecting the boxes represent the data being passed back and forth.)

During the *design phase*, the model is manipulated into a proposed solution. This solution may take the form of a flow chart, a PDL (Preliminary Design Language), or even pseudocode. Whatever the form, it looks more like a computer language but is still readable by humans. During the *coding phase,* the solution is converted to code.

At this point, you're either saying "I don't do all that!" or "This is true even in structured programming." To the first comment I say, "Yes you do, whether you know it or not." Even if you don't put all this stuff on paper, you have to go through these steps (or something like them) to solve any nontrivial programming problem.

To the second comment I say, "You're right." You have to go through these steps in a structured language as well, but the process is more difficult. Here's the argument: One result of analysis is the identification of the essential abstractions (read "classes") of the problem. Because you can't code classes in a structured language, the design and the model are more different in a structured language than they are in an object-oriented language. Another way to say "more different" in this context is "conceptually more distant." (Conceptual distance refers to the length of the mental jump you make to get from one phase of development to the other.)

Increased conceptual distance introduces more errors in the design. It also makes it more difficult to see the abstractions the designer was using when solving the problem, which in turn makes the resulting program more difficult to understand and maintain.

An Example Analysis and Design Problem

To see how object-oriented analysis and design (OOA&D, as we in the know call it) works, let's solve a problem down to the rough design level. (Generating the code at this point wouldn't add much to our understanding of the problem.)

Our task is to write the tuner controller for the new PaleColor 500 TV set. This controller will be connected to the TV hardware, as shown in Figure 12-1.

The controller takes input from both the infrared sensor (for the remote) and the front panel of the TV. (Did you remember that you can still control most sets without a remote?) The viewer can select either the channel to tune to or NEXT or PREV (for the next or previously stored channel in the channel list). When a channel is selected, the controller sends the frequency to the tuner and then displays the channel by enabling the display character generator for 5 seconds.

Quick analysis and design: a structured approach

Let's start with a type of structured analysis and design that's probably already familiar to you. A very high-level PDL of the main function looks like the following:

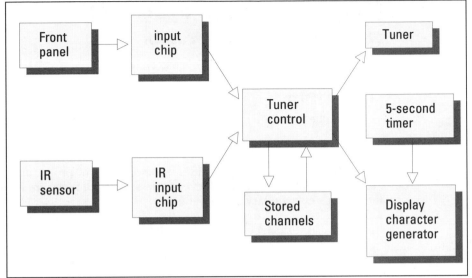

Figure 12-1:
The hardware inter-connections for our TV tuner controller.

```
INITIALIZE THE IR SENSOR

INITIALIZE THE FRONT PANEL

LOOP
    DO
        READ IR SENSOR
        READ FRONT PANEL
    UNTIL INPUT DETECTED
    PARSE INPUT

    IF NEXT
        INCREMENT NEXT CHANNEL POINTER
        IF BEYOND END OF CHANNEL LIST
            SET POINTER TO BEGINNING OF LIST
        GET CHANNEL POINTED AT

    IF PREV
        DECREMENT NEXT CHANNEL POINTER
        IF PRIOR TO BEGINNING OF LIST
            SET POINTER TO END OF LIST
        GET CHANNEL POINTED AT
    CONVERT CHANNEL TO FREQUENCY
    SEND FREQUENCY TO TUNER
    SEND CHANNEL TO CHARACTER DISPLAY GENERATOR
    SET TIMER TO TURN CHARACTER DISPLAY GENERATOR OFF IN 5 SEC.S
ENDLOOP
```

Notice how much this design centers on verbs. Every sentence begins with either *IF* or a verb. This is typical of functional design because it centers on what to do and not on the abstractions inherent in the problem.

Quick analysis and design: an object-oriented approach

In object-oriented analysis and design, we perform the following steps:

- Find the classes
- Describe the classes and the relationships between them
- Use the classes to structure the program

Finding the classes is mostly a matter of experience. The programmer starts with a list of candidate classes and then considers which of these are fundamental and which are secondary or derivative.

Candidate classes can be found among the following:

- Tangible or visible things, such as televisions or microwaves
- Roles, such as TV viewer or coach potato
- Events, such as tuning the TV or turning it off
- Interactions, such as the IR communication path between the remote and the TV

For more complicated programs, programmers must undertake a complete domain analysis. They must immerse themselves in the problem domain, learn the lingo of the domain experts, and study solutions to similar problems (whether computer-based or not), looking for the key abstractions. (They must be sure to take note of which abstractions worked and which did not.)

For simple problems, it is often useful to go through a statement of the problem and list the nouns. Here's a list from our TV tuner controller problem:

```
Controller
Input
InfraredSensor
FrontPanel
TV
Viewer
Channel
Channel list
Tuner
Display Character Generator
```

Now that we have a list, we need to figure out which terms might be useful. (The hardware connection diagram might help with this task.) We are building the *Controller*, so this is a possible class. The nouns *Viewer* and *TV* appear to be valid classes also, but at a higher level of abstraction. That is, the *Controller* is part of the *TV,* which is used by the *Viewer.* The remaining nouns might be valid classes, so we will leave them as candidates for now.

Now it's time to describe the classes and their relationships. This is an iterative process, so the two parts to this step — describing the classes and describing their relationships — should be considered simultaneously. In general, the validity of key abstractions doesn't change, but the border between them might move back and forth. That is, a particular capability allocated to one class might be moved to another.

There are several ways to describe classes and their relationships, but most involve expensive CASE tools that you don't have. (Don't worry, they don't work that well yet anyway.) However, one clever approach is called the Class-Responsibility-Collaboration (CRC) Method.[1] It is simple, and everything you need is available in your kitchen.

The CRC method characterizes each class by the following:

- *Class name.* Select candidate classes as described (or use any other technique you like). Use names that clearly describe the responsibility of each class (that is, don't use wishy-washy names).

- *Responsibilities.* Each class does something. Describe each class using a short phrase with an active verb. Refine the verb, if necessary, to describe unambiguously what the class does. These verbs eventually become member functions.

- *Collaborators.* Each class relies on other classes, called collaborators, to implement the complete design. By noting the collaborators for each class, you deepen your understanding of the role each class plays. Note also which member functions these collaborators need access to.

Start by writing the class name in the upper left corner of a 3-by-5 index card. Below this, write the initial responsibility list (use pencil because this will change). Along the right side, note the collaborator classes that the class depends on.

The properties of each class can be jockeyed back and forth until you think you have a good description of the essential abstractions of the problem.

When assigning responsibilities, use terse, strongly worded verbs. Use the same verb in different classes to do the same thing. For example, both class *IRSensor* and *FrontPanel* have the responsibility *read.* Classes that have no responsibilities should be deleted because they don't do anything.

---

[1] Proposed by Ward Cunningham and described in "Think Like an Object," Kent Beck, *UNIX Review,* October, 1991.

An OO solution to our problem

Using the candidate classes in the preceding section, I came up with the CRC cards shown in Figure 12-2. From this we can see that *Controller* does not make a very good class. It depends on every class in the system, which indicates that it is probably conceived functionally. In addition, its responsibilities are "do everything." *Controller* incorporates the entire solution. We will let this be our main program, which uses the other classes to solve the problem.

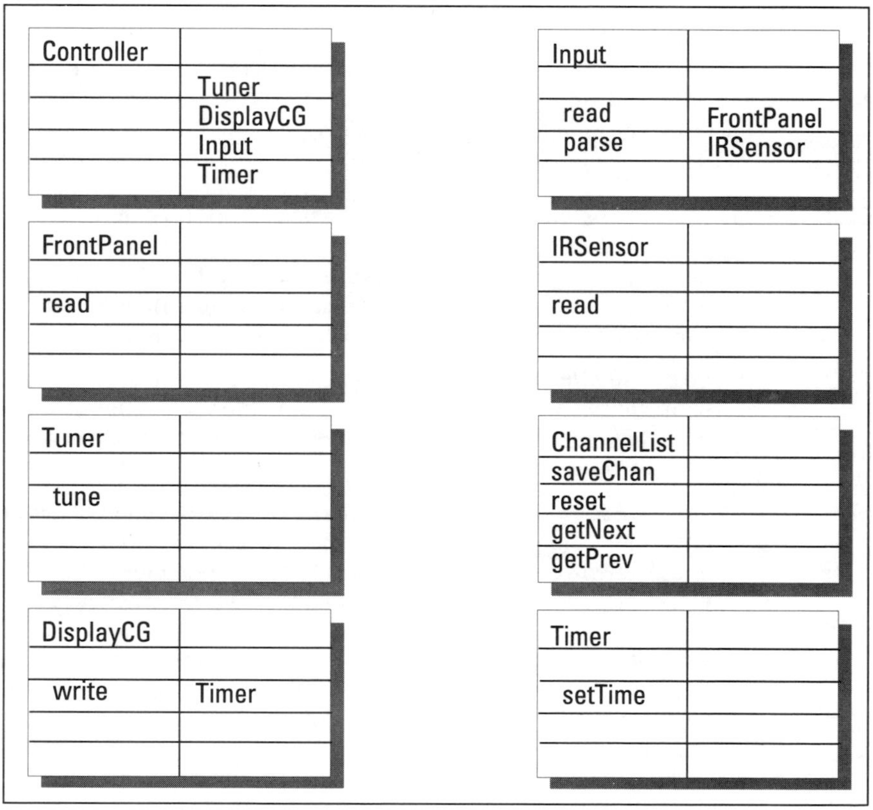

Controller		
	Tuner	
	DisplayCG	
	Input	
	Timer	

Input		
read	FrontPanel	
parse	IRSensor	

FrontPanel	
read	

IRSensor	
read	

Tuner	
tune	

ChannelList	
saveChan	
reset	
getNext	
getPrev	

DisplayCG	
write	Timer

Timer	
setTime	

Figure 12-2: CRC cards for our TV tuner problem.

Let's look at *main()* and one of the classes to get a feel for what the complete solution would look like:

```
DECLARE INPUT OBJECT
LOOP
    DO
        INPUT.READ
    UNTIL INPUT DETECTED
    INPUT.PARSE
```

```
        CONVERT CHANNEL TO FREQUENCY
        TUNER.SEND FREQUENCY
        DISPLAYCG.WRITE
    ENDLOOP
```

The *Input* class looks like the following:

```
    CONSTRUCTOR:
        DECLARE IRSENSOR
        DECLARE FRONTPANEL
    READ:
        DO
            IRSENSOR.READ
            FRONTPANEL.READ
        UNTIL INPUT DETECTED
        RETURN INPUT
    PARSE:
        PARSE THE INPUT STREAM
```

(We are a bit hampered by the fact that we haven't gone very far in our study of constructors. In the next part, we see how to build the *Input* class so that it works for any number and type of input devices.)

The PDL for *Controller* is simpler than the functional PDL presented earlier. You could argue that we got this simplicity by pushing more of the code into functions. (These functions are the member functions of the classes.) This is not completely correct, however.

Consider that details about how data will be read from the IR sensor appear at the highest level of the functional PDL. At this level, how the IR sensor hardware is handled is useless extra informational baggage for the reader. Further, if this hardware changes (which it undoubtedly will as soon as Hyundai starts making a cheaper one), even code at this level will have to be modified.

Consider the object-oriented PDL. We can see that all we are interested in doing is "reading input." The details of the IR sensor, if one is even present, are of no interest at this level. These details, along with details of parsing the input, are left to the *Input* class, where they belong. If the IR sensor hardware changes, we need to change only the part of the *Input* class that deals with the IR sensor. (C++ helps us here as well, as we will see later.) And if we have done our job well, those changes will not propagate outside the class.

Conclusion

As Grady Booch said (I'm such a name dropper), "The identification of classes and objects is the fundamental issue in object-oriented design; identification involves both discovery and invention."[2] This last is very important. The act of identifying classes teaches you something about the problem — you organize your thoughts and figure out the essential abstractions. (Why do you think biology students spend all their time studying taxonomies of plants and animals?)

As you learn, don't be afraid to reevaluate your classes. If necessary, try different classes. If you choose the wrong ones, they will tell you. They will be difficult to envision because they will be difficult to describe. In addition, such classes will have lots of member functions without a clear purpose. Classes with many collaborators are suspicious. A large number of friend functions is another tip-off that something's amiss.

Get the classes right and you'll know it just as fast. The classes are easy to visualize and adaptable to changing conditions. There won't be too many member functions and their purpose will be clear. The clouds will part and rainbows will shine. Your sex life will improve and your premature balding will reverse itself, as if by magic.

But wait, there's more. Next, we learn how to add class to our sample budget program.

---

[2] Grady Booch, *Object Oriented Design with Applications,* Benjamin-Cummings, 1991.

A Budget with Class: BUDGET3.CPP

*L*ooking at the BUDGET program, it's easy to see what the class candidates are: *Checking* and *Savings*. We already know that it's a good idea to make data members protected, so a few access functions are necessary in case a non-member function needs the account number or balance.

Like all classes, *Checking* and *Savings* need a constructor to initialize objects to legal values (mostly to a balance of zero). Two additional member functions are also necessary: *deposit()* and *withdrawal()*. We need some way to associate an account number with the object, so I have introduced a member function called *init()*.

Finally, I added one other member function called *display()* to display the current object. This is not a requirement, but it is common to let the object display itself rather than rely on an external function to do it. (Those other functions would need knowledge of the class's internals to know how to display it properly, and that's something we want to avoid.)

Here is the resulting program:

```
//BUDGET3.CPP - Budget program with real classes for
//              the first time. Now we transform the
//              C structs into classes. This is starting
//              to look like something.

#include <iostream.h>

//the maximum number of accounts one can have
const int maxAccounts = 10;

//Checking - this describes checking accounts
class Checking                            //Note 1
{
  public:
    Checking()                            //Note 2
    {
        accountNumber = 0;
        balance = 0.0;
    }
    void init()                           //Note 3
    {
```

continued

```
        cout << "Enter account number:";
        cin  >> accountNumber;
    }

    //access functions                    //Note 4
    int accountNo()
    {
        return accountNumber;
    }
    float acntBalance()
    {
        return balance;
    }

    //transaction functions               //Note 5
    void deposit(float amount)
    {
        balance += amount;
    }
    void withdrawal(float amount);

    //display function for displaying self on 'cout'
    void display()                        //Note 6
    {
        cout << "Account " << accountNumber
             << " = "      << balance
             << "\n";
    }

  protected:                              //Note 7
    unsigned accountNumber;
    float    balance;
};
//withdrawal - this member function is too big to
//             be inlined
void Checking::withdrawal(float amount)
{
    if (balance < amount )
    {
        cout << "Insufficient funds: balance " << balance
             << ", check "                      << amount
             << "\n";
    }
    else
    {
        balance -= amount;

        //if balance falls too low, charge service fee
        if (balance < 500.00)
        {
            balance -= 0.20F;
        }
    }
}

//Savings - you can probably figure this one out
struct Savings
```

```cpp
{
  public:
   Savings()
   {
      accountNumber = 0;
      balance = 0.0;
      noWithdrawals = 0;
   }
   void init()
   {
      cout << "Enter account number:";
      cin  >> accountNumber;
   }

   //access functions
   int accountNo()
   {
      return accountNumber;
   }
   float acntBalance()
   {
      return balance;
   }

   //transaction functions
   void deposit(float amount)
   {
      balance += amount;
   }
   void withdrawal(float amount);

   //display function - display self to cout
   void display()
   {
      cout << "Account "              << accountNumber
           << " = "                   << balance
           << " (no. withdrawals = " << noWithdrawals
           << ")\n";
   }

  protected:
   unsigned accountNumber;
   float    balance;
   int      noWithdrawals;
};
void Savings::withdrawal(float amount)
{
   if (balance < amount)
   {
      cout << "Insufficient funds: balance " << balance
           << ", withdrawal "                << amount
           << "\n";
   }
   else
   {
      if (++noWithdrawals > 1)
      {
```

continued

```
                balance -= 5.00F;
            }
            balance -= amount;
        }
}

//prototype declarations
void process(Checking &checking);
void process(Savings &savings);

//checking and savings account objects
Checking chkAcnts[maxAccounts];         //Note 8
Savings svgAcnts[maxAccounts];

//main - accumulate the initial input and output totals
int main()
{
    /*loop until someone enters an 'X' or 'x'*/
    int noChkAccounts = 0;     //count the number of accounts
    int noSvgAccounts = 0;
    char    accountType;       //S or C

    unsigned keepLooping = 1;
    while (keepLooping)
    {
        cout << "Enter S for Savings, "
                "C for Checking, X for exit\n";
        cin >> accountType;

        switch (accountType)
        {
            case 'c':
            case 'C':
                if (noChkAccounts < maxAccounts) {
                    chkAcnts[noChkAccounts].init(); //Note 9
                    process(chkAcnts[noChkAccounts]);
                    noChkAccounts++;
                }
                else
                {
                    cout << "No more room for checking accounts\n";
                }
                break;

            case 's':
            case 'S':
                if (noSvgAccounts < maxAccounts)
                {
                    svgAcnts[noSvgAccounts].init();
                    process(svgAcnts[noSvgAccounts]);
                    noSvgAccounts++;
                }
                else
                {
                    cout << "No more room for savings accounts\n";
                }
                break;
```

```
            case 'x':
            case 'X':
                keepLooping = 0;
                break;

            default:
                cout << "I didn't get that.\n";
        }
    }

    //now present totals
    float chkTotal = 0;         //total of all checking accounts
    cout << "Checking accounts:\n";
    for (int i = 0; i < noChkAccounts; i++)
    {
        chkAcnts[i].display();              //Note 10
        chkTotal += chkAcnts[i].acntBalance();
    }
    float svgTotal = 0;         //total of all savings accounts
    cout << "Savings accounts:\n";
    for (i = 0; i < noSvgAccounts; i++)
    {
        svgAcnts[i].display();
        svgTotal += svgAcnts[i].acntBalance();
    }

    float total = chkTotal + svgTotal;
    cout << "Total for checking accounts = " << chkTotal << "\n";
    cout << "Total for savings accounts  - " << svgTotal << "\n";
    cout << "Total worth                 = " << total << "\n";
    return 0;
}

//process(Checking) - input the data for a checking account*/
void process(Checking &checking)
{
    cout << "Enter positive number for deposit,\n"
            "negative for check, 0 to terminate";

    float transaction;
    do
    {
        cout << ":";
        cin  >> transaction;

        //deposit
        if (transaction > 0)
        {
            checking.deposit(transaction);
        }

        //withdrawal
        if (transaction < 0)
        {
            checking.withdrawal(-transaction);
        }
    } while (transaction != 0);
}
```

continued

```
//process(Savings) - input the data for a savings account
void process(Savings &savings)
{
    cout << "Enter positive number for deposit,\n"
            "negative for withdrawal, 0 to terminate";

    float transaction;
    do
    {
        cout << ":";
        cin  >> transaction;

        //deposit
        if (transaction > 0)
        {
            savings.deposit(transaction);
        }

        //withdrawal
        if (transaction < 0)
        {
            savings.withdrawal(-transaction);
        }
    } while (transaction != 0);
}
```

Executing this program with the same input as before generates the same output as the previous version. (If it didn't, I'd be worried.)

```
Enter S for Savings, C for Checking, X for exit
S
Enter account number:123
Enter positive number for deposit,
negative for withdrawal, 0 to terminate:200
:-50
:-50
:0
Enter S for Savings, C for Checking, X for exit
C
Enter account number:234
Enter positive number for deposit,
negative for check, 0 to terminate:200
:-25
:-20
:0
Enter S for Savings, C for Checking, X for exit
X
Checking accounts:
Account 234 = 154.600006
Savings accounts:
Account 123 = 95 (no. withdrawals = 2)
Total for checking accounts = 154.600006
Total for savings accounts  = 95
Total worth                 = 249.600006
```

Starting with class *Checking* (*Note 1*), we can see each of the member functions mentioned earlier. The constructor (*Note 2*) zeros out the account number and the balance. Initializing the balance to zero is critical; otherwise, every account would start with a random amount of money in it.

The *init()* member function (*Note 3*) assigns the object an account number. The access functions (*Note 4*) simply return the account number or the balance. The two transaction functions (*Note 5*) implement the deposit and withdrawal rules that apply to checking accounts. Because the *deposit()* function is quite simple, it has been implemented inline. The *withdrawal()* function, however, has been written as an outline function.

The *display()* function (*Note 6*) outputs the important data members to the standard output. The data members have been protected (*Note 7*) to keep prying fingers off.

The class *Savings* is virtually identical to the class *Checking*. *Checking* and *Savings* objects are allocated from a global array and therefore constructed before *main()* starts (at *Note 8*). Function *main()* looks similar, except for the format used to call member functions (*Note 9*) and the fact that data members must be accessed through access functions (*Note 10*).

The *process()* functions are considerably simpler because their class-specific code has been moved into the class.

I encourage you to enter this program and single-step through it. Nothing else will give you the feel for what's going on faster than seeing the program in action. (Be sure and set the "Outline inline functions" option as explained in Chapter 6 so that you can see the member functions single-step.) ■

25-Minute Workout

*T*his part has only one exercise. The time has come to sink or swim. Write a program that does the following.

Model a set of courses and students. Students have names. Students can enroll in courses. Students are given a grade (between 0 and 4) in each class. Courses can have different numbers of semester hours.

After all the students have been graded, the program should then spit out the following:

- The average grade in each course
- Each student's grade in each course
- The student's average grade for all classes
- The student's grade in each course curved by the average of all grades in the class

Write your solution in C++. (I didn't really need to say that, did I?)

Here are a few tips for solving this problem. One, use an object-oriented approach. Protect your data members as much as possible.

Two, study the requirements to find the candidate classes. Then examine the output requirements to determine the member functions you will need. Make CRC cards if it helps.

Three, use the following simple curving formula:

```
curved grade = 3.0 * (actual grade / average)
```

This makes the average grade 3.0. However, make sure the grade of any single student does not exceed 4.0.

Four, concentrate on what classes you need to solve this problem. To keep the program as short as possible, you can hardcode the actual course objects and student objects that you will need to test your classes. Just make sure that you provide enough courses and students to show that the classes work. ∎

Answer

Here's my analysis of the problem. The two classes I chose from the description were *Course* and *Student*. Armed with these candidate classes, I returned to the problem description to look for verbs to be turned into member functions. I found the following:

- Students enroll in courses
- Students are graded
- The program averages all grades in each course
- The program returns each student's grade in each course
- The program averages each student's grades from all courses in which that student is enrolled
- The program calculates the average curved grade by the average grade in the class

To enroll a student in a course and perform the necessary averages, I concluded that each *Student* object needed to know what courses it was enrolled in (like a course list) and each *Course* needed to know what students it had (like a student roll). To keep things simple, I used an array and set a maximum number of courses per student and a maximum number of students in each course. So that these maximums were not exceeded, I also needed *noStudents* to class *Course* and *noCourses* to *Student*.

I needed also a *Student::add(Course&)* to add a course to the student's course list and a *Course::add(Student&)* to add the student to the course's student roll. These two functions handled the *enroll* verb mentioned in the preceding list.

It wasn't important to me whether the application accessed these two functions through the *Student* class or the *Course* class; I chose *Student*. To keep me from forgetting and getting it wrong in use, I made *Course::add()* protected.

Students are graded in the preceding list implied the need for a grade function in *Student* or *Course*. Is the grade a student receives in a course a property of the student or a property of the course? I couldn't find a good answer to that one, except that historically grades are kept in little books (or little computer databases, nowadays) associated with the course. Thus, I decided to add the member function *Course::grade(Student&, grade)*. I also added member functions *grade(Student&)* to return a student's grade and *grade()* to return the average of all students in the course, as stipulated by the requirements.

One final member function in *Course*, *findStudent()*, is used in several member functions to find a student in the roll. These functions which are needed only internally should be left protected to keep the class's surface area as small as possible.

Semester hours is obviously a property of *Course*, requiring a data member and a member function to set it. The student's name is a property of *Student*, requiring a data member and function pair as well.

The following is my solution to the problem along with a description of how it works. Realize that your solution may be different; there is no single right solution as long as you're trying to think like an object.

```cpp
//PROB3.CPP  My solution to the Part III Workout

#include <iostream.h>
#include <string.h>

const int maxStudents = 20;  //max no. of students in one class
const int maxCourses = 6;    //max no. of courses student can take

class Student;                          //Note 1

class Course
{
   friend class Student;
  public:
   Course( )                            //Note 2
   {
      noStudents = 0;
      semesterHours = 3.0;  //default is 3.0
   }
   ~Course( )
   {
      //nothing to do here
   }

   //hours - return or set the number of hours in this class
   int hours( )
   {
      return semesterHours;
   }
   int hours(int newValue)
   {                                    //Note 3
      int oldValue = semesterHours;     //it's customary to...
      semesterHours = newValue;
      return oldValue;                  //...return old value
   }

   //grade - return the average for the class or the grade of a
   //         single student or set the grade of a single student
   float grade( );                      //Note 4
   float grade(Student &s);
   void  grade(Student &s, float grade);

  protected:
   //member functions
   //add - add a student to the roll
   int add(Student &s);
```

continued

```
        //findStudent - find student in role
        int findStudent(Student &s);

        //data members
        Student *pStudents[maxStudents];
        float    classGrade[maxStudents];
        int      semesterHours;
        int      noStudents;
};

class Student
{
  public:
    Student( )
    {
        //just zero out everything
        noCourses = 0;
        sName[0] = '\0';
    }
    ~Student( )
    {
        //nothing to do
    }

    //return grade in a given course or average in all courses
    float grade(Course &c)                //Note 5
    {
        return c.grade(*this);
    }
    float grade( );

    //return the grade compared to the class average
    float curvedGrade(Course &c);

    //add a student to a course
    void add(Course &c);

    //name - read and set name
    char *name( )
    {
        return sName;
    }
    void  name(char *pName);

  protected:
    char     sName[20];
    Course *pClasses[maxCourses];
    int      noCourses;
};

//-------------Course member functions--------------------
//grade - return the average for the class
float Course::grade( )
{
    //if there are no students, forget it now
    if (noStudents == 0)
    {
        return 0.0;
    }
```

```
      //add 'em all and return the average
      float accumGrade = 0.0;
      for (int i = 0; i < noStudents; i++)
      {
         accumGrade += classGrade[i];
      }
      return accumGrade / noStudents;
   }

//grade(Student*) - return the grade of a single student
float Course::grade(Student &s)
{
   //first look the student up in the student roll
   int offset = findStudent(s);

   //return student's grade or 0 if the student wasn't found
   return (offset >= 0) ? classGrade[offset] : 0.0;
}

//grade(Student, grade) - set the grade of a single student
void Course::grade(Student &s, float grade)
{
   int offset = findStudent(s);
   if (offset >= 0)
   {
      classGrade[offset] = grade;
   }
}

//add   add a student to the class roll; return 1 if
//      it works and a zero otherwise
int Course::add(Student &s)
{
   if (noStudents >= maxStudents)
   {
      cout << "No more room in class...maybe next semester\n";
      return 0;
   }
   pStudents[noStudents++] = &s;
   return 1;
}

//findStudent - find a student in the look-up table;
//              return offset or -1 if can't find
int Course::findStudent(Student &s)
{
   for (int i = 0; i < noStudents; i++)
   {
      if (pStudents[i] == &s)
      {
         return i;
      }
   }
   return -1;
}
```

continued

```
//--------------Student member functions-------------------
//grade( ) - return the average grade for all courses
float Student::grade( )
{
   int hours;
   int noHours = 0;
   float accumGrade = 0.0;
   for (int i = 0; i < noCourses; i++)
   {
      hours = pClasses[i]->hours( );
      accumGrade += pClasses[i]->grade(*this) * hours;
      noHours += hours;
   }
   return (noHours) ? (accumGrade / noHours): 0.0;
}

//add - add a student to a class
void Student::add(Course &c)
{
   if (noCourses >= maxCourses)
   {
      cout << "no more room in the inn\n";
      return;
   }
   if (c.add(*this))
   {
      pClasses[noCourses++] = &c;
   }
}

//curvedGrade - return the grade curved by the average
float Student::curvedGrade(Course &c)
{
   //set the average to 3.0
   float g = 3.0 * grade(c) / c.grade( );

   //don't let it go over 4.0
   if (g > 4.0)
   {
      g = 4.0;
   }
   return g;
}

//name(char*) - store the name provided
void  Student::name(char *pName)
{
   strncpy(sName, pName, sizeof(sName) - 1);
   sName[sizeof(sName) - 1] = '\0';
}

//--------------------test program------------------------
int main( )
{
   //declare a course
   Course geo101;
```

```
//give it a couple of students
Student harry, anne;
harry.name("Harry");
harry.add(geo101);
anne.name("Anne");
anne.add(geo101);

//grade them
geo101.grade(harry, 3.0);
geo101.grade(anne, 2.5);

//now let's look at the averages
cout<<"average geo101 grade = "<<geo101.grade( )          <<"\n";
cout<<"anne's grade         = "<<anne.grade(geo101)       <<"\n";
cout<<"anne's curved grade  = "<<anne.curvedGrade(geo101)<<"\n";

//let's look at harry's other course
Course engl201;
engl201.hours(4.0);
harry.add(engl201);
engl201.grade(harry, 2.0);
cout << "harry's average grade = " << harry.grade( ) << "\n";

return 0;
}
```

In this solution, I decided that the classes *Student* and *Course* could be built dependent on each other. There is little chance of using class *Student* without *Course* or vice versa in some future solution. (A student without a course or a course without any students doesn't make much sense.) To be able to make *Student* a friend of *Course*, the class needed to be declared, hence the early declaration (*Note 1*).

Starting with class *Course*, the constructor starts the course with an empty roll and a default of 3 semester hours (*Note 2*). The *Course::hours()* functions are standard. Notice, however, that when you change a data member value, returning the old value is an unwritten rule in C++ programming (*Note 3*). The *Course::grade()* members are present (*Note 4*), with *Course::add()* listed as protected, as promised.

Continuing to class *Student*, we find the same types of members. One interesting point (if you will look out the right side of the bus, ladies and gentlemen): *Student* has a grade function to return an individual grade (*Note 5*). This is a duplicate of *Course::grade(Student&)*; all it does is call that worthy function, but that's okay. As we noted, the grade is just as much a property of the *Student* as it is of the *Course*. The application shouldn't need to worry about where the data is stored. (Also note that to call the function *Course::grade()*, the function *Student::grade()* makes a direct reference to *this*.)

The code in the member functions is not particularly notable. The member function *Course::findStudent()* looks up a student in the roll. If it can find the student, it returns the offset. Otherwise, it returns -1. All the other functions include checks for a negative return from *Course::findStudent()*.

The *main()* program is childishly simple (as are most of my programs). I just declare a few courses, sign up a few students, grade them, and then print the individual grades, the curved grades, and the averages. The output from the program appeared as follows:

```
average geo101 grade  = 2.75
anne's grade          = 2.5
anne's curved grade   = 2.727273
harry's average grade = 2.428571
```

Now, wasn't that fun?

Part IV

Warming to the Water: Getting Comfortable with Classes

In This Part...

Part III introduced us to the concept of classes, in particular protected members, member functions, and constructors. In this part, we delve further into these concepts and introduce a few more to prepare us for the next big step, inheritance, which is covered in Part V.

Chapter 13
Making Constructive Arguments

. . . .

In This Chapter

▶ Making argumentative constructors

▶ Overloading the constructor

▶ Creating objects using these constructors

▶ Invoking member constructors

▶ Order of construction and destruction

. . . .

*Y*ou may have noticed that the constructors in Part III did not completely relieve the need for an initialization member function. The constructors had no arguments, so they had no choice but to initialize the object as "empty." In some cases, an initialization function was required to go back and "fill" the object with useful data.

If we could have passed arguments to the constructor, we could have avoided this clumsy two-step process. In this chapter, we investigate doing just that.

Constructors Outfitted with Arguments

C++ allows the programmer to define a constructor with arguments. For example:

```
#include <iostream.h>
#include <string.h>
class Student
{
   Student(char *pName)
   {
      cout << "constructing student " << pName << "\n";
      strncpy(name, pName, sizeof(name));
      name[sizeof(name) - 1]  = '\0';
   }
   //...other public members go here
   protected:
```

continued

```
    char   name[40];
    int    semesterHours;
    float  gpa;
};
```

Why do I need them?

Something as straightforward as adding arguments to the constructor shouldn't require much justification, but let me take a shot at it anyway. First, allowing arguments to constructors is convenient. It's a bit silly to make the programmer construct an empty object and then immediately call an initialization function to store data in it. A constructor with arguments is like one-stop shopping — sort of a full-service constructor.

There's another, more important reason to provide arguments to constructors: An empty object may not make sense. Remember that a constructor's job is to construct a legal object (legal as defined by the class). If an empty object is not legal, the constructor isn't doing its job.

For example, a bank account without an account number is probably not legal. (C++ doesn't care one way or the other, but the bank might get a bit excited.) We could construct a numberless *BankAccount* object and then require that the application use some other member function to initialize the account number prior to use. In fact, this is exactly what we did earlier in our BUDGET program. However, this breaks our rules by letting information about the bank account leak into the application.

How do they work?

Conceptually, the idea of adding an argument is simple. A constructor is a member function and member functions can have arguments. Ergo constructors can have arguments.

Remember, though, that you don't call the constructor like a normal function. Therefore, the only way to pass arguments to the constructor is when the object is created. For example, the following program creates an object *s* of class *Student* by calling the *Student(char*)* constructor. The object *s* is destructed when the function *main()* returns.

```
#include <iostream.h>
#include <string.h>
class Student
{
  public:
    Student(char *pName)
    {
```

```
        cout << "constructing student " << pName << "\n";
        strncpy(name, pName, sizeof(name));
        name[sizeof(name) - 1] = '\0';
        semesterHours = 0;
        gpa = 0.0;
    }
  ~Student()
    {
        cout << "destructing " << name << "\n";
    }

    //...other public members...
  protected:
    char   name[40];
    int    semesterHours;
    float gpa;
};

int main()
{
    Student s("Danny");        //construct little Danny
    return 0;
}                              //now, get rid of him
```

The constructor looks like the constructors shown in Part III except for the addition of the *char** argument *pName*. The constructor initializes the data members to their empty startup values, except for the data member *name*, which gets its initial value from *pName*.

The object *s* is created in *main()*. The argument to be passed to the constructor appears in the declaration of *s*, right next to the name of the object. Thus, the student *s* is given the name *Danny* in this declaration. The closed brace invokes the destructor on poor little Danny.

Executing the program generates the following output:

```
constructing student Danny
destructing Danny
```

Many of the constructors in this chapter violate our "functions with more than three lines shouldn't be inlined" rule. I decided to make them inline anyway because I think they're easier to follow that way.

When outlined, constructors and destructors appear as follows:

```
#include <iostream.h>
#include <string.h>
class Student
{
  public:
    //declarations only
    Student(char *pName);
  ~Student();

    //...other public members...
```

continued

```
   protected:
     char   name[40];
     int    semesterHours;
     float gpa;
};

//definitions (notice no return type)
Student::Student(char *pName)
{
    cout << "constructing student " << pName << "\n";
    strncpy(name, pName, sizeof(name));
    name[sizeof(name) - 1] = '\0';
    semesterHours = 0;
    gpa = 0.0;
}

//check out this destructor declaration
//      - does this look bizarre or what?
Student::~Student()
{
    cout << "destructing " << name << "\n";
}
```

As your experience in C++ grows, you should have no trouble mentally convert-ing from one form to the other. ■

A constructor can have as many arguments as you want. Consider the following constructor taken from class *Student*:

```
class Student
{
  public:
    Student(char *pName, int xfrHours, float xfrGPA)
    {
        cout << "constructing student " << pName << "\n";
        strncpy(name, pName, sizeof(name));
        name[sizeof(name) - 1] = '\0';
        semesterHours = xfrHours;
        gpa = xfrGPA;
    }
    //...remainder same as before...
}
```

Now when a *Student* object is created, three arguments must be provided:

```
int main()
{
    Student s("Clara", 16, 3.5);
    return 0;
}
```

Here student *s* starts out life with the name Clara, 16 semester hours, and an initial GPA of 3.5 (not bad).

Placing Too Many Demands on the Carpenter, or Overloading the Constructor

While we are drawing parallels between constructors and other, more normal member functions, let's draw one more: Constructors can be overloaded. C++ chooses the proper constructor based on the arguments in the declaration. For example, the class *Student* can have all three constructors shown in the following snippet at the same time:

```cpp
#include <iostream.h>
#include <string.h>
class Student
{
  public:
   Student()
   {
      cout << "constructing student no name\n";
      semesterHours = 0;
      gpa = 0.0;
      name[0] = '\0';
   }
   Student(char *pName)
   {
      cout << "constructing student " << pName << "\n";
      strncpy(name, pName, sizeof(name));
      name[sizeof(name) - 1]  = '\0';
      semesterHours = 0;
      gpa = 0;
   }
   Student(char *pName, int xfrHours, float xfrGPA)
   {
      cout << "constructing student " << pName << "\n";
      strncpy(name, pName, sizeof(name));
      name[sizeof(name) - 1]  = '\0';
      semesterHours = xfrHours;
      gpa = xfrGPA;
   }
   ~Student()
   {
      cout << "destructing student\n";
   }

   //...other public members...
   protected:
    char  name[40];
    int   semesterHours;
    float gpa;
};

//the following invokes each constructor in turn
int main()
{
   Student noName;
```

continued

```
        Student freshMan("Smel E. Fish");
        Student xfer("Upp R. Classman", 80, 2.1);
        return 0;
    }
```

Because the object *noName* appears with no arguments, it is constructed using the constructor *Student::Student( )*. This constructor is called the *default*, or *void*, *constructor*. (I prefer the latter name, but the former is more common so I'll use it in this book.) The *freshMan* is constructed using the constructor that has only a *char** argument, and the *xfer Student* uses the constructor with three arguments.

Notice how similar all three constructors are, particularly the last two. By adding defaults to the last constructor, all three constructors can be combined into one. For example, the following class combines all three constructors into a single, clever constructor:

```
#include <iostream.h>
#include <string.h>
class Student
{
  public:
    Student(char *pName  = "no name",
            int xfrHours = 0,
            float xfrGPA = 0.0)
    {
        cout << "constructing student " << pName << "\n";
        strncpy(name, pName, sizeof(name));
        name[sizeof(name) - 1] = '\0';
        semesterHours = xfrHours;
        gpa = xfrGPA;
    }
   ~Student()
    {
        cout << "destructing student\n";
    }

    //...other public members...
  protected:
    char  name[40];
    int   semesterHours;
    float gpa;
};

int main()
{
    Student noName;
    Student freshMan("Smell E. Fish");
    Student xfer("Upp R. Classman", 80, 2.5);
    return 0;
}
```

Now all three objects are constructed using the same constructor; defaults are provided for nonexistent arguments in *noName* and *freshMan*.

In earlier versions of C++, you could not create a default constructor by providing defaults for all the arguments. The default constructor had to be a separate explicit constructor. Although this restriction has been lifted (it seems to have had no good basis), some older compilers might still impose it. ▪

The rules for deciding which constructor to use are the same as those for resolving calls to other overloaded functions. For example, the following class has a problem:

```
class Student
{
  public:
    Student(char *pName);
    Student(char *pName, float grade = 0.0);
};

int main()
{
    Student freshMan("Smell E. Fish"); //which constructor?
    return 0;
}
```

This generates a compiler error because the compiler can't decide which constructor to call, the *Student(char*)* constructor or the *Student(char*, float)* constructor with *float* defaulted to zero.

Default Default Constructors

As far as C++ is concerned, every class must have a constructor; otherwise, you couldn't create any objects of that class. If you don't provide a constructor for your class, C++ should probably just generate an error, but it doesn't. To provide compatibility with existing C code, which knows nothing about constructors, C++ automatically provides a default constructor (sort of a "default default constructor") that sets all the data members of the object to binary zero.

If your class already has a constructor, C++ doesn't provide the automatic default constructor. (Having tipped your hand that this isn't a C program, C++ doesn't feel obliged to go to any extra work to ensure compatibility.)

The result is: If you define a constructor for your class but you also want a default constructor, you must define it yourself. ▪

Some code snippets will help demonstrate this. The following is legal:

```
class Student
{
```

```
    //...all the same stuff as before but no constructors
};

int main()
{
    Student noName;
    return 0;
}
```

noName is declared with no arguments, so C++ invokes the default constructor to construct it. Because the programmer has not already defined any constructors for class *Student*, C++ provides a default constructor that zeros out any data members that *Student* might have.

The following code snippet does not compile properly:

```
class Student
{
  public:
    Student(char *pName);
};

int main()
{
    Student noName;
    return 0;
}
```

The seemingly innocuous addition of the *Student(char*)* constructor precludes C++ from automatically providing a *Student()* constructor with which to build object *noName*. This example generates the following error message from the Borland C++ compiler. (The error message from any other compiler would be similar.)

```
Could not find a match for 'Student::Student()'
```

The compiler is telling you that it can't find a constructor to match the declaration. Adding a default constructor solves the problem:

```
class Student
{
  public:
    Student(char *pName);
    Student();                     //manually provided default constructor
};

int main()
{
    Student noName;                //used to build this object
    return 0;
}
```

This is why C++ programmers earn really big bucks!

Declaration ambiguity

Look again at the way the *Student* objects were declared in the earlier example:

```
Student noName;
Student nameOnly("Smell E. Fish");
Student lotsAData("Upp R. Classman", 80, 2.5);
```

All of the *Student* objects except *noName* are declared with parentheses surrounding the arguments to the constructor. Why is *noName* declared without parentheses?

To be neat and consistent, you might think you could have declared *noName* as follows:

```
Student noName();
```

Unfortunately, this is allowed, but it does not have the intended effect. Instead of declaring an object *noName* of class *Student* to be constructed with the default constructor, this declares a function that returns an object of class *Student* by value. Surprise! (I think I need a raise.)

The following two declarations demonstrate how similar the new C++ format for declaring an object is to that of declaring a function. (I think this was a mistake, but what do I know?) The only difference is that the function declaration contains types in the parentheses, whereas the object declaration contains objects:

```
Student thisIsAFunc(int);
Student thisIsAnObject(10);
```

If the parentheses are empty, there is nothing to differentiate between an object and a function. To retain compatibility with C, C++ chose to make a declaration with empty parentheses a function. (A safer alternative would have been to force the keyword *void* in the function case, but that would not have been compatible with existing C programs.)

Constructing Class Members

In the examples so far, all data members have been of simple types, such as *int* and *float*. With simple types, it's sufficient to assign a value to the variable within the constructor. But what if our class contains data members of a user-defined class? Consider the following example:

```
#include <iostream.h>
#include <string.h>

int nextStudentId = 0;
class StudentId
{
  public:
    StudentId()
    {
        value = ++nextStudentId;
        cout << "Assigning student id " << value << "\n";
    }
  protected:
    int value;
};

class Student
{
  public:
    Student(char *pName  = "no name")
    {
        cout << "Constructing student " << pName << "\n";
        strncpy(name, pName, sizeof(name));
        name[sizeof(name) - 1]  = '\0';
    }
  protected:
    char  name[40];
    StudentId id;
};

int main()
{
    Student s("Randy");
    return 0;
}
```

A student ID is assigned to each student as the *student* object is constructed.
In this example, IDs are handed out sequentially using the global variable
nextStudentId.

This *Student* class contains a member *id* of class *StudentId*. The constructor for
Student can't assign a value to this *id* member because *Student* does not have
access to the protected members of *StudentId*. We could make *Student* a friend
of *StudentId*, but that violates our "you take care of your business, I'll take care
of mine" philosophy. Somehow we need to invoke the constructor for *StudentId*
when *Student* is constructed.

C++ does this for us automatically in this case, invoking the default constructor
StudentId::StudentId() on *id*. This occurs after the *Student* constructor is called
but before control passes to the first statement in the constructor. (Single step
the preceding program in the debugger to see what I mean. As always, be sure
that inline functions are forced outline.) The output from executing this simple
program follows:

```
Assigning student id 1
Constructing student Randy
```

Notice that the message from the *StudentId* constructor appears before the output from the *Student* constructor.

(By the way, with all these constructors performing output, you might think that constructors must output something. Most constructors don't output a darned thing. Book constructors do because readers usually don't take the good advice provided by authors and single step the programs.)

If the programmer does not provide a constructor, the default constructor provided by C++ automatically invokes the default constructors for any data members. The same is true come harvesting time. The destructor for the class automatically invokes the destructor for any data members that have destructors. The C++ provided destructor does the same.

Okay, this is all great for the default constructor. But what if we wanted to invoke a constructor other than the default? Where do we put the object? To demonstrate, let's assume that instead of calculating the student ID, it is provided to the *Student* constructor, which passes the ID to the constructor for class *StudentId*.

Let me first show you what doesn't work. Consider the following program:

```cpp
#include <iostream.h>
#include <string.h>

class StudentId
{
  public:
    StudentId(int id = 0)
    {
       value = id;
       cout << "Assigning student id " << value << "\n";
    }

  protected:
    int value;
};

class Student
{
  public:
    Student(char *pName  = "no name", int ssId = 0)
    {
       cout << "Constructing student " << pName << "\n";
       strncpy(name, pName, sizeof(name));
       name[sizeof(name) - 1]  = '\0';
```

continued

```
        //don't try this at home kids. It doesn't work
        StudentId id(ssId);    //construct a student id
    }
  protected:
    char  name[40];
    StudentId id;
};

int main()
{
    Student s("Randy", 1234);
    cout << "This message from main\n";
    return 0;
}
```

The constructor for *StudentId* has been changed to accept a value externally (the default value is necessary to get the example to compile, for reasons which will become clear shortly). Within the constructor for *Student*, the programmer (that's me) has (cleverly) attempted to construct a *StudentId* object named *id*.

If we look at the output from this program, we notice a problem:

```
Assigning student id 0
Constructing student Randy
Assigning student id 1234
Destructing id 1234
This message from main
Destructing id 0
```

First, the constructor appears to be invoked twice, once with zero and a second time with the expected 1234. Then we notice that the 1234 object gets destructed before the output string in *main()*. Apparently this object is destructed within the constructor itself.

The explanation for this rather bizarre behavior is clear. The data member *id* already exists by the time the body of the constructor is entered. Rather than constructing the existing data member *id*, the declaration provided in the constructor creates a local object of the same name. This local object is destructed upon returning from the constructor.

Somehow we need a different mechanism to indicate "construct the existing member; don't create a new one." This mechanism needs to appear before the open brace, before the data members are declared. For this, C++ defined a new construct as follows:

```
class Student
{
  public:
```

```
    Student(char *pName  = "no name", int ssId = 0) : id(ssId)
    {
        cout << "Constructing student " << pName << "\n";
        strncpy(name, pName, sizeof(name));
        name[sizeof(name) - 1] = '\0';
    }
  protected:
    char  name[40];
    StudentId id;
};
```

Notice in particular the first line of the constructor. Here's something we haven't seen before. The *:* means that what follows are calls to the constructors of data members of the current class. To the C++ compiler, this line reads: "Construct the member *id* using the argument *ssId* of the *Student* constructor. Whatever data members are not called out in this fashion are constructed using the default constructor."

This new program generates the expected result:

```
Assigning student id 1234
Constructing student Randy
This message from main
Destructing id 1234
```

The *:* syntax must also be used to assign values to *const* or reference type members. Consider the following silly class:

```
class SillyClass
{
  public:
    SillyClass(int& i) : ten(10), refI(i)
    {
    }
  protected:
    const int ten;
    int& refI;
};

int main()
{
    int i;
    SillyClass sc(i);
    return 0;
}
```

After the constructor for *SillyClass* has been entered, the data members *ten* and *refI* have already been created. This is analogous to declaring a *const* or reference variable in a function. Such variables must be assigned a value when declared.

In fact, any data member can be declared using the preceding syntax, but *const* and reference variables must be declared in this way.

There is a displeasing lack of symmetry in initialization declaration formats. When declaring variables in a class, you must use the parenthetical style if you want to initialize the variables. When declaring simple variables in a function, however, you must use the "assignment style." When declaring objects of a user-defined type within a function, either style is allowed. For example:

```
class SillyClass
{
  public:
    int d;
    SillyClass() : d(10)        //parenthetical style required...
    {                           //...for data members
        d = 10;                 //this is assignment...
    }                           //...not initialization
};

int main()
{
    int i = 10;                 //this is initalization
    int j(10);                  //this is not legal under most
                                //compilers
    AClass ac1 = 10;            //both allowed as long as...
    AClass ac2(10);             //...AClass(int) exists
    return 0;
}
```

The declarations of *ac1* and *ac2* are identical to enhance compatability with C. I can accept the existence of both initialization styles (*AClass ac2(10);* and *AClass ac1= 10;*) for class objects for historical reasons. But why not allow the parenthetical style (*int j(10);*) for simple objects outside constructors, especially considering that it's mandated in constructors?

Borland C++ 4.0 allows both formats to be used in the latter case:

```
int main()          //both allowed under BC++ 4.0:
{
    int i = 10;      //conventional format
    int j(10);       //more C++-like format
    return 0;
}
```

Some other C++ compilers do not support the parenthetical format for simple types — not even Borland's own Turbo C++ 3.0 compiler. ■

Order of Construction

When there are multiple objects, all with constructors, the programmer usually doesn't care about the order in which things are built. If one or more of the constructors have side effects, however, the order can make a difference.

The rules for the order of construction are as follows:

- Locals and static objects are constructed in the order in which their declarations are invoked.
- Static objects are constructed only once.
- All global objects are constructed before *main()*.
- Global objects are constructed in no particular order.
- Members are constructed in the order in which they are declared in the class.
- Destructors are invoked in the reverse order from the constructors.

Let's consider each of these rules in turn.

Local objects are constructed in order

Local objects are constructed in the order in which the program encounters their declaration. Normally this is the same as the order in which the objects appear in the function, unless your function jumps around particular declarations. (By the way, jumping around declarations is a bad thing to do. It confuses the reader and the compiler.)

Static objects are constructed only once

Static objects are similar to other local variables except that they are constructed only once. This is to be expected because they retain their value from one invocation of the function to the next. However, unlike C, which is free to initialize statics when the program begins, C++ must wait until the first time control passes through the static's declaration to perform the construction. Consider the following trivial program:

```
#include <iostream.h>
#include <string.h>
class DoNothing
{
  public:
    DoNothing(int initial)
    {
        cout << "DoNothing constructed with a value of "
             << initial
             << "\n";
    }
};

void fn(int i)
```

continued

```
{
    static DoNothing dn(i);
    cout << "In function fn with i = " << i << "\n";
}

int main()
{
    fn(10);
    fn(20);
    return 0;
}
```

Executing this program generates the following results:

```
DoNothing constructed with a value of 10
In function fn with i = 10
In function fn with i = 20
```

Notice that the message from the function *fn()* appears twice, but the message from the constructor for *DoNothing* appears only the first time *fn()* is called.

All global objects are constructed before main ()

As mentioned in our review of C in Part I, all global variables go into scope as soon as the program starts. Thus, all global objects are constructed before control is passed to *main()*.

This can cause a real debugging headache. Some debuggers try to execute up to *main()* as soon as the program is loaded and before they hand over control to the user. This makes perfect sense for C because no user code is ready to execute until *main()* is entered. For C++, however, this can be a problem because the constructor code for all global objects has already been executed by the time you get control. If one of them has a fatal bug, you never even get control. In this case, the program appears to die before it even starts!

We can approach this problem in several ways. One is to test each constructor on local objects before using them on globals. If that doesn't solve the problem, you can try adding output statements to the beginning of all suspected constructors. The last output statement you see probably came from the flawed constructor. ■

Crashing constructors called from global objects was a problem at one time with the stand-alone Turbo Debugger. Now, however, there is an Execute startup code option in the Open File window. Turn this option off before you open the *EXE* file you want to debug. Rather than starting with the normal *main()* and seeing C++ source code, you will be presented with the assembly language window with the instruction pointer pointing to some useless instruction. (This is the first instruction in your program, but you won't recognize it because it's part of the C++ startup code.) Open the module (by choosing the Open command in the View menu or by pressing F3) and set breakpoints in all the suspicious constructors. Then set a breakpoint at the first instruction in *main()* and let 'er rip. You should be able to "single step" through each global constructor.

Borland's IDE debugger and all Microsoft debuggers don't have a problem with crashing constructors called from global objects because they don't attempt to start execution of anything until you tell them to. Load up the executable and set breakpoints in all the constructors as directed previously to find the culprit. ▪

Global objects are constructed in no particular order

Figuring out the order of construction of local objects is easy. An order is implied by the flow of control. With globals, there is no such flow to give order. All globals go into scope simultaneously, remember? Okay, you argue, why can't the compiler just start at the top of the file and work its way down the list of global objects? That would work fine for a single file (and I presume that's what most compilers do).

Unfortunately, most programs in the real world consist of several files that are compiled separately and then linked. Because the compiler has no control over the order in which these files are linked, it cannot affect the order in which global objects are constructed from file to file.

Most of the time this is pretty ho-hum stuff. Once in a while, though, it can generate bugs that are extremely difficult to track down. (It happens just often enough to make it worth mentioning in a book.)

Consider the following example:

```
//in Student.H:
class Student
{
  public:
    Student (unsigned id) : studentId(id)
    {
    }
    const unsigned studentId;
};
class Tutor
{
  public:
    Tutor(Student &s)
```

continued

```
    {
        tutoredId = s.studentId;
    }
  protected:
    unsigned tutoredId;
};


//in FILE1.CPP
//set up a student
Student randy(1234);


//in FILE2.CPP
//assign that student a tutor
Tutor   jenny(randy);
```

Here the constructor for *Student* assigns a student ID. The constructor for *Tutor* records the ID of the student to help. The program declares a student *randy* and then assigns that student a tutor *jenny*.

The problem is that we are making the implicit assumption that *randy* gets constructed before *jenny*. Suppose that it was the other way around. Then *jenny* would get constructed with a block of memory that had not yet been turned into a *Student* object and, therefore, had garbage for a student ID.

This example is not too difficult to figure out and more than a little contrived. Nevertheless, problems deriving from global objects being constructed in no particular order can appear in very subtle ways. To avoid this problem, don't allow the constructor for one global object to refer to the contents of another global object. ■

Members are constructed in the order in which they are declared

Members of a class are constructed according to the order in which they are declared within the class. This is not quite as obvious as it might sound. Consider the following example:

```
class Student
{
  public:
    Student (unsigned id, unsigned age) : sAge(age), sId(id)
    {
    }
    const unsigned sId;
    const unsigned sAge;
};
```

In this example, *sId* is constructed before *sAge* even though it appears second in the constructor's initialization list. The only time you could probably detect any difference in the construction order is if both of these were members of classes that had constructors and these constructors had some mutual side effect.

Destructors are invoked in the reverse order of the constructors

Finally, no matter what order the constructors kick off, you can be assured that the destructors are invoked in the reverse order. (It's nice to know that there's at least one rule in C++ that has no if's, and's or but's.)

Conclusion

The rules we have studied so far apply to the care and feeding of conventional objects. What about objects that are allocated off the heap? C++ has separate mechanism to handle this type of memory allocation and deallocation. This mechanism is the topic of the next chapter.

Chapter 14

More New and Improved Keywords

· ·

In This Chapter

▶ The newest thing in heap maintenance: *new* and *delete*

▶ Constructing and destructing heap objects

▶ Allocating and deallocating big arrays from the heap

· ·

The heap manipulation tools *malloc()* and *free()* are important tools in the C programmer's tool box. Although heap manipulation is no less important to the C++ programmer, the English-standard *malloc()* and *free()* tools don't fit on C++'s metric bolts.

The *new* Keywords: Now You're *free ()* to delete *malloc ()*

C++ provides alternates for the *malloc()* and *free()* Standard C library calls to allocate memory off the heap. The replacement for *malloc()* is called *new*; the replacement for *free()* is *delete*. Both *new* and *delete* are keywords rather than library functions.

Why do I need them?

The *malloc()* mechanism was great for C's purposes, but it's unusable from C++'s standpoint for one simple reason: It can't invoke the constructor. Consider the following code snippet:

```
void fn()
{
   Student *pS;      //this doesn't call any constructor
   pS = (Student*)malloc(sizeof Student); //neither does this
   //...party on, dudes...
   free(pS);         //this doesn't call the destructor either
}
```

The declaration of the pointer *pS* doesn't call the constructor for *Student* because *pS* doesn't point to anything.

If the constructor is to be called, it must happen at the *malloc()* call when memory is first allocated. Unfortunately, however, *malloc()* is just a function call and doesn't have enough information to call a constructor. (For example, *malloc()* wouldn't know which constructor to call; there's nothing in the arguments it receives to tell it the class of the block of memory it's trying to allocate.)

We could make the programmer initialize the memory into a *Student* separately, as follows:

```
void fn()
{
    Student *pS;
    //allocate memory block
    *pS = (Student*)malloc(sizeof Student);
    //now initialize it into a Student
    pS->init();
    //...party time...
}
```

Anyone who's stayed awake this far knows what's wrong with this: The class shouldn't rely on the application to remember to do the class's work.

What we need is a new construct that first calls *malloc()* and then calls the proper constructor on the returned block of memory. Hey, that's exactly what *new* is. Similarly, *delete* calls the destructor before calling *free()* to return the memory to the heap.

How do they work?

In use, the *new* and *delete* mechanism is straightforward. Compare this to the preceding example:

```
void fn()
{
    Student *pS;
    //allocate heap memory and construct it
    pS = new Student;
    //...excellent...
    //put it back and invoke the destructor
    delete pS;
}
```

Notice that it's not necessary to cast the pointer returned from *new* to the proper type. *new* knows the type of the object it's trying to allocate — it must know in order to invoke the proper constructor. The pointer returned from *new* always has the type of the argument to the right of *new*.

Arguments to the constructor are passed by adding them to the class name. Thus spake Zarathustra:

```
void fn()
{
    Student *pS;
    //allocate a student with a name and an id
    pS = new Student("Randy", 1234);
    //...and so on...
}
```

Allocating Arrays

It is possible to allocate arrays of objects off the heap. The following code snippet demonstrates how this is accomplished:

```
void fn(int noOfObjects)
{
    Student *pS;
    pS = new Student[noOfObjects];
    //...dance to the music...
}
```

This allocates an array of *noObjects* students. The default constructor is invoked on each object in the array starting with *pS[0]*, progressing to *pS[1]*, and so on. It is not possible to invoke any other constructor when allocating arrays.

A problem arises on the delete side because *delete* can't tell the difference between a pointer to a single object and a pointer to an array of objects. An empty pair of brackets tells *delete* that this is an array:

```
void fn(int noOfObjects)
{
    Student *pS;
    pS = new Student[noOfObjects];
    //...dance to the music...
    //delete the array
    delete[] pS;
}
```

The destructor is invoked separately for each object in the array. Without the brackets, only the first object in the array would be destructed and returned to the heap. ■

This somewhat peculiar syntax came about historically. Originally, the programmer had to indicate how many members in the array to destruct, as shown in the following:

```
void fn(int noOfObjects)
{
   //...just like above
   //delete the array
   delete[noOfObjects] pS;
}
```

The more natural looking *delete pS[noOfObjects];* would have meant delete the *noOfObjects*'th member of the array.

As C++ developed, people realized that keeping track of the size of the array was a big problem. The array might be allocated in one place in the program and not deallocated for quite some time. To save the programmer the effort, C++ saves the length of the array, but the programmer still has to tell C++ to look for this information — hence the empty brackets.

Nowadays, if you include the length of the array in the brackets, most C++ compilers (including both Borland compilers and Visual C++) ignore the value you put there and act as if the brackets were empty. ∎

In addition to only destructing the first object in the array, both Borland C++ and Turbo C++ overwrite lower memory if you forget to put the brackets on the *delete* statement when deleting an array. (You get a "Null pointer assignment" message in any of the small data models.) Visual C++ does not seem to suffer from this "feature." ∎

new and *delete* were introduced to handle class objects, but they can be used also for intrinsic types such as *char* and *int*. For example, the following snippet allocates an array of *char*s:

```
char *someFn(int length)
{
   char *pS = new char[length];
   //who knows what evil lurks in the hearts of men?
   return pS;
}
```

This is slightly neater than the *malloc()* syntax because it avoids the cast. In addition, why use two mechanisms, if one will do? ∎

Conclusion

As we saw, the programmer can allocate objects off the heap with the new keyword *new*, rather than allocate unspecified blobs of memory with *malloc()*. This capability is critical to C++; otherwise it would be impossible to invoke the proper constructor when memory is allocated.

Often, heap memory is allocated and its address stored in one of the data members of the class. This pointer represents a problem if we attempt to make a copy of that object. In the next chapter, we will explore this problem — along with its solution.

Chapter 15

The Copy Copy Copy Constructor

• •

In This Chapter

▶ Introducing the copy constructor

▶ Making copies

▶ Having copies made for you automatically

▶ Shallow copies versus deep copies

▶ Avoiding all those copies

• •

There is one other constructor that deserves particular attention. This constructor, known as the *copy constructor*, is used to make copies of objects.

The Copy Constructor

A copy constructor is a constructor that has the name *X::X(X&)*, where *X* is any class name. That is, it is the constructor of class *X* which takes as its argument a reference to an object of class *X*. Now I know that this sounds really useless, but just give me a chance to explain why C++ needs such a beastie.

Why do I need it?

Think for a moment about what happens when you call a function like the following:

```
void fn(Student fs)
{
    //...same scenario; different argument...
}
int main()
{
    Student ms;
    fn(ms);
    return 0;
}
```

As you know, a copy of the object *ms* — and not the object itself — is passed to the function *fn()*. With C, the procedure is pretty simple: C just makes a binary copy of the object on the stack and passes that to the function.

This is not acceptable in C++. First, as I have pointed out, it takes a constructor to create an object, even a copy of an existing object. Second, what if we don't want a simple copy of the object? (Let's ignore the "why?" of this for a little while.) We need to be able to specify how the copy should be constructed.

Thus, the copy constructor is necessary in the preceding example to create a copy of the object *ms* on the stack during the call of function *fn()*. (This particular copy constructor would be *Student::Student(Student&)* — say that three times quickly.)

How does it work?

There's no better way to understand how the copy constructor works than to see one in action. Consider the following *Student* class:

```
#include <iostream.h>
#include <string.h>
class Student
{
  public:
   //conventional constructor
   Student(char *pName  = "no name", int ssId = 0)
   {
      cout << "Constructing new student " << pName << "\n";
      strncpy(name, pName, sizeof(name));
      name[sizeof(name) - 1]  = '\0';
      id = ssId;
   }

   //copy constructor
   Student(Student &s)
   {
      cout << "Constructing Copy of " << s.name << "\n";
      strcpy(name, "Copy of ");
      strcat(name, s.name);
      id = s.id;
   }
  ~Student()
   {
      cout << "Destructing " << name << "\n";
   }
  protected:
   char   name[40];
   int    id;
};

//fn - receives its argument by value
```

```
void fn(Student s)
{
    cout << "In function fn()\n";
}

int main()
{
    Student randy("Randy", 1234);
    cout << "Calling fn()\n";
    fn(randy);
    cout << "Returned from fn()\n";
    return 0;
}
```

The output from executing this program follows:

```
Constructing new student Randy
Calling fn()
Constructing Copy of Randy
In function fn()
Destructing Copy of Randy
Returned from fn()
Destructing Randy
```

Starting with *main()*, we can see how this program works. The normal constructor generates the first message. *main()* generates the *calling...* message. C++ calls the copy constructor to make a copy of *randy* to pass to *fn()*, which generates the next line of output. The copy is destructed at the return from *fn()*. The original object, *randy*, is destructed at the end of *main()*.

The copy constructor here is flagged with comments. It looks like a normal constructor except that it takes its input from another object rather than from several separate arguments.

(Notice that this copy constructor does a little bit more than just make a copy of the object; it tacks the phrase *Copy of* to the front of the name. That was for your benefit. Normally, copy constructors should restrict themselves to just making copies. But, if the truth be known, they can do anything they want.)

The Automatic Copy Constructor

Like the default constructor, the copy constructor is important. Important enough that C++ thinks no class should be without one. If you don't provide your own copy constructor, C++ generates one for you. (This is different than the default constructor, which C++ provides unless your class has *any* constructors defined for it.)

The copy constructor provided by C++ performs a member-by-member copy of each data member. Originally, the copy constructor that C++ provided performed a bitwise copy. The difference is that a member-by-member copy invokes any copy constructors that might exist for the members of the class whereas a bitwise copy does not. We can see the effects of this difference in the following example:

```
#include <iostream.h>
#include <string.h>

class Student
{
  public:
   Student(char *pName  = "no name")
   {
      cout << "Constructing new student " << pName << "\n";
      strncpy(name, pName, sizeof(name));
      name[sizeof(name) - 1]  = '\0';
   }
   Student(Student &s)
   {
      cout << "Constructing Copy of " << s.name << "\n";
      strcpy(name, "Copy of ");
      strcat(name, s.name);
   }
   ~Student()
   {
      cout << "Destructing " << name << "\n";
   }
  protected:
   char  name[40];
};


class Tutor
{
  public:
   Tutor(Student &s) : student(s) //invoke copy constructor...
   {                              //...on member student
     cout << "Constructing tutor\n";
   }
  protected:
   Student student;
};

void fn(Tutor tutor)
{
   cout << "In function fn()\n";
}
int main()
{
   Student randy("Randy");
   Tutor tutor(randy);
   cout << "Calling fn()\n";
   fn(tutor);
   cout << "Returned from fn()\n";
   return 0;
}
```

Executing this program generates the following output:

```
Constructing new student Randy
Constructing Copy of Randy
Constructing tutor
Calling fn()
Constructing Copy of Copy of Randy
In function fn()
Destructing Copy of Copy of Randy
Returned from fn()
Destructing Copy of Randy
Destructing Randy
```

Constructing the object *randy* invokes the *Student* constructor, which outputs the first line.

The object *tutor* is created by invoking the constructor *Tutor(Student&)*. This constructor initializes the data member *Tutor::student* by invoking the copy constructor for *Student* explicitly. This generates the next line of output.

The call to function *fn()* requires a copy of *tutor* to be created. Because I did not provide a copy constructor for *Tutor*, the default copy constructor (provided by C++) copies each member. This invokes the copy constructor for class *Student* to copy the data member *tutor.student*.

 Some really old implementations of C++ might still perform bitwise copies. If you want to make sure that the copy constructors of the data members are invoked, provide a copy constructor that explicitly invokes them, as follows:

```
class Student
{
  public:
    Student(Student& s);      //copy constructor for Student

    //...other stuff...
};

class Course
{
  public:
    Class(Class &c) : s(c.s)  //explicitly invoke copy constructor
    {
       //whatever
    }

  protected:
    Student s;
};
```

Here we see that the class *Course* contains a member *s* of class *Student*. Class *Student* also defines a copy constructor. This copy constructor should be invoked for the data member *s*, so the programmer has written a copy constructor for *Course* that explicitly invokes this constructor. ∎

Shallow Copies versus Deep Copies

Performing a member-by-member copy seems the obvious thing to do in a copy constructor. Other than adding the capability to tack silly things like *Copy of* to the front of students' names, when would we ever want to do anything but a member-by-member copy?

Consider what happens if the constructor allocates an asset such as memory off the heap. If the copy constructor simply makes a copy of that asset without allocating its own, we end up with a troublesome situation: two objects thinking they have exclusive access to the same asset. This gets nastier when the destructor is invoked for both objects and they both try to put the same asset back. To make this more concrete, consider the following example class:

```
#include <iostream.h>
#include <string.h>
class Person
{
  public:
   Person(char *pN)
   {
      cout << "Constructing " << pN << "\n";
      pName = new char[strlen(pN) + 1];
      if (pName != 0)
      {
         strcpy(pName, pN);
      }
   }
   ~Person()
   {
      cout << "Destructing " << pName << "\n";
      //let's wipe out the name just for the heck of it
      pName[0] = '\0';
      delete pName;
   }
  protected:
   char *pName;
};

int main()
{
   Person p1("Randy");
   Person p2 = p1;        //invoke the copy constructor...
   return 0;              //...equivalent to Person p2(p1);
}
```

Here, the constructor for *Person* allocates memory off the heap to store the person's name, rather than put up with some arbitrary limit imposed by a fixed-length array. The destructor dutifully puts this heap memory back as it should. The main program simply creates one person, *p1*, and then makes a copy of that person, *p2*. We see the problem by examining the output:

```
Constructing Randy
Destructing Randy
Destructing
Null pointer assignment
```

We get one constructor output message but two destructor messages. That's not too surprising, because C++ provided the copy constructor used to build *p2* and it performs no output. However, the second destructor message is screwed up. Our constructor is called once and allocates a block of memory off the heap to hold the person's name. The copy constructor provided by C++ copies that address into the new object without allocating a new block.

When the objects get destructed, the destructor for *p2* gets at the block first. This destructor clears out the name and then releases the block. When *p1* comes along, the memory has been released and the name has been wiped out already. This explains the screwed up name and the *Null pointer assignment* message.

The message *Null pointer assignment* is Borland and Turbo C's way of telling you that you screwed up a pointer and wrote to location 0 in the default data segment. Other compilers have different messages. ■

The problem is shown in Figure 15-1. The object *p1* is copied into the new object *p2*, but the assets are not. Thus, *p1* and *p2* end up pointing to the same assets (in this case, heap memory). This is known as a *shallow copy* because it just "skims the surface," copying the members themselves.

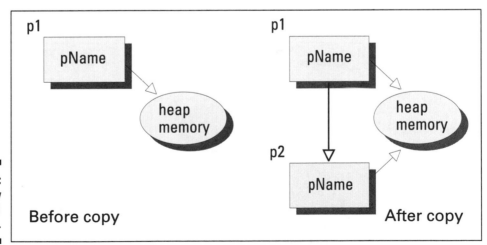

Figure 15-1:
Shallow
copy of p1
to p2.

What's needed is a copy constructor that allocates to the new object its own assets. Let's add one of these to *Person* and see how it looks. The following shows an appropriate copy constructor for class *Person*.

```
class Person
{
  public:
    //copy constructor allocates a new heap block
    Person(Person &p)
    {
       cout << "Copying " << p.pName << " into its own block\n";
       pName = new char[strlen(p.pName) + 1];
       if (pName != 0)
       {
          strcpy(pName, p.pName);
       }
    }
    //...everything else the same...
}
//...same here as well...
```

Here we see that the copy constructor allocates its own memory block for the name and then copies the contents of the source object name into this new name block. See Figure 15-2. Deep copy is so named because it reaches down and copies all the assets. (Okay, the analogy is pretty strained, but that's what they call it.)

The output from this program is as follows:

```
Constructing Randy
Copying Randy into his own block
Destructing Randy
Destructing Randy
```

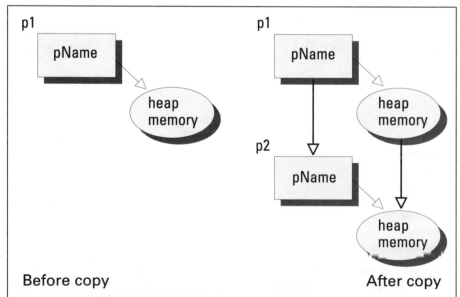

Figure 15-2:
Deep copy
of p1 to p2.

Heap memory is not the only asset that requires a deep copy constructor, but it is the most common. Open files, ports, and allocated hardware (such as printers) also require deep copies. These are the same types of assets that destructors must return. Thus, a good rule of thumb is that if your class requires a destructor to deallocate assets, it also requires a copy constructor. ■

It's a Long Way to Temporaries

 I have mentioned that copies are generated when objects are passed by value. Copies are created under other conditions as well, such as when objects are returned by value. Consider the following example:

```
Student fn();                    //returns object by value
int main()
{
    Student s;
    s = fn();                    //call to fn() creates temporary
    //how long does the temporary returned by fn()...
    //...last?
    return 0;
}
```

The function *fn()* returns an object by value. Eventually, the returned object is copied to *s*, but where does it reside until then?

C++ creates a temporary object into which it stuffs the returned object. (Temporaries are created in other ways as well.) "Okay," you say, "C++ creates the temporary but how does it know when to destruct the temporary?" (How clever you are for asking just the right question.) In this example, it doesn't make much difference because we'll be through with the temporary when the copy constructor copies it into *s*. But what if *s* were defined as a reference:

```
int main()
{
    Student &refS = fn();
    //...now what?...
    return 0;
}
```

Now it makes a big difference how long temporaries live because *refS* exists for the entire function. The C++ rules committees are still arguing, but so far the rule is: Temporaries created by the compiler are valid throughout the extended expression in which they were created and no further. In the following function, I have marked the point at which the temporary is no longer valid:

```
Student fn1();
int fn2(Student&);
int main()
{
```

(continued)

```
int x;
//create a Student object by calling fn1(). Pass that
//object to the function fn2(). fn2() returns an integer
//that is used in some silly calculation. All this time,
//the temporary returned from fn() is valid.
x = 3 * fn2(fn1()) + 10;
//the temporary returned from fn1() is now no longer valid
//...other stuff...
return 0;
}
```

This makes the reference example invalid, because the object may go away before *refS* does, leaving *refS* referring to a non-object.

It may have occurred to you that all this copying of objects hither and yon can be a bit time-consuming. What if you don't want to make copies of everything? The most straightforward solution is to pass objects to functions and return objects from functions by reference. This knocks out the majority of cases.

But what if you're still not convinced that C++ isn't out there craftily constructing temporaries that you know nothing about? Or what if your class allocates unique assets that you don't want copied? What do you do then?

You can simply add an output statement to your copy constructor. The presence of this message warns you that a copy has just been made. Another approach is to declare the copy constructor protected, as follows:

```
class Student
{
  protected:
   Student(Student&s){}
  public:
   //...everything else normal...
};
```

This precludes any external functions, including C++, from constructing a copy of your *Student* objects. (This does not affect the capability of member functions to create copies.)

Conclusion

The copy constructor together with the default constructor (discussed earlier) form the dynamic duo of constructors that every class should have and every C++ programmer should understand. In this chapter, we saw how temporary objects may be created by C++ automatically. In the next chapter, we see other ways in which temporary objects are created and how constructors are used in the process.

Chapter 16
Changing an Object's Type

• •

In This Chapter

▶ Anonymous programming, or creating objects with no names

▶ How do I convert an object from the class it is to the class I want it to be?

▶ Using constructors to perform type conversion

• •

*G*enerally, when you create an object, it has a name and a variable associated with it so that you can refer to the object by name. However, in the last chapter we saw how C++ can create objects which have no name using the copy constructor. This is not a capability limited to C++.

In this chapter we will see how you can also use any of a class's constructors to create objects without a name. We will also see how these nameless objects can act as a sort of type conversion.

Nameless Objects

The programmer creates an object without assigning it a name by invoking the constructor directly. For example:

```
void fn()
{
   //create a nameless object of type Student
   Student("Randy", 1234);
   //...carry on...
}
```

Why do I need them?

Creating a nameless object may seem like a worthless thing to do, but it can be useful. For example, we might be interested in the side effects of the class rather than the object itself. Or we might want to use the object in an expression, as in the following example:

```
class Student
{
  public:
    Student(char *pName);
};
class Course
{
  public:
    void enroll(Student&);
    //...other members like before...
};

//enrollStudent - enroll a student with a given name
//                in the specified course
void enrollStudent(Course *pC, char *pName)
{
    pC->enroll(Student(pName)); //create and use object at once
}
```

Here the function *enrollStudent( )* needs a *Student* to pass to the *Course::enroll( )* function. I could have first created an object with a name and then passed that object to the *enroll* function. In this case, the function *enrollStudent( )* would appear as follows:

```
//enrollStudent - enroll a student with a given name
//                in the specified course
void enrollStudent(Course *pC, char *pName)
{
    Student s(pName);        //this time first create the object...
    pC->enroll(s);           //...and then use it
}
```

Using a nameless object merely dispenses with the variable. (I know this doesn't sound profound, but stick with me. We will see shortly that there's more to the story.)

How do they work?

The following are all mechanisms for creating nameless objects:

```
class Student
{
  public:
    Student(char *pName);
};
void fn(Student&s);
int main()
{
    Student &refS = Student("Randy");
    Student s = Student("Jenny");
    fn(Student("Danny"));
    return 0;
}
```

The first declaration in *main()* generates a reference to a nameless *Student* object. This is no different than declaring an object in the conventional fashion.

The second declaration appears to first construct a nameless object using the *Student(char*)* constructor outlined and then copy that object into the *Student* object *s*. The definition of C++ (the Annotated Reference Manual, or ARM, until the ANSI standard is released) says that a compiler may do just that, if it wants. However, the standard also says that the compiler may avoid the extraneous nameless object and just construct the *s* object as if it had been declared as follows:

```
int main()
{
   Student s("Jenny");   //alternate for s above
   //...continue as before...
}
```

The third case, the call *fn(Student("Danny"))*, constructs a nameless object for the purpose of passing the object to the function.

Type Conversion Using Constructors

Sometimes, the type of the object the programmer has and the type of the object the programmer needs are not the same. For example, we might want to multiply a *float* times an *int*. We can convert the *int* to a *float* by specifying a cast. (We can also cast a *float* to an *int*.) But this isn't necessary because C++ automatically converts the *int* into a *float* for us.

We don't have to tell C++ how to convert from an *int* to a *float*. C++ already understands how to convert from one intrinsic type to another. It doesn't understand *a priori* how to convert to or from a user-defined type, but we can tell it how.

Consider a constructor such as *Student(char*)*. This constructor takes a *char** and uses it to produce an object of class *Student*. In a way, this is like a type conversion. In other words, it's as if the constructor *Student(char*)* tells C++ how to convert a *char** into a *Student*. Well, that's the way C++ sees it.

In other words, the following is legal:

```
class Student
{
  public:
    Student(char*);
};
void fn(Student s);
```

continued

```
int main()
{
   fn("Danny");        //what exactly are we calling here?
   return 0;
}
```

Let me direct your attention to the call to *fn()* in *main()*. The programmer is attempting to pass a character string, that is, a *char**. However, there is no function *fn(char*)*. (If there were, C++ would call that function without any further ado.) Rather than just give up, C++ sees whether it can convert the argument into something it can use to make the call to some other overloaded function *fn()*.

C++ notices that there is a function *fn(Student&)* and that there is also a constructor *Student(char*)* that can convert a *char** into a *Student*. Putting two and two together, C++ uses *char** to construct a *Student* object with which to make the call.

C++ treats the call to *fn()* as if it had been written as follows:

```
//...all this stuff stays the same...
int main()
{
   fn(Student("Danny"));  //call to constructor made explicit
   return 0;
}
```

(Except for the comment, this call to *fn()* looks like the call in the seemingly useless example at the beginning of the chapter. I told you it had a purpose.)

C++ has used the constructor to convert an object from one type to another. It will attempt to do this any time it can. The limitations are as follows:

- ✔ C++ must use constructors with only a single argument (or with all arguments defaulted except for one). This is a syntactical problem more than a technical problem.
- ✔ If ambiguities arise, C++ throws up its electronic hands and gives up.

The following code snippet demonstrates how ambiguities can arise:

```
class Student
{
  public:
    Student(char *pName  = "no name");
};
class Teacher
{
  public:
    Teacher(char *pName  = "no name");
};
```

```
void addCourse(Student&s);
void addCourse(Teacher&t);

int main()
{
   addCourse("Prof. Dingleberry");
   return 0;
}
```

Here we can see that C++ could convert the *char** to a *Student* and call *addCourse(Student&)*. Or it could convert the *char** to a *Teacher* to call *addCourse(Teacher&)*. With no way to resolve the ambiguity, C++ has no choice but to generate an error.

To correct the ambiguity, we must add an explicit call to the intended constructor:

```
int main()
{
   addCourse(Teacher("Prof. Dingleberry"));
   return 0;
}
```

Consider how similar the preceding call to the constructor is to a cast. Here we have cast *char** into *Teacher*. The similarity is more than superficial. C++ considers this to be a new format for specifying a cast. This new format can be used for intrinsic casts, plus the old format can be used for constructor conversions, as shown in the following:

```
void fn(int *pI)
{
   float x = 10.5;
   int i = int(x);             //same as i = (int)x;
   addCourse(Teacher("Prof. Dingleberry")); //new format
   addCourse((Teacher)"Prof. Dingleberry"); //same as above
   char *pC = (int*)pI;   //older format must be used when
                          //casting pointers
}
```

Some people prefer the newer format because it looks like the format for invoking the constructor. Others prefer the older, more familiar format. Note, however, that you must use the older format when casting from one pointer type to another due to the syntactical confusion that * by itself would cause. ∎

Older versions of Turbo C++ cannot make this mental leap on their own. An explicit cast is required.

In addition, Visual C++ refuses to implicitly create a temporary object that can be modified by the called function. Thus, our example on page 215 could not have been declared *fn(Student &s)*. However, it could have been declared *fn(Student const &s)*. Making the conversion explicit also solves the problem. ∎

Conclusion

Type conversion is a necessary part of any language. The conversion provided by constructors is a wonderfully (and surprisingly) elegant mechanism for providing this capability.

I'm getting a little tired of writing about constructors and I know you're getting tired of reading about them. As important as constructors are, there are other aspects to C++ programming. In the next chapter, we move on to consider one of them, the static class member.

Chapter 17

Static Members: Can Fabric Softener Help?

In This Chapter

▶ How do I declare static member data?

▶ What about static member functions?

▶ Why can't my static member function call my other member functions?

*L*et's turn our attention away from constructors for a moment (at last). The members we have seen so far have all been on a "per object" basis. For example, each student has his or her own name.

You can also declare a member to be shared by all objects of a class by declaring that member static. The term *static* applies to both data members and member functions, although the meaning is slightly different. This chapter describes these differences, beginning with static data members.

Static Data Members

Data members are made common to all members of a class by declaring them *static*. Such members are called static data members.

Why do I need them?

Most properties are properties of the object. Using our well-worn (one might say, threadbare) student example, properties such as name, ID number, and courses are specific to the individual student. However, some properties are shared by all students, for example, the number of students currently enrolled, the highest grade of all students, or a pointer to the first student in a linked list.

It is possible to store this type of class information in global variables. The problem is that global variables are "outside" the class. We would like to bring this type of class information inside the class boundaries, where it can be protected. This is the idea behind static members.

I don't like the term *static* in this context. I don't see much similarity between static in this sense and static variables declared in a function — or static functions, for that matter. Other object-oriented languages call these *class members* because they describe the entire class. These languages call normal members *instance members* or *object members* because they describe individual objects. C++ programmers occasionally use these terms as well because they are more descriptive. ∎

How do they work?

A static data member is one that has been declared with the *static* storage class. For example:

```
class Student
{
  public:
   Student(char *pName  = "no name")
   {
      strcpy(name, pName);
      noOfStudents++;
   }
   ~Student()
   {
      noOfStudents--;
   }
   int number()
   {
      return noOfStudents;
   }
  protected:
   static int noOfStudents;
   char name[40];
};
Student s1;
Student s2;
```

The data member *noOfStudents* is not part of either *s1* or *s2*. That is, for every object of class *Student* there is a separate *name*, but there is only one *noOfStudents*, which all *Student*s must share. If we used an assembly language debugger to look into *s1* or *s2*, we would see space allocated only for *name* and not for *noOfStudents*.

"Well then," you ask, "if the space for *noOfStudents* is not allocated in any of the objects of class *Student*, where is it allocated?" The answer is, "It isn't." You have to specifically allocate space for it, as follows:

```
int Student::noOfStudents = 0;
```

This somewhat peculiar-looking syntax allocates space for the static data member and initializes it to zero. Static data members can be initialized only at the file level (that is, they can't be initialized from within a function).

That's because all static data members must be initialized before any constructors can be executed, and the constructors for global variables execute before *main()* is called. See how this all fits?

The name of the class is required for any member when it appears outside its class boundaries. ◼

In the old days (pre-1991), some C++ compilers, including Turbo C++ 1.0, allocated space automatically. This was written out of the standard, and Borland stopped doing it as of version 2.0. ◼

Referencing static data members

The access rules for static members are the same as the access rules for normal members. From within the class, static members are referenced like any other class member. Public static members can be referenced from outside the class as well. Both types of reference are shown in the following code snippet:

```
class Student
{
  public:
    Student()
    {
       noOfStudents++;        //reference from inside the class
       //...other stuff...
    }

    static int noOfStudents;
    //...other stuff like before...
};
void fn(Student &s1, Student &s2)
{
    //reference public static
    cout << "No of students "
         << s1.noOfStudents //reference from outside the class
         << "\n";
}
```

In *fn()*, *noOfStudents* is referenced using the object *s1*. But *s1* and *s2* share the same member *noOfStudents* — how did I know to choose *s1*? Why didn't I use *s2* instead? It doesn't make any difference. You can reference a static member using any object of that class. For example:

```
//...class defined the same as before...
void fn(Student &s1, Student &s2)
{
   //the following produce identical results
   cout << "No of students " << s1.noOfStudents << "\n";
   cout << "No of students " << s2.noOfStudents << "\n";
}
```

In fact, you don't need an object at all. You can use the class name directly instead, if you prefer, as in the following:

```
//...class defined the same as before...
void fn(Student &s1, Student &s2)
{
   //the following produce identical results
   cout << "No of students "
        << Student::noOfStudents
        << "\n";
}
```

If you use an object name, C++ uses only the class of the object.

The object used to reference a static member is not evaluated even if it's an expression. For example, consider the following case:

```
class Student
{
  public:
    static int noOfStudents;
    Student& nextStudent();
    //...other stuff the same...
};
void fn(Student &s)
{
    cout << s.nextStudent().noOfStudents << "\n"
}
```

The member function *nextStudent( )* is not actually called. All C++ needs to access *noOfStudents* is the return type, and it can get that without bothering to evaluate the expression. This is true even if *nextStudent( )* should do other things, such as wash windows or shine your shoes. None of those things will get done.

Although the example is obscure, it does happen. That's what you get for trying to cram too much stuff into one expression. ▪

Uses for static data members

There are probably umpteen uses for static data members, but let me touch on three common ones. First, you can use static members to keep count of the number of objects floating about. In the *Student* class, for example, the count is initialized to zero, the constructor increments it, and the destructor decrements it. Remember, however, that this count reflects the number of *Student* objects (including any temporaries) and not necessarily the number of students.

A closely related use for a static member is as a flag to indicate whether a particular action has occurred yet. For example, a class *Radio* may need to initialize hardware before sending the first tune command but not before subsequent tunes. A flag indicating that this is the first tune is just the ticket.

Finally, a very common use for static members is to contain the pointer to the first member of a linked list. If we wanted to keep all *Student* objects in a linked list, for example, we might do something like the following:

```cpp
#include <iostream.h>
#include <string.h>
class Student
{
  public:
   Student(char *pName);
  ~Student();
  protected:
   static Student *pFirst;
   Student *pNext;
   char name[40];
};
Student *Student::pFirst = 0;

//put the member function definitions here
Student::Student(char *pName)
{
   strncpy(name, pName, sizeof name);
   name[sizeof name - 1] = '\0';
   //add myself to beginning of list
   pNext = pFirst;
   pFirst = this;
}
Student::~Student()
{
   //remove myself from list
   //if I'm first, then...
   if (pFirst == this)
   {
      //...then list is whatever's after me; otherwise,...
      pFirst = pNext;
   }
   else
   {
     //...look for me...
     for (Student *pS = pFirst; pS; pS = pS->pNext)
     {
        //..once you find me...
        if (pS->pNext == this)
        {
```

continued

```
            //...remove me
            pS->pNext = pNext;
            break;
        }
    }
}
```

(I decided that this destructor had exceeded the bounds of good inline taste and have made it an outline function.)

Each object of class *Student* contains a pointer *pNext* that points to the next object in the linked list. In addition, the class contains a static member *pFirst* that points to the first member of the list (or contains a zero if the list is empty). Graphically, this looks something like Figure 17-1.

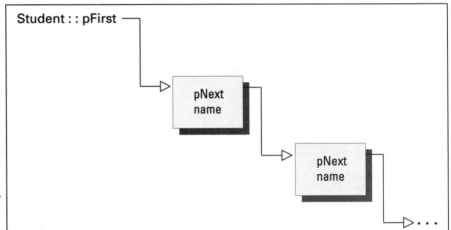

Figure 17-1:
Linked list of
Student
objects.

The constructor is straightforward. Each new object is added onto the beginning of the list. The destructor is a good deal more complicated because it must look for the current object (**this*) in the list and remove it. (In a production class, there should be test code to generate an error if the destructor can't find *this* in the linked list.)

Static Member Functions

Like static data members, static member functions are associated with a class and not with any particular object of that class. This means that like a reference to a static data member, a reference to a static member function does not require an object. If an object is present, only its type is used.

Thus, both calls to the static member function *number()* in the following example are legal:

```
#include <iostream.h>
#include <string.h>
class Student
{
  public:
    static int number()
    {
        return noOfStudents;
    }
    //...other stuff the same...
  protected:
    char name[40];
    static int noOfStudents;
};
int Student::noOfStudents = 0;
int main()
{
    Student s;
    cout << s.number() << "\n";
    cout << Student::number() << "\n";
    return 0;
}
```

Notice how the static member function can access the static data member. However, a static member function is not directly associated with any object, so it does not have default access to any non-static members. Thus, the following would not be legal:

```
class Student
{
  public:
    //the following is not legal
    static char *sName()
    {
        return name;        //which name? there is no object
    }
    //...other stuff the same...
  protected:
    char name[40];
    static int noOfStudents;
};
```

That is not to say that static member functions have no access to non-static data members. Consider the following useful function:

```
#include <iostream.h>
#include <string.h>
class Student
{
  public:
    //same constructor and destructor as earlier
```

continued

```
    Student(char *pName);
   ~Student();

   //findName - return student w/specified name
   static Student *findName(char *pName);
  protected:
   static Student *pFirst;
   Student *pNext;
   char name[40];
};
Student* Student::pFirst = 0;
//findName - return the Student with the specified name.
//           Return zero if no match.
Student* Student::findName(char *pName)
{
   //loop thru the linked list...
   for (Student *pS = pFirst; pS; pS = pS->pNext)
   {
      //...if we find the specified name...
      if (strcmp(pS->name, pName) == 0)
      {
         //...then return the object's address
         return pS;
      }
   }
   //...otherwise, return a zero (item not found)
   return (Student*)0;
}

int main()
{
   Student s1("Randy");
   Student s2("Jenny");
   Student s3("Kinsey");
   Student *pS = Student::findName("Jenny");
   return 0;
}
```

The function *findName()* has access to *pFirst* because it's shared by all objects. Being a member of class *Student*, *findName()* has access also to *name*, but the call must specify the object to use (that is, whose name). There is no default object associated with a static member function. It doesn't help to call the static member function with an object. For example:

```
//...same as before...
int main()
{
   Student s1("Randy");
   Student s2("Jenny");
   Student s3("Kinsey");
   Student *pS = s1.findName("Jenny");
   return 0;
}
```

The *s1* is not evaluated and not passed to *findName()*. Only its class is used to decide which *findName()* to call.

What is *this* about, anyway?

I've mentioned *this* a few times, but let's look at it again just for grins. *this* is a pointer to the "current" object. It's used when no other object name is specified. In a normal member function, *this* is the implied first argument to the function. For example:

```
class SC
{
  public:
          void nFn(int a); //like SC::nFn(SC *this, int a)
    static void sFn(int a); //like SC::sFn(int a)
};
void fn(SC &s)
{
    s.nFn(10); //--converts to--> SC::nFn(&s, 10);
    s.sFn(10); //--converts to--> SC::sFn(10);
}
```

That is, the function *nFn()* is interpreted almost as if it were declared *void SC::nFn(SC *this, int a)*. The call to *nFn()* is converted by the compiler as shown, with the address of *s* passed as the first argument. (You can't actually write the call this way; this is only what the compiler is doing.)

Within the function, *SC::nFn()* references to other non-static members automatically use the *this* argument as the pointer to the current object. When *SC::sFn()* was called, no object address was passed. Thus, it has no *this* pointer to use when referencing non-static functions. This is why we say that a static member function is not associated with any current object.

Conclusion

As we've seen, static members allow all objects of the same class to share a common member. That's why static members are called class members (as opposed to normal object members) in other object-oriented languages.

With this chapter, we have finished cleaning up the messy details associated with the introduction of classes. The decks have now been cleared for the payoff: inheritance, the topic of Part V.

Maintaining a More Reasonable Budget: BUDGET4.CPP

*A*dding some of the features presented in Part IV will jazz up our budget program, creating a more attractive result. I've added the following:

- ✔ More reasonable constructors to build accounts

- ✔ *new* and *delete* to avoid any limitations on the number of accounts

- ✔ Static members to retain class information

Without further ado, here is the program we've all come to know and love:

```
//BUDGET4.CPP - Budget program with expanded constructors,
//              new (and improved) heap management, and
//              static members. The Checking and Savings
//              classes should have a destructor to remove
//              the object from the list, but the destructors
//              aren't included to save space.

#include <iostream.h>
#include <stdlib.h>

//Checking - this describes checking accounts
class Checking
{
  protected:
   Checking(Checking &c)
   {
      cout << "No creating funds\n";
   }

  public:                               //Note 1
   Checking(unsigned accNo, float initialBalance = 0.0);

   //access functions
   int accountNo()
   {
      return accountNumber;
   }
```

continued

```
            float acntBalance()
            {
                return balance;
            }
            static Checking *first()
            {
                return pFirst;
            }
            Checking *next()
            {
                return pNext;
            }
            static int noAccounts()
            {
                return count;
            }

            //transaction functions
            void deposit(float amount)
            {
                balance += amount;
            }
            void withdrawal(float amount);

            //display function for displaying self on 'cout'
            void display()
            {
                cout << "Account " << accountNumber
                     << " = "        << balance
                     << "\n";
            }

          protected:
            //keep accounts in a linked list so there's no limit
            static Checking *pFirst;            //Note 2
                   Checking *pNext;

            static int count;            //number of accounts
            unsigned   accountNumber;
            float      balance;
        };

        //allocate space for statics
        Checking *Checking::pFirst = 0;          //Note 3
        int       Checking::count  = 0;

        //define constructor
        Checking::Checking(unsigned accNo, float initialBalance)
        {
            accountNumber = accNo;
            balance = initialBalance;

            //add this to end of list and count it
            count++;
            if (pFirst == 0)                   //Note 4
            {
                pFirst = this;      //empty list; make it first
            }
```

```cpp
        else                     //list not empty; look for last
        {
            for (Checking *pC = pFirst; pC->pNext; pC = pC->pNext)
            {                     //do nothing (we're just looking...
            }                     //...for the last element in the list)
            pC->pNext = this;     //tack us onto end
        }
        pNext = 0;                //we're always last
}

//withdrawal - now the withdrawal function
void Checking::withdrawal(float amount)
{
    if (balance < amount )
    {
        cout << "Insufficient funds: balance " << balance
             << ", check "                      << amount
             << "\n";
    }
    else
    {
        balance -= amount;
        //if balance falls too low, charge service fee
        if (balance < 500.00)
        {
            balance -= 0.20F;
        }
    }
}

//Savings - you can probably figure this one out
class Savings
{
  protected:
    Savings(Savings &s)
    {
        cout << "No creating funds\n";
    }

  public:
    Savings(unsigned accNo, float initialBalance = 0.0);

    //access functions
    int accountNo()
    {
        return accountNumber;
    }
    float acntBalance()
    {
        return balance;
    }
    static Savings *first()
    {
        return pFirst;
    }
    Savings *next()
    {
        return pNext;
    }
```

continued

```cpp
        static int noAccounts()
        {
           return count;
        }

        //transaction functions
        void deposit(float amount)
        {
           balance += amount;
        }
        void withdrawal(float amount);

        //display function - display self to cout
        void display()
        {
           cout << "Account "              << accountNumber
                << " = "                   << balance
                << " (no. withdrawals = " << noWithdrawals
                << ")\n";
        }

      protected:
       //keep savings accounts in linked list as well
       static Savings *pFirst;
              Savings *pNext;

       static int count;                 //number of accounts
       unsigned   accountNumber;
       float      balance;
       int        noWithdrawals;
    };

    //allocate space for statics
    Savings *Savings::pFirst = 0;
    int      Savings::count  = 0;

    //define constructor
    Savings::Savings(unsigned accNo, float initialBalance)
    {
       accountNumber = accNo;
       balance = initialBalance;
       noWithdrawals = 0;

       //add this to end of list and count it
       count++;
       if (pFirst == 0)
       {
          pFirst = this;          //empty list; make it first
       }
       else                       //list not empty; look for last
       {
          for (Savings *pS = pFirst; pS->pNext; pS = pS->pNext)
          {
          }
          pS->pNext = this;       //make last point to us
       }
       pNext = 0;                 //and we point to nothing
    }
```

```cpp
//withdrawal - perform a Savings withdrawal
void Savings::withdrawal(float amount)
{
   if (balance < amount)
   {
      cout << "Insufficient funds: balance " << balance
           << ", withdrawal "                 << amount
           << "\n";
   }
   else
   {
      if (++noWithdrawals > 1)
      {
         balance -= 5.00F;
      }
      balance -= amount;
   }
}

//prototype declarations
unsigned getAccntNo();
void process(Checking &checking);
void process(Savings &savings);
void outOfMemory();

//main - accumulate the initial input and output totals
int main()
{
   /*loop until someone enters an 'X' or 'x'*/
   Checking *pC;
   Savings  *pS;

   char      accountType;      //S or C

   unsigned keepLooping = 1;
   while (keepLooping)
   {
      cout << "Enter S for Savings, "
              "C for Checking, X for exit\n";
      cin  >> accountType;

      switch (accountType)
      {
         case 'c':
         case 'C':                         //Note 5
            pC = new Checking(getAccntNo());
            if (pC == 0)
            {
               outOfMemory();
            }
            process(*pC);
            break;

         case 's':
         case 'S':                         //Note 5
            pS = new Savings(getAccntNo());
            if (pS == 0)
```

continued

```
                                {
                                    outOfMemory();
                                }
                                process(*pS);
                                break;

                        case 'x':
                        case 'X':
                            keepLooping = 0;
                            break;

                        default:
                            cout << "I didn't get that.\n";
                    }
                }

                //now present totals
                float chkTotal = 0.0;
                float svgTotal = 0.0;
                cout << "Checking accounts:\n";      //Note 6
                for (pC = Checking::first(); pC; pC = pC->next())
                {
                    pC->display();
                    chkTotal += pC->acntBalance();
                }
                cout << "Savings accounts:\n";       //Note 6
                for (pS = Savings::first(); pS; pS = pS->next())
                {
                    pS->display();
                    svgTotal += pS->acntBalance();
                }

                float total = chkTotal + svgTotal;
                cout << "Total for checking accounts = " << chkTotal << "\n";
                cout << "Total for savings accounts  = " << svgTotal << "\n";
                cout << "Total worth                 = " << total << "\n";
                return 0;
            }

//getAccntNo - return the account number entered
unsigned getAccntNo()
{
    unsigned accntNo;
    cout << "Enter account number:";
    cin  >> accntNo;
    return accntNo;
}

//process(Checking) - input the data for a checking account*/
void process(Checking &checking)
{
    cout << "Enter positive number for deposit,\n"
            "negative for check, 0 to terminate";

    float transaction;
    do
    {
```

```
        cout << ":";
        cin  >> transaction;

        //deposit
        if (transaction > 0)
        {
            checking.deposit(transaction);
        }

        //withdrawal
        if (transaction < 0)
        {
            checking.withdrawal(-transaction);
        }
    } while (transaction != 0);
}

//process(Savings) - input the data for a savings account
void process(Savings &savings)
{
    cout << "Enter positive number for deposit,\n"
            "negative for withdrawal, 0 to terminate";

    float transaction;
    do
    {
        cout << ":";
        cin  >> transaction;

        //deposit
        if (transaction > 0)
        {
            savings.deposit(transaction);
        }

        //withdrawal
        if (transaction < 0)
        {
            savings.withdrawal(-transaction);
        }
    } while (transaction != 0);
}

//outOfMemory - generate out of memory message and quit
void outOfMemory()
{
    cout << "Out of memory\n";
    abort();
}
```

A substantial part of this program is the same as BUDGET3.CPP. (How can you improve an old workhorse like that?) Notice, however, the addition of a more meaningful constructor to *Checking* (*Note 1*). In addition, the elements *pFirst* and *pNext* (*Note 2*) allow for the savings account members to be stored in a linked list rather than in an array.

A linked list does not suffer the array's restriction of limiting the number of accounts to a predeclared number. *pFirst* is static because it points to the first member in the list and is a property of the class. *pNext* is not static because it points to the next member in the list as seen from each object. The space for *pFirst* and the other static, *count*, are allocated outside the class (*Note 3*). The class *Savings* has the same additions as *Checking*.

The constructor for *Checking* must now add the current object to the linked list. It does this by looping to the end of the list and then adding the current object, *this* (*Note 4*). (Tacking *this* onto the front is easier but it makes all the objects appear in reverse order in the list, which is inconvenient.) The constructor for *Savings* is virtually identical to that for *Checking*.

No destructors are provided because objects are not dynamically destructed in this application. An example of a destructor that removes objects from a linked list was provided in Chapter 17.

In the main program, new accounts are created by invoking *new* with the new constructors (*Note 5*). *new* first allocates memory off the heap, and then passes that memory to the constructor, which adds it to the linked list.

One final change is in the way the program moves through the list of accounts (*Note 6*). When the accounts were maintained in an array, it was sufficient to initialize a pointer to the first account and then increment the pointer through the array.

With a linked list, the program starts with the first element (that is, the element pointed to by *pFirst*) and then links through the list. On each iteration through the loop, the program moves from the current object to the next object (as pointed to by *pNext*). Because both *pFirst* and *pNext* are protected, access functions are used to retrieve these values. The loop is exhausted when the address of the next object is zero. (Iterating through a linked list reminds me of Tarzan's favorite method of travel. He starts out at his treehouse and swings from one vine to the next. When he runs out of vines and falls to the ground, he, like the loop, is finished.)

25-Minute Workout

Once again, it's time to start sweating. Get out your keyboards and put away your notes. You have 25 minutes — and no cheating.

1

a. Write a constructor for the class *Student* in the program you wrote for the Part III Workout. (You did write that program, didn't you?) This constructor should not make any restrictions on the length of the name. Hint: Use *new*.

b. Consider the following class:

```
class Motor
{
    public:
     Motor(int noCylinders, float displacement);
};
class Car
{
    public:

     //this constructor is not complete
     Car(int color, float displacement,
         int noDoors = 4, int noCylinders = 6)
     {
         //stuff goes here
     }
    protected:
     Motor motor;
     int    paintColor;
     int    numberDoors;
};
```

Complete the constructor for *Car*. Don't forget to initialize the member *motor*.

c. In the following declaration of *student*, what constructor call is invoked on which members?

```
Student otherStudent("Danny");
Student student[5] = {"Randy", otherStudent, "Trudy"};
```

d. What does the following do?

```
class Student
{
    public:
     Student(char *pName);
     Student()
     {
         Student("no name");
     }
};
```

e. Assuming that the intent in *1d* was to avoid having two constructors, how could you do this correctly? There are several ways to do this.

2

a. Why is the constructor *Student::Student(Student)* illegal? Hint: In older versions of the compiler in which the constructor is not illegal, invoking this constructor is always fatal.

b. Why was the copy constructor in BUDGET4 declared protected? Hint: What asset is it trying to protect?

3

a. What's wrong with the following *count()* function? Hint: This is a subtle problem.

```
class Student
{
  public:
    static int count;
};
int Student::count;

//count - count how many students between first and last
void count(Student *pFirst, Student *pLast)
{
    Student *pS = pFirst;
    pS->count = 0;          //start with 0
    while (pS != pLast)     //until we get to the last one
    {
      pS++->count += 1;     //count each one
    }                       //leave count with student count
}
```

b. How many bytes of memory are used by *s*? (Assume that a *char* is one byte and that an *int* is two bytes.)

```
class Student
{
  public:
    char name[40];
    static int count;
};
Student s[10];
```

Answers

Hey, go back and try working the problems first!

1

a. Here's the constructor for *Student* with no limitations on name length:

```
#include <string.h>
class Student
```

```
{
  public:
   Student()
   {
      //just zero out everything
      noCourses = 0;
      pName = 0;
   }
   Student(char *pN)
   {
      noCourses = 0;
      int length = strlen(pN) + 1;
      pName = new char[length];
      if (pName)
      {
         strcpy(pName, pN);
      }
   }
  ~Student()
   {
      delete pName;
   }
   //...other member functions the same...
  protected:
   char    *pName;
   Course *pClasses[maxCourses];
   int      noCourses;
};
```

This constructor first calls *strlen* to count the number of characters in the nameprovided. It then allocates that much memory from the heap. If the memory request is granted, it copies the name into the heap block. (Don't forget to check to make sure that the memory pointer returned from a heap request is valid before using it!) Note that the class *Student* now needs a destructor to return the heap block when the object "goes away."

b. The point of this question is to get you to construct the member *motor* correctly. (Should the constructor for *Car* be called *Detroit*?)

```
Car::Car(int color, float displacement,
      int doors, int noCylinders) :
      motor(noCylinders, displacement)
{
   paintColor = color;
   numberDoors = doors;
}
```

c. Here's the play-by-play:

student[0]	*Student("Randy")*
student[1]	*Student(otherStudent)*
student[2]	*Student("Jenny")*
student[3]	*Student()*
student[4]	*Student()*

d. This was probably an attempt to consolidate code by having the default constructor call the *char** constructor with "no name" as the name. This does not work, however. It constructs locally a nameless object with the name "no name." (That's a fitting name for a nameless object, don't you think?) This object is destructed on the next line, the closed brace.

e. There are several ways that the programmer could have created the desired effect. One way is to default the name field as follows:

```
class Student
{
  public:
    Student(char *pName = "no name");
};
```

Another approach is to build a separate protected function that both constructors can call:

```
class Student
{
  public:
    Student(char *pName)
    {
        init(pName);
    }
    Student()
    {
        init("no name");
    }
  protected:
    void init(char *pName);
};
```

This is the most flexible solution because it works for any combination of argument types.

a. Suppose this constructor was not illegal and someone defined it. Now suppose what would happen if someone tried to use one of these beasties. For example:

```
void fn(Student &original)
{
    Student copy(original);
}
```

C++ needs to make a copy of *original*. Finding the preceding constructor, it says "Aha, I can use this constructor to make a copy of *original* so I'll call it." "But wait," the compiler says, "first I'll need to make a copy of the argument to the constructor because it's passed by value."

So the compiler starts looking for a constructor for that purpose. Does it find it? Of course; it finds *Student(Student)*. "Aha," it says, "I can use this constructor to make a copy of the copy of *original*, so I'll call it." "But wait," the compiler says, "first I'll need to make a copy of the argument to the constructor because it's passed by value." So it finds *Student(Student)*, and so on ad computer nauseum. This would be an infinite loop if it weren't for the fact that it eventually blows up the stack. To avoid this silliness, the designers of C++ just decided to make it illegal.

b. The copy constructor in BUDGET4 was declared protected to keep the application from making copies of any accounts. If an account object were copied, this would copy the balance, effectively creating cash. (Did anybody say embezzlement?) Protecting the copy constructor precludes this from happening.

3

a. Because *count* is a static member of *Student*, the subexpression *pS++* in the expression *pS++->count* is never evaluated. (Only the class of subexpression *ps++* is important.) Thus, *pS* never changes and the loop is infinite.

b. *s* is 400 bytes or 402 bytes, depending on how you look at it. That is, each element of *s* is 40 *char*s, which is 40 bytes, and there are 10 of them, plus the single static *int count* for the entire class *Student*. The point is that it's not 420 because the member *count* appears only once — not 10 times.

Part V
Plunging In: Inheritance

The 5th Wave   By Rich Tennant

WITH OBJECT-ORIENTED PROGRAMMING,
I UNDERSTAND THE "ENCAPSULATION"
AND "INHERITANCE" PART PRETTY WELL.
IT'S THAT DARN "CLUTTERMORPHISM"
THAT STUMPS ME.

In This Part...

In our discussions of object-oriented philosophy in Part III, two main features of real-world solutions were seemingly not shared by functional programming solutions.

The first is the capability to treat objects separately. I presented the example of a microwave oven to whip up a snack. The microwave oven provides an interface (the front panel) that I use to control the oven, without worrying about its internal workings. This is true even if I know all about how the darn things work (which I don't).

A second aspect to real-world solutions is the capability to categorize like objects, recognizing and exploiting their similarities. If my recipe calls for an oven of any type, I should be okay because a microwave is an oven.

I have already presented the mechanism that C++ uses to implement the first feature, the class. To support the second aspect of object-oriented programming, C++ uses a concept known as inheritance, which extends classes. Inheritance is the topic of Part V.

Chapter 18
Inheritance (How Do I Get Mine?)

In This Chapter

▶ The meaning of inheritance

▶ Inheriting a base class

▶ Constructing the base class

▶ Exploring meaningful relationships: the IS_A versus the HAS_A relationship

*I*n this chapter, we discuss *inheritance,* which is the capability of one class of things to inherit capabilities or properties from another class. For example, I am a human (except when I first wake up in the morning). I inherit from the class Human certain properties, such as my ability to converse (more or less) intelligently and my dependence on air, water, and carbohydrate-based nourishment. These properties are not unique to humans. The class Human inherited the dependencies on air, water, and nourishment from the class Mammal, of which it is a member.

The capability to pass down properties is a powerful one. It allows us to describe things in an economical way. For example, when my son asks "What's a duck?" I can say, "It's a bird that goes quack." Despite what you might think, that answer conveys a considerable amount of information to him. He knows what a bird is, and now he knows all those same things about a duck plus the duck's additional property of "quackness."

Object-oriented languages express this inheritance relationship by allowing one class to inherit from another. Thus, OO languages can generate a model that is closer to the real world (remember that real-world stuff!) than the model generated by languages that do not support inheritance.

C++ allows one class to inherit another class as follows:

```
class Student
{
};
class GraduateStudent : public Student
{
};
```

Here, a *GraduateStudent* inherits all the members of a *Student*. Thus, a *GraduateStudent* IS_A *Student*. Of course, *GraduateStudent* may also contain members unique to a *GraduateStudent*.

Why Do I Need Inheritance?

There are several reasons why inheritance was introduced into C++. Of course, the major reason is the capability to express the inheritance relationship. (I'll return to that in a moment.) A minor reason is to reduce the amount of typing. Suppose we have a class *Student*, and we are asked to add a new class called *GraduateStudent*. Inheritance can drastically reduce the number of things we have to put in the class. All we really need in the class *GraduateStudent* are things that describe the differences between students and graduate students.

A more important, related issue is that major buzzword of the 90s, *reuse*. Software scientists have realized for some time that it doesn't make much sense to start from scratch with each new project, rebuilding the same software components.

Compare the situation in software to other industries. How many car manufacturers start from ore to build a car? And even if they did, how many would start completely over from ore with the next model? Practitioners in other industries have found it makes more sense to start from screws, bolts, nuts, and even larger off-the-shelf components such as motors and compressors.

Unfortunately, except for very small functions, like those found in the Standard C library, it's rare to find much reuse of software components. One problem is that it's virtually impossible to find a component from an earlier program that does exactly what you want. Generally, these components require "tweaking."

There's a rule of thumb that says, "If you open it, you've broken it." In other words, if you have to modify a function or class to adapt it to a new application, you will have to retest everything, not just the parts you add. Changes can introduce bugs anywhere in existing code. ("The one who last touched it is the one who gets to fix it.")

Inheritance allows existing classes to be adapted to new applications without the need for modification. The existing class is inherited into a new subclass that contains any necessary additions and modifications.

This carries with it a third benefit. Suppose we inherit from some existing class. Later we find that the base class has a bug that must be corrected. If we have modified the class to reuse it, we must manually check for, correct, and retest the bug in each application separately. If we have inherited the class without changes, we can probably adopt the fixed base class without further ado.

This IS_Amazing

To make sense out of our surroundings, humans build extensive taxonomies. Fido is a special case of dog which is a special case of canine which is a special case of mammal and so it goes. This shapes our understanding of the world.

To use another example, a student is a (special type of) person. Having said this, I already know a lot of things about students. I know they have social security numbers, they watch too much TV, and they daydream about living in the south during the winter and in the north during the summer. I know all these things because these are properties of all people.

In C++, we call this *inheritance*. We say that the class *Student* inherits from the class *Person*. We say also that *Person* is a *base class* of *Student* and *Student* is a *subclass* of *Person*. Finally, we say that a *Student* IS_A *Person* (using all caps is a common way of expressing

this unique relationship — I didn't make it up). C++ shares this terminology with other object-oriented languages.

Notice that although *Student* IS_A *Person*, the reverse is not true. A *Person* is not a *Student*. (A statement like this always refers to the general case. It could be that a particular *Person* is, in fact, a *Student*.) A lot of people who are members of class *Person* are not members of class *Student*. In addition, class *Student* has properties it does not share with class *Person*. For example, *Student* has a grade point average, but *Person* does not.

The inheritance property is transitive as well. For example, if I define a new class *GraduateStudent* as a subclass of *Student*, *GraduateStudent* must also be *Person*. It has to be that way: if a *GraduateStudent* IS_A *Student* and a *Student* IS_A *Person*, a *GraduateStudent* IS_A *Person*.

How Does Inheritance Work?

Let's return to the *GraduateStudent* example and fill it out with a few example members:

```
#include <string.h>
class Advisor
{
};

class Student
{
  public:
    Student(char *pName = "no name")
    {
      strncpy(name, pName, sizeof(name));
      average = semesterHours = 0;
    }
    void addCourse(int hours, float grade)
    {
```

continued

```
        average = (semesterHours * average + grade);
        semesterHours += hours;
        average = average / semesterHours;
      }
    int   hours( ) { return semesterHours;}
    float gpa( )   { return average;}

  protected:
    char   name[40];
    int    semesterHours;
    float  average;
};

class GraduateStudent : public Student
{
  public:
    qualifier( ) { return qualifierGrade;};
  protected:
    Advisor advisor;
    int qualifierGrade;
};

int main( )
{
    Student llu("Lo Lee Undergrad");
    GraduateStudent gs;
    llu.addCourse(3, 2.5);
    gs.addCourse(3, 3.0);
    return 0;
}
```

The class *Student* has been defined in a conventional fashion. The object *llu* is just like the other *Student* objects we've laid our baby blues on. The colon followed by *public Student* declares class *GraduateStudent* to be a subclass of *Student*.

The appearance of the keyword *public* implies that there is probably *protected* inheritance as well. All right, it's true. But I want to hold off discussing this type of inheritance until Part VI.

The object *gs*, as a member of a subclass of *Student*, can do anything that *llu* can do. It has *name*, *semesterHours*, and *average* data members and the *addCourse( )* member function. After all, *gs* quite literally IS_A *Student* — it's just a little bit more than a *Student*. (You'll get tired of me reciting this "IS_A" stuff before the book is over.)

Now consider the following scenario:

```
void fn(Student &s)
{
    //whatever fn it wants to have
}
int main( )
{
```

```
      GraduateStudent gs;
      fn(gs);
      return 0;
   }
```

Notice that the function *fn( )* expects to receive as its argument an object of class *Student*. The call from *main( )* passes it an object of class *GraduateStudent*. However, this is fine because once again (all together now) "a *GraduateStudent* IS_A *Student*."

Basically, the same condition arises when invoking a member function of *Student* with a *GraduateStudent* object. For example:

```
int main( )
{
   GraduateStudent gs;
   gs.addCourse(3, 2.5); //calls Student::addCourse( )
   return 0;
}
```

Constructing a Subclass

Even though a subclass has access to the protected members of the base class and could initialize them, we would like the base class to construct itself. In fact, this is what happens. Before control passes beyond the open brace of the constructor for *GraduateStudent*, control passes to the default constructor of *Student* (because no other constructor was indicated). If *Student* were based on another class, such as *Person*, the constructor for that class would be invoked before the *Student* constructor got control. Like a skyscraper, the object gets constructed starting at the basement class and working its way up the class structure one story at a time.

Just as with member objects, we sometimes need to be able to pass arguments to the base class constructor. We handle this in almost the same way as with member objects, as the following example shows:

```
class GraduateStudent : public Student
{
  public:
   GraduateStudent(char *pName = "no name",
                   Advisor &adv) : Student(pName),
                                   advisor(adv)
   {
      qualifierGrade = 0;
   }
   //...remainder as before...
};
void fn(Advisor &advisor)
```

continued

```
{
    GraduateStudent gs("Yen Kay Doodle", advisor);
    //...whatever this function does...
}
```

Here the constructor for *GraduateStudent* invokes the *Student* constructor, passing it the argument *pName*. The base class is constructed before any member objects; thus, the constructor for *Student* is called before the constructor for *Advisor*. After the constructor for *Advisor* is called for *advisor*, the constructor for *GraduateStudent* gets a shot at it.

Following our rule that destructors are invoked in the reverse order of the constructors, the destructor for *GraduateStudent* is given control first. After it's given its last full measure of devotion, control passes to the destructor for *Advisor* and then to the destructor for *Student*. If *Student* were based on a class *Person*, the destructor for *Person* would get control after *Student*.

This is logical. The blob of memory is first converted to a *Student* object. Then it is the job of the *GraduateStudent* constructor to complete its transformation into a *GraduateStudent*. The destructor simply reverses the process.

The HAS_A Relationship

Notice that the class *GraduateStudent* includes the members of class *Student* and *Advisor*, but in a different way. By defining a data member of class *Advisor*, we know that a *Student* has all the data members of an *Advisor* within it, yet we say that a *GraduateStudent* HAS_A *Advisor*. What's the difference between this and inheritance?

Let's use a car as an example. We could logically define a car as being a subclass of vehicle, and so it inherits the properties of other vehicles. At the same time, a car has a motor. If you buy a car, you can logically assume that you are buying a motor as well. (Unless you went to the used car lot where I got my last junk heap.)

Now if some friends asked you to show up at a rally on Saturday with your vehicle of choice and you came in your car, there would be no complaint because a car IS_A vehicle. But if you appeared on foot carrying a motor, they would have reason to be upset because a motor is not a vehicle. It is missing certain critical properties that vehicles share. It's even missing properties that cars share, such as electric clocks that don't work.

From a programming standpoint, it's just as straightforward. Consider the following:

```
class Vehicle
{
};
class Motor
{
};
class Car : public Vehicle
{
  public:
    Motor motor;
};
void VehicleFn(Vehicle &v);
void motorFn(Motor &m);
int main( )
{
    Car c;
    VehicleFn(c);     //this is allowed
    motorFn(c);       //this is not allowed
    motorFn(c.motor);//this is, however
    return 0;
}
```

The call *VehicleFn(c)* is allowed because *c* IS_A *Vehicle*. The call *motorFn(c)* is not because *c* is not a *Motor*, even though it contains a *Motor*. If what was intended was to pass the *motor* portion of *c* to the function, this must be expressed explicitly, as in the call *motorFn(c.motor)*.

One further distinction: the class *Car* has access to the protected members of *Vehicle*, but not to the protected members of *Motor*.

Conclusion

Understanding inheritance is critical to understanding the whole point behind object-oriented programming. It's also required in order to understand the next chapter. If you feel you've got it down, move on to Chapter 19. If not, you may want to reread this chapter.

Chapter 19

Virtual Member Functions: Are They for Real?

In This Chapter

▶ Overloading member functions in a subclass

▶ Polymorphism (alias late binding)

▶ I prefer to have my binding finished early. What's wrong with that?

▶ Are polymorphic nachos really safe?

▶ Special considerations with polymorphism

*I*t has always been possible to overload a member function in one class with a member function from another class. With inheritance, however, you can overload a base class member function with a member function in a subclass as well. Consider, for example, the following simple code snippet:

```
class Student
{
  public:
    //...all as it was before...
    float calcTuition();
};
class GraduateStudent : public Student
{
  public:
    float calcTuition();
};

int main()
{
    Student s;
    GraduateStudent gs;
    s.calcTuition();        //calls Student::calcTuition()
    gs.calcTuition();       //calls GraduateStudent::calcTuition()
    return 0;
}
```

As with any overloading situation, when the programmer refers to *calcTuition()*, C++ has to decide which *calcTuition()* is intended. Normally the class is sufficient to resolve the call, and this example is no different. The call *s.calcTuition()* refers to *Student::calcTuition()* because *s* is declared locally as a *Student*, whereas *gs.calcTuition()* refers to *GraduateStudent::calcTuition()*.

But what if the exact class of the object can't be determined at compile time? To demonstrate how this can occur, let's change the preceding program in a seemingly trivial way:

```
class Student
{
  public:
    //...all as it was before...
    float calcTuition() {
       return 0;
    }
};
class GraduateStudent : public Student
{
  public:
    float calcTuition()
    {
       return 0;
    }
};

void fn(Student &x)
{
    x.calcTuition();      //to which calcTuition() does this refer?
}
int main()
{
    Student s;
    GraduateStudent gs;
    fn(s);
    fn(gs);
    return 0;
}
```

Instead of calling *calcTuition()* directly, the call is now made through an intermediate function, *fn()*. Depending on how *fn()* is called, *x* can be a *Student* or a *GraduateStudent*. (Remember? A *GraduateStudent* IS_A *Student*.)

We would like *x.calcTuition()* to call *Student::calcTuition()* when *x* is a *Student* but call *GraduateStudent::calcTuition()* when *x* is a *GraduateStudent*. This is a capability you've probably never seen in a language and certainly haven't seen in C.

Normally, the compiler decides which function a call refers to at compile time. Even when the function is overloaded, which means C++ must use the arguments to help disambiguate the call, the decision is still made at compile time.

In the case described here, however, a decision cannot be made until run time when the actual type of the object can be determined.

The capability to decide at run time which of several overloaded member functions to call based on the actual type is called *polymorphism,* or *late binding.* The term polymorphism comes from *poly* (meaning multiple), *morph* (meaning change) and *ism* (meaning unintelligible Greek word). C++ supports polymorphism. (This is not very surprising by now; I wouldn't be spending all this time talking about polymorphism if C++ didn't support it.) Deciding which overloaded member functions to call at compile time is called *early binding* because that sounds like the opposite of late binding.

The type that we've been accustomed to until now is called the *declared type.* Another name for the actual type is the *run-time type.* Remember function *fn()* from the previous example? The run-time type of *x* is *Student* when *fn()* is called with *Student s* and *GraduateStudent* when *fn()* is called with *GraduateStudent gs.* The declared type of *x* is always *Student,* however, because that's what the declaration in *fn()* says. ▪

Polymorphism and late binding are not quite identical terms. Polymorphism refers to the capability of the call to decide between possible actions at run time. Late binding is the mechanism C++ uses to implement polymorphism. Other object-oriented languages may use different techniques. This book is limited to discussing C++ (and a bit of C), however, so I use the terms polymorphism and late binding synonymously. ▪

Why Do I Need Polymorphism?

Polymorphism is key to the power of object-oriented programming. It's so important that languages that don't support polymorphism cannot advertise themselves as OO languages. (I think it's in NAFTA somewhere — you can't import a language labeled OO if it doesn't support polymorphism.) Languages that support classes but not polymorphism are called *object-based languages.* Ada is an example of such a language.

Without polymorphism, inheritance has little meaning. Let me spring yet another example on you to show why. Suppose that I had written this really boffo program that used some class called, well, *Student.* After months of design, coding, and testing, I release this application to rave reviews from colleagues and critics alike. (There's even talk of starting a new Nobel Prize category for software, but I modestly brush such talk aside.)

Time passes and my boss asks me to add to this program the capability to handle graduate students who are similar but not identical to normal students.

(They don't have quite the same attention span.) Deep within the program, *someFunction()* calls the *calcTuition()* member function as follows:

```
void someFunction(Student &s)
{
    //...whatever it might do...
    s.calcTuition();
    //...continues on...
}
```

If C++ did not support late binding, I would need to edit *someFunction()* to something like the following to add class *GraduateStudent* :

```
#define STUDENT 1
#define GRADUATESTUDENT 2
void someFunction(Student &s)
{
    //...whatever it might do...
    //add some member type that indicates
    //the actual type of the object
    switch (s.type)
    {
        STUDENT:
            s.Student::calcTuition();
            break;
        GRADUATESTUDENT:
            s.GraduateStudent::calcTuition();
            break;
    }
    //...continues on...
}
```

I would add the member *type* to the class, which I would then set to *STUDENT* in the constructor for *Student* and to *GRADUATESTUDENT* in the constructor for *GraduateStudent*. The value of *type* would refer to the run-time type of *s*. I would then add the test in the preceding code snippet to call the proper member function depending on the value of this member.

That doesn't seem so bad, except for three things. First, this is only one function. Suppose *calcTuition()* is called from a lot of places and suppose that *calcTuition()* is not the only difference between the two classes. The chances are not good that I will find all the places that need to be changed.

Second, I must edit (read "break") code that was debugged, checked in, and working, introducing further opportunities for screwing up. Edits can be time consuming and boring, which usually makes my attention drift. Any one of my edits may be wrong or may not fit in with the existing code. Who knows?

Finally, after I've finished editing, redebugging, and retesting everything, I now have two versions to keep track of (unless I can drop support for the original version). This means two sources to edit when bugs are found (perish the thought) and some type of accounting system to keep them straight.

Then what happens when my boss wants yet another class added? (My boss is like that.) Not only do I get to repeat the process, but I'll have three copies to keep track of.

With polymorphism, there's a good chance that all I need to do is add the new subclass and recompile. I may need to modify the base class itself, but at least it's all in one place. Modifications to the application should be minimal to none.

This is yet another reason to leave data members protected and access them through public member functions. Data members cannot be polymorphically overloaded by a subclass, whereas a member function can. ∎

At some philosophical level there's an even more important reason for polymorphism. Remember how I made nachos in the oven? In this sense, I was acting as the late binder. The recipe read: Heat the nachos in the oven. It didn't read: If the type of oven is a microwave, do this; if the type of oven is conventional, do that; if the type of oven is convection, do this other thing. The recipe (the code) relied on me (the late binder) to decide what the action (member function) *heat* means when applied to the oven (the particular instance of class Oven) or any of its variations (subclasses), such as a microwave oven (Microwave). This is the way people think, and designing a language along these lines allows the software model to more accurately describe what people are thinking.

How Does Polymorphism Work?

Given all that I've said so far, it may be surprising that the default for C++ is early binding. The reason is simple. Polymorphism adds a small amount of overhead both in terms of data storage and code needed to perform the call. The founders of C++ were concerned that any additional overhead they introduced would be used as a reason not to adopt C++ as the systems language of choice, so they made the more efficient early binding the default.

To indicate polymorphism, the programmer must flag the member function with the C++ keyword *virtual*, as follows:

```
#include <iostream.h>
class Base
{
  public:
    virtual void fn()
    {
        cout << "In Base class\n";
    }
};
class SubClass : public Base
```

continued

```
{
  public:
    virtual void fn()
    {
        cout << "In SubClass\n";
    }
};

void test(Base &b)
{
    b.fn();              //this call bound late
}
int main()

{
    Base bc;
    SubClass sc;
    cout << "Calling test(bc)\n";
    test(bc);
    cout << "Calling test(sc)\n";
    test(sc);
    return 0;
}
```

The keyword *virtual* is what tells C++ that *fn()* is a polymorphic member function. That is to say, declaring *fn()* virtual means that calls to it will be bound late if there is any doubt as to the run-time type of the object with which *fn()* is called.

In the example snippet, *fn()* is called through the intermediate function *test()*. When *test()* is passed a *Base* class object, *b.fn()* calls *Base::fn()*. But when *test()* is passed a *SubClass* object, the same call invokes *SubClass::fn()*. (You *really* have to single step this in the debugger to believe it.)

Executing the program generates the following output:

```
Calling test(bc)
In Base class
Calling test(sc)
In SubClass
```

You need to declare the function virtual only in the base class. The "virtualness" is carried down to the subclass automatically. However, in this book I follow the coding standard of declaring the function virtual everywhere (virtually). ▪

Some programmers react skeptically to polymorphism. They immediately want to know how it works and how much it costs (in terms of overhead in time and space). If you want to know the internals of late binding and polymorphic calls, see the Appendix for a thorough explanation of late binding. ▪

Making Nachos the Polymorphic Way

Okay, now that we've seen some of the nitty gritty details of declaring a virtual function, let's return to our nacho example and see what it would look like in code. Consider the following code snippet:

```
#include <dos.h>              //needed for sleep()

class Stuff{};
class Nachos : public Stuff {};

//Oven - implements a conventional oven

class Oven
{
  public:
    virtual void cook(Nachos &nachos);

    //support functions that we need
    void turnOn();            //apply current
    void turnOff();           //turn off current

    void insert(Stuff &s);    //put stuff in oven
    void remove(Stuff &s);    //pull stuff out

  protected:
    float temp;
};

void Oven::cook(Nachos &nachos)
{
    //preheat oven
    turnOn();
    while (temp < 350)
    {
    }

    //now put nachos in for 15 minutes
    insert(nachos);
    sleep(15 * 60);

    //get them out and turn the oven off
    remove(nachos);
    turnOff();
}

class Microwave : public Oven {
  public:
    virtual void cook(Nachos &nachos);
    void rotateStuff(Stuff &s);
};
void Microwave::cook(Nachos &nachos)
{
    //no preheating necessary - temperature irrelevant
```

continued

```
        //put nachos in first
        insert(nachos);
        turnOn();

        //only cook for a minute (rotate in the middle)
        sleep(30);
        rotateStuff(nachos);
        sleep(30);

        //turn the oven off first (lest your hair fall out)
        turnOff();
        remove(nachos);
    }

    Nachos makeNachos(Oven &oven)
    {
        //get all the stuff together
        //and assemble the parts
        Nachos n;

        //now (here comes the critical part), cook it
        //(given whatever kind of oven you have)
        oven.cook(n);

        //return the results
        return n;
    }
```

Here we see the class *Nachos*, which is declared as a subclass of *Stuff* (meaning all the stuff you can cook). The class *Oven* is outfitted with the common functions *turnOn()*, *turnOff()*, *insert()*, and *remove()*. (The last two refer to the insertion and extraction of stuff from the oven.) In addition, the class *Oven* has a member function *cook(Nachos&)*, which has been declared virtual.

The function *cook(Nachos&)* has been declared virtual because it is implemented differently in the subclass *Microwave*, which inherits from the class *Oven*. The implementation of *Oven::cook(Nachos&)* preheats the oven to a temperature of 350 degrees, puts the nachos in, and cooks them for 15 minutes. It then removes said nachos before turning off the oven. The implementation of *Microwave::cook(Nachos&)*, by comparison, puts the nachos in, turns the power on for 30 seconds, rotates the nachos, and then waits another 30 seconds before turning the oven off and removing the nachos.

This is fine and dandy, but it is all just a buildup for the really interesting part. The function *makeNachos()* is passed an *Oven* of some type. Given that oven, it assembles all the parts into an object *n* and then cooks them by calling *oven.cook()*. Exactly which function is used, function *Oven::cook()* or function *Microwave::cook()*, depends on the real-time type of *oven*. The function *makeNachos()* has no idea — and doesn't want to know — what the run-time type of oven is.

Why is polymorphism such a good idea? First, it allows the maker of ovens —
and not the cooker of nachos — to worry about the details of how ovens work.
Our division of labor lays such details at the oven programmer's feet.

Second, polymorphism can greatly simplify the code. Look how simple
makeNachos() appears without any of the oven details. (I realize that it
wouldn't be too complicated even with the details, but remember that polymorphism works for real-world problems with their attendant complexity.) The
nacho functions can concentrate on nacho details. Finally, the result is extensible. When a new subclass *ConvectionOven* comes along with a new member
function *ConvectionOven::cook(Nachos&)*, we do not need to change one iota of
makeNachos() to incorporate the new function. Polymorphism automatically
includes the new function and calls it when necessary.

This is heady stuff. Reflect on what this means. Polymorphism is the key that
unlocks the power of inheritance.

When Is a Virtual Function Not?

Just because you think a particular function call is bound late doesn't mean it
is. C++ generates no indication at compile time of which calls it thinks are
bound early and late.

The most critical thing to watch for is that all the member functions in question
be declared identically, including the return type. If not declared with the same
arguments in the subclasses, the member functions are not overloaded polymorphically, whether or not they are declared virtual. For example, let's change
the previous function so that the arguments don't match exactly, and then rerun the program:

```
#include <iostream.h>
class Base
{
  public:
    virtual void fn(int x)
    {
        cout << "In Base class, int x = " << x << "\n";
    }
};
class SubClass : public Base
{
  public:
    virtual void fn(float x)
    {
        cout << "In SubClass, float x = " << x << "\n";
    }
};
```

continued

```
void test(Base &b)
{
   int i = 1;
   b.fn(i);          //this call not bound late
   float f = 2.0;
   b.fn(f);          //neither is this one
}

int main()
{
   Base bc;
   SubClass sc;
   cout << "Calling test(bc)\n";
   test(bc);
   cout << "Calling test(sc)\n";
   test(sc);
   return 0;
}
```

The only difference between this program and the earlier one is that *fn( )* in
Base is declared as *fn(int)*, whereas the *SubClass* version is declared *fn(float)*.
No error is generated because this program is legal. However, the results show
no sign of polymorphism:

```
Calling test(bc)
In Base class, int x = 1
In Base class, int x = 2
Calling test(sc)
In Base class, int x = 1
In Base class, int x = 2
```

Because the first call passes an *int*, it's not surprising that the compiler calls
fn(int) with both *bc* and *sc*. It is a little surprising that the *float* in the second
call is converted to an *int* and the same *Base::fn(int)* is called the second time
in *test( )*. This happens because the object *b* passed to *test( )* is declared as an
object of class *Base*. Without polymorphism, calls to *b.fn( )* in *test( )* refer to
Base::fn(int).

If the arguments don't match exactly, there is no late binding. ▪

The Borland compilers do generate the following warning:

```
SubClass::fn(float) hides virtual function Base::fn(int)
```

This draws the programmer's attention to the probable error. Microsoft Visual
C++, however, does not complain.

There is one exception to the preceding identical declaration rule. It's technical
and hasn't been officially adopted into the C++ Standard yet. Because it's likely
to be accepted, however, you might want to know it: If the member function in

the base class returns a pointer or reference to a base class object, an over

loaded member function in a subclass may return a pointer or reference to an object of the subclass. In other words, the following is allowed:

```
class Base
{
  public:
    Base* aFn();
};

class Subclass : public Base
{
  public:
    Subclass* aFn();
};
```

In practice this is quite natural. If a function is dealing with *Subclass* objects, it seems natural that it should continue to deal with *Subclass* objects. ∎

Virtual Considerations

Static member functions cannot be declared virtual. Because static member functions are not called with an object, there is no run-time object to have a type.

In the following example, *x* is not evaluated. Only its declared type is used to decide that the programmer wants to call *Base::staticFn()*:

```
void fn(Base &x)
{
    x.staticFn();          //x not evaluated here
    Base::staticFn();      //alternate way to call static...
                           //...no object provided
}
```

An object isn't even necessary, as the second call shows.

Specifying the class name in the call forces the call to bind early. For example, the following call is to *Base::fn()* because that's what the programmer indicated, even if *fn()* is declared virtual:

```
void test(Base &b)
{
    b.Base::fn();          //this call is not bound late
}
```

A virtual function cannot be inlined. To expand a function inline, the compiler must know which function is intended at compile time. Thus, although the example member functions so far have been declared in the class, all of them have been outline functions.

Constructors cannot be virtual because there is no (completed) object to use to determine the type. At the time the constructor is called, the memory that the object occupies is just an amorphous mass. It's only after the constructor has finished that the object is a member of the class in good standing.

By comparison, the destructor normally should be declared virtual. If not, you run the risk of improperly destructing the object, as in the following circumstance:

```
class Base
{
  public:
   ~Base();
};
class SubClass : public Base
{
  public:
   ~SubClass();
};
void finishWithObject(Base *pHeapObject)
{
   //...work with object...
   //now return it to the heap
   delete pHeapObject;  //this calls ~Base() no matter what...
}                       //...the run-time type of pHeapObject is
```

If the pointer passed to *finishWithObject()* really points to a *SubClass*, the *SubClass* destructor is not invoked properly. Declaring the destructor virtual solves the problem.

So when would you not want to declare the destructor virtual? There's only one case. Do you remember that I said that virtual functions introduce a "little" overhead? Let me be more specific. When the programmer defines the first virtual function in a class, C++ adds an additional, hidden pointer — not one pointer per virtual function, just one pointer if the class has any virtual functions. (See the Appendix for more detail on this pointer.) A class that has no virtual functions (and does not inherit any virtual functions from base classes) does not have this pointer.

Now one pointer doesn't sound like much, and it isn't unless the following two conditions are true:

✔ The class doesn't have many data members (so that one pointer represents a lot compared to what's there already)

✔ You intend to create a lot of objects of this class (otherwise, the overhead doesn't make any difference)

If these two conditions are both met and your class doesn't already have any virtual member functions, you might not want to declare the destructor virtual.

Normally, always declare the destructor virtual. If you don't declare the destructor virtual, document it! ■

Conclusion

If inheritance is the Green Hornet, polymorphism is definitely Kato. By itself, inheritance is nice but limited in capability. Combined with polymorphism, inheritance is a powerful programming aid. In the remaining pages of Part V, we will see how we can put this dynamic duo to work on our programs.

Chapter 20

Class Factoring
and Abstract Classes

● ●

In This Chapter

▶ Factoring common properties into a base class

▶ Using abstract classes to hold factored information

▶ Abstract classes and dynamic typing

● ●

So far we've seen how inheritance can be used to extend existing classes to new applications. Inheritance also affords the programmer the ability to combine common features from different classes in a process known as *factoring*.

Factoring

To see how factoring works, let's look back at the two classes used in our Budget example, *Checking* and *Savings*. These are shown graphically in Figure 20-1.

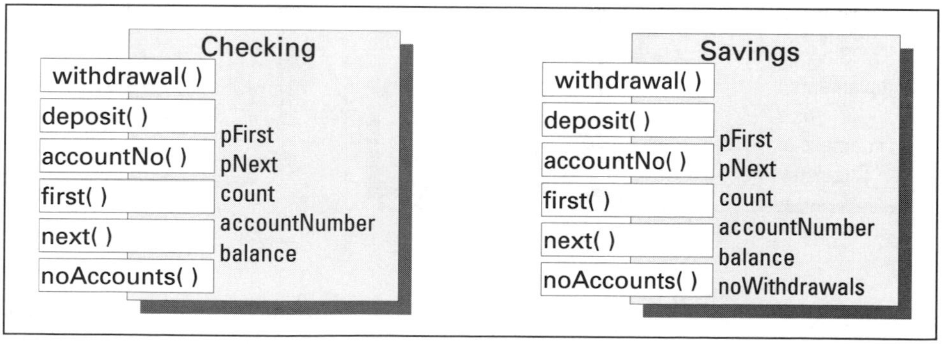

Figure 20-1:
Independent
classes
Checking
and
Savings.

To read this figure and the other figures that follow, remember the following:

- ✔ The big box is the class, with the class name at the top
- ✔ The names in boxes are member functions
- ✔ The names not in boxes are data members
- ✔ The names that extend partway out of the boxes are publicly accessible members; those that do not are protected
- ✔ A thick arrow represents the IS_A relationship
- ✔ A thin arrow represents the HAS_A relationship ■

You can see in Figure 20-1 that the *Checking* and *Savings* classes have a lot in common. Because they aren't identical, however, they must remain as separate classes. (In a real-life bank application, the two classes would be a good deal more different than in our simplistic example.) Still, there should be a way to avoid this repetition.

We could have one of these classes inherit from the other. *Savings* has the extra members, so it makes more sense to let it inherit from *Checking*, as shown in Figure 20-2. The class is completed with the addition of data member *noWithdrawals* and the virtual overloading of member function *withdrawal()*.

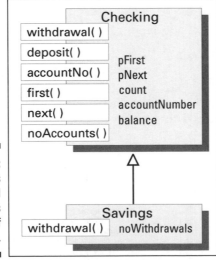

Figure 20-2:
Savings
implemented
as s
subclass of
Checking.

There's a lot going for this solution. It sure saves typing. In code, it looks like the following. (The implementation of member functions has been removed to save space.)

```
//Checking - this describes checking accounts; the
//            implementation of member functions has
//            been removed to save space
class Checking
{
  protected:
   Checking(Checking &c);

  public:
   Checking(unsigned accNo, float initialBalance = 0.0);
   //access functions
   int accountNo( );
   float acntBalance( );
   static Checking *first( );
   Checking *next( );
   static int noAccounts( );
   //transaction functions
   void deposit(float amount);
   virtual void withdrawal(float amount);

  protected:
   //keep accounts in a linked list so there's no limit
   static Checking *pFirst;
         Checking *pNext;
   static int count;          //number of accounts
   unsigned   accountNumber;
   float      balance;
};
//allocate space for statics
Checking *Checking::pFirst = 0;
int       Checking::count  = 0;

//Savings - base this on a Checking account
class Savings : public Checking
{
  public:
   Savings(unsigned accNo, float initialBalance = 0.0);
   virtual void withdrawal(float amount);
  protected:
   int          noWithdrawals;
};
```

Notice that the class *Checking* is unchanged. *Savings*, however, is a mere shadow of its former self. *Savings* contains only the differences between itself and *Checking*.

Although this solution is laborsaving, it's not completely satisfying. The main problem is that it, like the weight listed on my driver's license, misrepresents the truth. This inheritance relationship implies that a *Savings* account is a special type of *Checking* account, which is not the case.

"So what?" you say, "It works and it saves effort." True, but my reservations are more than stylistic trivialities. Such misrepresentations are confusing to the programmer, both today's and tomorrow's. Someday, a programmer unfamiliar with this program will have to read and understand what the code is doing. Misleading tricks are difficult to reconcile and understand.

In addition, such misrepresentations can lead to problems down the road. Suppose, for example, that our bank changes its policies with respect to checking accounts. Let's say it decides to charge a service fee on checking accounts only if the minimum balance dips below a given value during the month.

A change like this can be easily handled with minimal changes to the class *Checking*. Let's see, we'll have to add a new data member to the class *Checking*; let's call it *minimumBalance*.

But now we have a problem. Because *Savings* inherits from *Checking*, *Savings* gets this new data member as well. It has no use for this member because the minimum balance does not affect savings accounts. One extra data member may not be a big deal, but it does add confusion.

Changes like this accumulate. Today it's an extra data member, tomorrow it's a changed member function. Eventually the *Savings* account class is carrying a lot of extra baggage that is applicable only to *Checking* accounts.

How can we avoid these problems? The solution is to base both classes on a new class built specially for this purpose; let's call it *Account*. This class embodies all the features that a savings account and a checking account have in common, as shown in Figure 20-3.

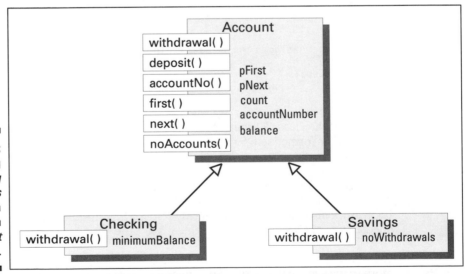

Figure 20-3:
Basing
Checking
and *Savings*
from a
common
Account
class.

In code, it looks like this:

```
//Account - this class embodies the properties common
//          to all bank accounts; the implementation
//          of member functions has been omitted to
//          save space
class Account
{
  protected:
   Account(Account &c);

  public:
   Account(unsigned accNo, float initialBalance = 0.0);
   //access functions
   int accountNo( );
   float acntBalance( );
   static Account *first( );
   Account *next( );
   static int noAccounts( );
   //transaction functions
   void deposit(float amount);
   virtual void withdrawal(float amount);

  protected:
   //keep accounts in a linked list so there's no limit
   static Account *pFirst;
          Account *pNext;
   static int count;         //number of accounts
   unsigned   accountNumber;
   float      balance;
};
//allocate space for statics
Account *Account::pFirst = 0;
int      Account::count  = 0;

//Checking - a checking account
class Checking : public Account
{
  public:
   Checking(unsigned accNo, float initialBalance = 0.0);
   virtual void withdrawal(float amount);
};

//Savings - a savings account
class Savings : public Account
{
  public:
   Savings(unsigned accNo, float initialBalance = 0.0);
   virtual void withdrawal(float amount);
  protected:
   int        noWithdrawals;
};
```

How does this solve the problems? First, this is a more accurate description of the real world (whatever that is). In our concept of things (or at least in my concept of things), there really is something known as an account. Savings accounts and checking accounts are specializations of this more fundamental concept.

In addition, the class *Savings* is insulated from changes to the class *Checking* (and vice versa). If the bank institutes a fundamental change to all accounts, we can modify *Account* and all subclasses will automatically inherit the change. But if the bank changes its policy only for checking accounts, the savings accounts remain insulated from the change.

This process of culling out common properties from similar classes is called *factoring*. This is an important feature of object-oriented languages for the reasons described so far plus one more: reduction in redundancy.

In software, as in tummies, needless bulk is bad. The more code you generate, the more you have to debug. It's not worth staying up nights generating clever code just to save a few lines here or there — that type of cleverness usually boomerangs. But factoring out redundancy through inheritance can legitimately reduce the programming effort.

Factoring is legitimate only if the inheritance relationship corresponds to reality. Factoring together a class *Mouse* and *Joystick* because they're both hardware pointing devices is legitimate. Factoring together a class *Mouse* and *Display* because they both make low-level operating system calls is not. ■

Factoring can and usually does result in multiple levels of abstraction. For example, a program written for a more developed bank may have a class structure such as that shown in Figure 20-4.

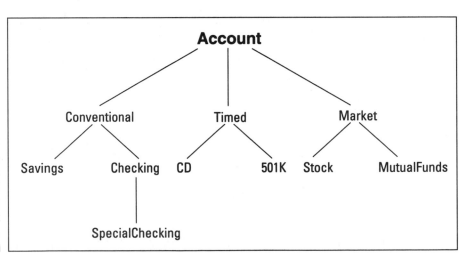

Figure 20-4:
A more
developed
bank
account
hierarchy.

Here we see that another class has been inserted between *Checking* and *Savings* and the most general class, *Account*. This class, called *Conventional*, incorporates features common to conventional accounts. Other account types, such as stock market accounts, are also foreseen.

Such multitiered class structures are common and desirable as long as the relationships they express correspond to reality. Note, however, that there is no one correct class hierarchy for any given set of classes.

Suppose that our bank allows account holders to access checking and stock market accounts remotely. Withdrawals from other account types can be made only at the bank. Although the class structure in Figure 20-4 seems natural, that shown in Figure 20-5 is also justifiable given this information. The programmer must decide which class structure best fits the data and leads to the cleanest, most natural implementation.

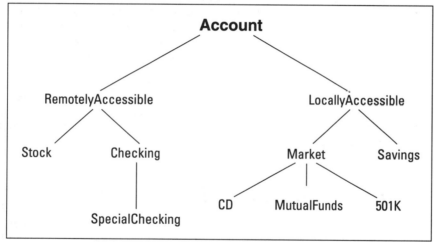

Figure 20-5: Alternate class hierarchy to the one in Figure 20-4.

Abstract Classes

As intellectually satisfying as factoring is, it introduces a problem of its own. Let's return one more time to the bank account classes, specifically the common base class *Account*. Let's think for a minute about how we might go about defining the different member functions defined in *Account*.

Most *Account* member functions are no problem because both account types implement them in the same way. *withdrawal()* is different, however. The rules for withdrawing from a *Savings* account are different than those for withdrawing from a *Checking* account. Thus, we would expect *Savings::withdrawal()* to be implemented differently than *Checking::withdrawal()*. But the question I want to ask is, how do we implement *Account::withdrawal()*?

"No problem," you say. "Just go to your banker and ask 'What are the rules for making a withdrawal from an account?' " The reply is, "What type of account? Savings or checking?" "From an account," you say, "just an account." Blank look.

The problem is that the question doesn't make sense. There's no such thing as "just an account." All accounts (in this example) are either checking accounts or savings accounts. The concept of an account is an abstract one that factors out properties common to the two concrete classes. It is incomplete, however, because it lacks the critical property *withdrawal()*. (After we get further into the details, we'll find other properties that a simple account lacks.)

Let me borrow an example from the animal kingdom. We can observe the different species of warm-blooded, baby-bearing animals and conclude that there is a concept Mammal. We can derive classes from mammal, such as canine, feline, and hominid. It is impossible, however, to find anywhere on earth a pure mammal, that is, a mammal that isn't a member of some species. Mammal is a high-level concept that we have created — no instances of mammal exist.

We don't want the programmer to create an object of class *Account* or class *Mammal* because we wouldn't know what to do with it. To address this problem, C++ allows the programmer to declare a class that cannot be instanced with an object. The only use for such a class is that it can be inherited. Such a class is called an *abstract* class.

How do they work?

An abstract class is a class with one or more pure virtual functions. A *pure virtual function* is a virtual member function that is marked as having no implementation. It has no implementation because we don't know how to implement it. For example, we don't know how to perform a *withdrawal()* in class *Account*. The concept doesn't make sense. However, we can't just not include a definition of *withdrawal()* because C++ will assume that we forgot to define the function and give us a link error stating that the function is missing (and presumed forgotten).

The syntax for declaring a function pure virtual — and letting C++ know that the function has no definition — is demonstrated in the following class *Account*:

```
//Account - this class is an abstract class
class Account
{
  protected:
    Account(Account &c);
```

```
public:
 Account(unsigned accNo, float initialBalance = 0.0);
 //access functions
 int accountNo( );
 float acntBalance( );
 static Account *first( );
 Account *next( );
 static int noAccounts( );
 //transaction functions
 void deposit(float amount);

 //the following is a pure virtual function
 virtual void withdrawal(float amount) = 0;

protected:
 //keep accounts in a linked list so there's no limit
 static Account *pFirst;
         Account *pNext;
 static int count;          //number of accounts
 unsigned    accountNumber;
 float       balance;
};
```

The = *0* after the declaration of *withdrawal( )* indicates that the programmer does not intend to define this function. The declaration is a placeholder for the subclasses. The subclasses of *Account* are expected to overload this function with a concrete function.

I think this notation is silly, and I don't like it any more than you do. But it's here to stay, so we'll just have to learn to live with it. There is a reason, if not exactly a justification, for this notation. Every virtual function must have an entry in a special table. (See the Appendix for an explanation of this table.) This entry contains the address of the function. The entry for a pure virtual function is zero. ∎

An abstract class cannot be instanced with an object; that is, you can't make an object out of an abstract class. That is, the following declaration is not legal:

```
void fn( )
{
   //declare an account with 100 dollars
   Account acnt(1234, 100.00);//this is not legal
   acnt.withdrawal(50);       //what would you expect this to do?
}
```

If the declaration were allowed, the resulting object would be incomplete, lacking in some capability. For example, what should the preceding call do? Remember, there is no *Account::withdrawal( )*.

Abstract classes serve as base classes for other classes. An *Account* contains all the properties that we associate with a generic bank account. We can create other types of bank accounts by inheriting from *Account*, but they cannot be instanced with an object.

Making an honest class out of an abstract class

The subclass of an abstract class remains abstract until all pure virtual functions have been overloaded. The class *Savings* is not abstract because it overloads the pure virtual function *withdrawal( )* with a perfectly good definition. An object of class *Savings* knows how to perform *withdrawal( )* when called on to do so. The same is true of class *Checking*: The class is not virtual because the function *withdrawal( )* overloads the pure virtual function in the base class.

A subclass of an abstract class can remain abstract, however. Consider the follow classes:

```
class Display
{
  public:
    virtual void initialize( ) = 0;
    virtual void write(char *pString) = 0;
};

class Monochrome : public Display
{
    //overload both member functions with "real" functions
    virtual void initialize( );
    virtual void write(char *pString);
};

class ColorAdapter : public Display
{
    //overload the only function we know how to at this point
    virtual void write(char *pString);
};

class VGA : public ColorAdapter
{
    virtual void initialize( );
};

void fn( )
{
    Monochrome mc;
    VGA vga;
    //...what the function chooses to do from here...
}
```

The class *Display*, intended to represent video PC displays, has two pure virtual functions: *initialize( )* and *write( )*. We cannot implement either function for adapters in general. The different types of video cards do not initialize or write in the same way.

One of the subclasses, *Monochrome*, is not abstract. This is a particular type of video adapter that the programmer knows how to program. Therefore, the class *Monochrome* has overloaded both *initialize()* and *write()* appropriately for this adapter.

VGA, another one of the subclasses, is also not abstract. Here again, the programmer knows how to program the adapter. In this case, however, there is a level of abstraction between the generic *Display* and the specific case of the *VGA* display. The VGA is a special case of all color adapters, of which CGA and EGA are also members.

For this discussion, let's assume that all color adapter video cards are written to in the same way but that each must be initialized in its own way. (This isn't necessarily true, but let's assume it is.) To express the common write property, we introduce the class *ColorAdapter* to implement the *write()* function (along with any other properties that all *ColorAdapter*s have in common). We do not overload the member function *initialize()*, however, because the different *ColorAdapter*s do not have this property in common.

Therefore, even though the function *write()* has been overloaded, the class *ColorAdapter* is still abstract because the *initialize()* function has yet to be overloaded.

Because *VGA* inherits from *ColorAdapter*, it has to overload only the one missing member function, *initialize()*, to complete the definition of *Display* adapter. The function *fn()* is therefore free to instance and use a *VGA* object.

Overloading the last pure virtual function with a normal member function makes the class complete (that is, non-abstract). Only non-abstract classes can be instanced with an object. ■

Originally, every pure virtual function in a subclass had to be overloaded, even if the function was overloaded with another pure virtual function. Eventually, the people that count realized that this was as silly as it sounds and dropped the requirement. Older compilers may still require it though. ■

Passing abstract classes

Because you can't instance an abstract class, it may sound odd that it is possible to declare a pointer or a reference to an abstract class. With polymorphism, however, this isn't as crazy as it sounds. Consider the following code snippet:

```
void fn(Account *pAccount);    //this is legal
void otherFn( )
{
    Savings s;
    Checking c;

    //this is legitimate because Savings IS_A Account
```

continued

```
    fn(&s);
    //same here
    fn(&c);
}
```

Here, *pAccount* is declared as a pointer to an *Account*. However, it is understood that when the function is called, it will be passed the address of some non-abstract subclass object such as *Savings* or *Checking*.

All objects received by *fn()* will be of either class *Savings* or class *Checking* (or some future non-abstract subclass of *Account*). The function is assured that we will never pass an actual object of class *Account*, because we could never create one to pass in the first place.

Why do I need pure virtual functions?

If *withdrawal()* can't be defined, why not leave it out? Why not define the function in *Savings* and *Checking* and keep it out of *Account*? In many object-oriented languages, you can do just that. But C++ wants to be able to check that you really know what you're doing.

Like ANSI C, C++ is a strongly typed language. When you refer to a member function, C++ insists that you prove that the member function exists in the class you specified. This avoids unfortunate run-time surprises when a referenced member function turns out to be missing.

Let's make the following minor changes to *Account* to demonstrate the problem:

```
class Account
{
    //just like before but without withdrawal( ) declared
};
class Savings : public Account
{
  public:
    virtual void withdrawal(float amnt);
};

void fn(Account *pAcc)
{
    //withdraw some money
    pAcc->withdrawal(100.00);   //this call is not allowed
                                //withdrawal( ) is not a member
                                //of class Account
};
int main( )
{
    Savings s;   //open an account
    fn(&s);
    //...continues on...
}
```

Suppose that you open a savings account *s* with $500 in it. You then pass the address of that account to the function *fn()*, which attempts to make a withdrawal. Because the function *withdrawal()* is not a member of *Account*, however, the compiler generates an error.

Now let's see how pure virtual functions correct the problem. Here's the same situation with *Account* declared as an abstract class:

```
class Account
{
  public:
    //just like preceding
    //declare withdrawal pure virtual
    virtual void withdrawal(float amnt) = 0;
};
class Savings : public Account
{
  public:
    virtual void withdrawal(float amnt);
};

void fn(Account *pAcc)
{
    //withdraw some money
    pAcc->withdrawal(100.00);   //now it works
};
int main( )
{
    Savings s;    //open an account
    fn(&s);
    //...same as before...
}
```

The situation is the same except the class *Account* includes a member function *withdrawal()*. Now when the compiler checks to see if *pAcc->withdrawal()* is defined, it sees the definition of *Account::withdrawal()* just as it expects. The compiler is happy. You are happy.

The pure virtual function is a placeholder in the base class for the subclass to overload with its own implementation. Without that placeholder in the base class, there is no overloading.

Determining the Run-Time Type

With all this IS_A and IS_NOT_A going on, it's sometimes difficult to keep straight who REALLY_IS_A and who isn't. Consider the following function:

```
void fn(Account &account)
{
    //...whatever processing...
    //is this account a Savings or Checking account?
}
```

The declaration says that *fn()* is designed to accept any type of account, be it a savings account or a checking account. Fine. But what if the function decides it wants to know the run-time type of the account it's dealing with? How can it do that?

Believe it or not, this is a contentious issue among OO types. The first answer to the question, and the one that I most agree with, is "It shouldn't!" If the function includes code to check for a particular type, it may be ruining the extensibility inherent in inheritance with late binding.

Suppose there was a function *runtimeType()* that returned the run-time type of an object. Now consider how it might be used:

```
void fn(Account &account)
{
    //process closing accounts
    //use a switch based on dynamic type
    switch(runtimeType(account))
    {
      case SAVINGS:
          //close savings account
          break;
      case CHECKING:
          //close checking account
          break;
    }
}
```

Here the function accepts an *Account*. But when it's time to process the closing of the different account types, the function decides to branch depending on the run-time type returned by *runtimeType()*.

This program executes fine but the wide-awake reader will see the problem. Sooner or later, the requirements will change and a new class will be added, for example, *NewSavings*. Now the programmer must remember to go back to *fn()* — and to all the other places where a branch is made based on the value returned from *runtimeType()* — and edit it to add the new case. This is functional programming in OO clothing.

Anytime you find yourself writing an *if* or a *switch* statement based on the run-time type of an object, stop and see if you can't find another, more extensible solution to the problem. ∎

Often the problem can be avoided by converting the different cases into virtual member functions of the class. In the preceding example, a clever object-oriented program would have done the following:

```
class Account
{
  public:
    //...other stuff the same...
```

```
      //code to handle account closings
      //overloaded in subclasses
      virtual closeAccount( ) = 0;
};

void fn(Account &account)
{
    //process closing accounts
    account.closeAccount( );
}
```

Here the account closing code is put into a member function that is part of the class. Calling a virtual function has the same decision-making power of a *switch* or an *if* statement. However, when a new class such as *NewSavings* arrives in town, it comes with its own *closeAccount()* member function. Existing functions such as *fn()* don't require any change to accommodate these new arrivals.

But let's say you're determined to know the run-time type, and I can't dissuade you. The most straightforward approach is to define a data member to store the type. Consider the following example program:

```
#include <iostream.h>
class Account
{
  public:
    enum Type {ACCOUNT, CHECKING, SAVINGS};
    Account(unsigned accNo, float initialBalance = 0.0)
    {
        type = ACCOUNT;        //set the run-time type
    }
    Type runtimeType( )
    {
        return type;
    }
  protected:
    Type type;
};
class Checking : public Account
{
  public:
    Checking(unsigned accNo, float initialBalance = 0.0) :
        Account(accNo, initialBalance)
    {                          //set the run-time type;...
        type = CHECKING;       //...overwrite the value put there...
    }                          //...by Account's constructor
};
class Savings : public Account
{
  public:
    Savings(unsigned accNo, float initialBalance = 0.0) :
        Account(accNo, initialBalance)
    {
        type = SAVINGS;        //same as with Checking
    }
};
```

continued

```
void fn(Account &a)
{
   switch(a.runtimeType( ))
   {
     case Account::SAVINGS:
        cout << "This is a savings account\n";
        break;
     case Account::CHECKING:
        cout << "This is a checking account\n";
        break;
     default:
        cout << "I don't know what this thing is\n";
   }
};
int main( )
{
   Savings s(1234);
   cout << "Calling fn( ) with s\n";
   fn(s);
   Checking c(2345);
   cout << "Calling fn( ) with c\n";
   fn(c);
   return 0;
}
```

The *enum* defined in *Account* provides numerical values for the different sub-classes. (Declaring *enum* in the class gives it class scope, which avoids conflicts with other *enum*s.) The constructor for each of the subclasses assigns the proper value to the data member *type*. This member can then be queried to determine which constructor was executed on the object and, therefore, the dynamic type of the object.

The output from this program appears as follows:

```
Calling fn( ) with s
This is a savings account
Calling fn( ) with c
This is a checking account
```

Notice that the *switch()* in *fn()* includes a default case that outputs a warning if the run-time type is not recognized. This is important. When you add *NewSavings*, the program branches to the default condition if you forget to include the new type in the *switch* statement. The default condition's output statement will at least alert you to the oversight.

Conclusion

Now that we've seen inheritance enhanced with a scoop of late binding and a dollop of pure virtualness, let's see how these features combine to convert our example BUDGET program into a truly object-oriented program.

Using Inheritance to Rationalize the Budget: BUDGET5.CPP

*T*he addition of classes created quite a bit of change from BUDGET2 to BUDGET3. By comparison, the changes from version 3 to 4 were more cosmetic. Here you will notice quite a change as we add inheritance to create BUDGET5. I think you'll like the results.

In this version we add the following:

- ✔ Use of inheritance to highlight the similarities between checking and savings accounts and to avoid redundancy
- ✔ Use of virtual member functions to increase readability and expandability
- ✔ Creation of a pure virtual class to capture the commonalties between checking and savings accounts

Until now, we were forced to maintain the two classes *Checking* and *Savings* as separate entities. Although we were painfully aware of the similarities between the two, we were unable to express that relationship.

Now, with the help of our new OO superhero inheritance and its sidekick polymorphism, we can rationalize these two classes into a single class *Account*, which captures the commonalities between these two classes. The result is a much smaller and simpler program:

```
//BUDGET5.CPP - Budget program with inheritance and
//              late binding (aka, polymorphism).  Notice
//              how much smaller the program is now that the
//              redundancy has been removed.  A single
//              function can now handle both checking and
//              savings accounts (and any other accounts that
//              we might invent in the future).

#include <iostream.h>
#include <stdlib.h>
#include <ctype.h>
```

continued

```
//Account - this abstract class incorporates properties
//           common to both account types: Checking and
//           Savings. However, it's missing the concept
//           withdrawal(), which is different between the two
class Account
{
  protected:
   Account(Account &c)
   {
      cout << "No creating funds\n";
   }

  public:
   Account(unsigned accNo, float initialBalance = 0.0);

   //access functions
   int accountNo()
   {
      return accountNumber;
   }
   float acntBalance()
   {
      return balance;
   }
   static Account *first()
   {
      return pFirst;
   }
   Account *next()
   {
      return pNext;
   }
   static int noAccounts()
   {
      return count;
   }

   //transaction functions
   void deposit(float amount)
   {
      balance += amount;
   }                                      //Note 1
   virtual void withdrawal(float amount) = 0;

   //display function for displaying self on 'cout'
   void display()
   {
      cout << "Account " << accountNumber
           << " = "       << balance
           << "\n";
   }

  protected:
   //keep accounts in a linked list so there's no limit
   static Account *pFirst;              //Note 2
           Account *pNext;
```

```
    static int count;          //number of accounts
    unsigned    accountNumber;
    float       balance;
};

//allocate space for statics         //Note 2
Account  *Account::pFirst = 0;
int       Account::count  = 0;

Account::Account(unsigned accNo, float initialBalance)
{
    accountNumber = accNo;
    balance = initialBalance;

    //add this to end of list and count it
    count++;
    if (pFirst == 0)
    {
        pFirst = this;        //empty list; make it first
    }
    else                      //list not empty; look for last
    {
        for (Account *pA = pFirst; pA->pNext; pA = pA->pNext)
        {
        }
        pA->pNext = this;     //tack us onto end
    }
    pNext = 0;                //we're always last
}

//Checking - this class contains properties unique to
//           checking accounts.  Not much left, is there?
class Checking : public Account
{
  public:
    //here the constructor is defined inline
    Checking(unsigned accNo, float initialBalance = 0.0) :
        Account(accNo, initialBalance)        //Note 3
    {
    }

    //overload pure virtual functions
    virtual void withdrawal(float amount);    //Note 4
};

void Checking::withdrawal(float amount)       //Note 5
{
    if (balance < amount )
    {
        cout << "Insufficient funds: balance " << balance
             << ", check "                      << amount
             << "\n";
    }
    else
    {
        balance -= amount;
```

continued

```
            //if balance falls too low, charge service fee
            if (balance < 500.00)
            {
                balance -= 0.20F;
            }
        }
}


//Savings - same story as Checking except that it also
//           has a unique data member
class Savings : public Account
{
  public:
    //here the constructor is defined as a separate function
    //just to show you the difference
    Savings(unsigned accNo, float initialBalance = 0.0);

    //transaction functions
    virtual void withdrawal(float amount);


  protected:
    int         noWithdrawals;
};
                                            //Note 6
Savings::Savings(unsigned accNo, float initialBalance) :
    Account(accNo, initialBalance)
{
    noWithdrawals = 0;
}
void Savings::withdrawal(float amount)
{
    if (balance < amount)
    {
        cout << "Insufficient funds: balance " << balance
             << ", withdrawal "                << amount
             << "\n";
    }
    else
    {
        if (++noWithdrawals > 1)
        {
            balance -= 5.00F;
        }
        balance -= amount;
    }
}

//prototype declarations
unsigned getAccntNo();
void process(Account &account);          //Note 7
void outOfMemory();

//main - accumulate the initial input and output totals
```

```cpp
int main()
{
    /*loop until someone enters 'X' or 'x'*/
    Account *pA;                          //Note 8
    char     accountType;    //S or C

    unsigned keepLooping = 1;
    while (keepLooping)
    {
        cout << "Enter S for Savings, "
                "C for Checking, X for exit\n";
        cin  >> accountType;

        switch (accountType)
        {
            case 'c':
            case 'C':
                pA = new Checking(getAccntNo());;//Note 9
                if (pA == 0)
                {
                    outOfMemory();
                }
                process(*pA);
                break;

            case 's':
            case 'S':
                pA = new Savings(getAccntNo()); //Note 9
                if (pA == 0)
                {
                    outOfMemory();
                }
                process(*pA);
                break;

            case 'x':
            case 'X':
                keepLooping = 0;
                break;

            default:
                cout << "I didn't get that.\n";
        }
    }

    //now present totals                 //Note 10
    float total = 0.0;
    cout << "Account totals:\n";
    for (pA = Account::first(); pA; pA = pA->next())
    {
        pA->display();
        total += pA->acntBalance();
    }
    cout << "Total worth  = " << total << "\n";
    return 0;
}
```

continued

```
//getAccntNo - return the account number entered
unsigned getAccntNo()
{
    unsigned accntNo;
    cout << "Enter account number:";
    cin  >> accntNo;
    return accntNo;
}

//process(Account) - input the data for an account*/
void process(Account &account)
{
    cout << "Enter positive number for deposit,\n"
            "negative for withdrawal, 0 to terminate";

    float transaction;
    do
    {
        cout << ":";
        cin  >> transaction;

        //deposit
        if (transaction > 0)
        {
            account.deposit(transaction);
        }

        //withdrawal
        if (transaction < 0) {
            account.withdrawal(-transaction);   //Note 11
        }
    } while (transaction != 0);
}

//outOfMemory - generate out-of-memory message and quit
void outOfMemory()
{
    cout << "Out of memory\n";
    abort();
}
```

The first batter out of the dugout is now class *Account*. In appearance, it's the same as the earlier classes *Savings* and *Checking*. Because *withdrawal()* is declared pure virtual (see *Note 1*), we know that *Account* is abstract and cannot be instanced.

The first non-abstract class is *Checking*. This class is quite small, consisting of only an empty constructor (*Note 3*) and a *withdrawal()* to overload the pure virtual member function from the base class (*Note 4*). The implementation of *Checking::withdrawal()* appears at *Note 5*.

Class *Savings* is similar, except in this case I implemented the constructor as a non inline member function to demonstrate the difference (*Note 6*).

Following the class definitions, you can see that we no longer have the function redundancy. The one function *process(Account&)* has replaced both *process(Checking&)* and *process(Savings&)* (*Note 7*). There is the same reduction in redundancy in *main()*. A single pointer, *pA* (declared at *Note 8*), can point to either a *Checking* account object or a *Savings* account object (*Note 9*).

Skipping ahead to *process()* for a second, we can see that the function is generic. Late binding occurs in the innocuous-looking call to *withdrawal()* (*Note 11*). When the object *account* refers to a *Checking* account, this call invokes *Checking::withdrawal()*. When *account* refers to a *Savings* account, this same call ends up at *Savings::withdrawal()*.

After the account objects have been built, they are displayed in the same way as before:

```
Enter S for Savings, C for Checking, X for exit
S
Enter account number:123
Enter positive number for deposit,
negative for withdrawal, 0 to terminate:200
:-50
:-50
:0
Enter S for Savings, C for Checking, X for exit
C
Enter account number:234
Enter positive number for deposit,
negative for withdrawal, 0 to terminate:200
:-25
:-20
:0
Enter S for Savings, C for Checking, X for exit
X
Account totals:
Account 123 = 95
Account 234 = 154.600006
Total worth  = 249.600006
```

BUDGET4 used the members *pFirst* and *pNext* to keep the account objects in a linked list, thereby removing any artificial limitations that a fixed-sized array might impose. BUDGET5, however, places *pFirst* and *pNext* in the parent class *Account* (*Note 2*). This implies that both *Savings* and *Checking* accounts are linked into the same list, so they are displayed together (*Note 10*). The output reflects this. One of the example problems in the Workout section is to split these linked lists.

25-Minute Workout

*1*t's review time again. (Dawg!) Set that calisthenics timer and see if you know as much as you think you do. As always, I have provided answers if you get stuck.

1

a. In BUDGET5, both account types (*Checking* and *Savings)* use the same display function. In previous versions of BUDGET, however, savings accounts display the number of withdrawals. Make the savings accounts do so again. Hint: Use virtual functions and make minimal changes to the classes.

b. The bank wants a new *Savings* account that acts just like a conventional *Savings* account if the balance is below $750. However, as long as the balance stays at or above that magical number, the bank won't charge a fee. Without changing the existing classes, add a new class to BUDGET5 to handle this change.

c. BUDGET5 also displays *Savings* and *Checking* accounts mixed together. Separate the two types of accounts while they are displayed, as they were in previous versions of BUDGET. Hint: There are two approaches here. One is to keep the two accounts in separate lists. The second is to recognize which is which when they're in the same list. Try both approaches.

2 Factor the following concrete classes into some type of hierarchy. You will want to create new classes to represent abstract concepts.

Citroen CV2 (small air-cooled 2-door)
Sedan
Pickup
Station wagon
Panel truck
18 wheeler

Answers

1

a. The solution I chose was to give *Savings* its old *display()* function back. To do this I made the following additions (things that remained the same are not shown):

```
class Account

{
    //everything else the same as before
    virtual void display( );    //make this a virtual function
};

//display - generic display function
//          (virtual fns can't be inline)
void Account::display( )
{
    cout << "Account "           << accountNumber
         << " = "                << balance
         << "\n";
}

//Savings class with addition of display function
class Savings : public Account
{
  public:
    //everything else the same here, too
    virtual void display( );    //add this declaration
};

//display - unique display function for Savings
void Savings::display( )
{
    cout  << "Account "           << accountNumber
          << " = "                << balance
          << " (no. withdrawals = " << noWithdrawals
          << ")\n";
}
```

I declared *Account::display()* to be virtual so that I could overload it in the subclass *Savings*. I then added the *Savings::display()* function from BUD-GET4 to *Savings*. Now, when *main()* displays the different accounts, the proper *display()* function is chosen automatically, depending on the account type. The output of savings accounts now appears with information on the number of withdrawals, as before:

```
Account totals:
Account 123 = 95 (no. withdrawals = 2)
Account 234 = 154.600006
Total worth  = 249.600006
```

b. My class, *NewSavings*, appears as follows:

```
//NewSavings - implement a new savings account that charges
//             no withdrawal fee if balance is >= 750
class NewSavings : public Savings
{
  public:
    NewSavings(unsigned accNo, float initialBalance = 0.0) :
        Savings(accNo, initialBalance) {}
```

```
            //transaction functions++
            virtual void withdrawal(float amount);
    };
                                                    //Note 6
        void NewSavings::withdrawal(float amount)

    {
        if (balance < amount)
        {
            cout << "Insufficient funds: balance " << balance
                 << ", withdrawal "                 << amount
                 << "\n";
        }
        else
        {
            //if the balance is less than 750...
            if (balance < 750.00F)
            {
                //...treat just like old savings account;
                Savings::withdrawal(amount);    //Note 1
            }
            //...otherwise,...
            else
            {
                //...no service charge (Yeah!)
                balance -= amount;
            }
        }
    }
```

Here we see that once again the member function *withdrawal()* is overloaded by one, which has the desired effect. Notice, however, that if the balance is below $750, this new *withdrawal()* calls the old *Savings::withdrawal()* (*Note 1*). Remember that including the name of the class in the call forces it to bind early even if the function is declared virtual.

c. Let's start with the separate list approach. This program does not differ much from the BUDGET5 program presented earlier, but the changes are scattered over much of the program. Therefore, to avoid confusion, I've repeated the entire program here:

```
//BUDGET5.1c - this version splits the linked list into two
//             by establishing two different pFirst pointers,
//             one to the first Checking account object and
//             the other to the first Savings account object.
//
//             This is the solution to problem 1c.
//

#include <iostream.h>
#include <stdlib.h>
#include <ctype.h>
```

continued

```
//Account - this abstract class incorporates properties
//          common to both account types Checking and
//          Savings; however, it's missing the concept
//          withdrawal() which is different between the two
class Account
{
  protected:
   Account(Account &c)
   {
      cout << "No creating funds\n";
   }

   //this function adds an object to the list pointed
   //at by the argument provided to the function
   void addToList(Account * &pFirst);               //Note 1

  public:
   Account(unsigned accNo, float initialBalance = 0.0F);

   //access functions
   int accountNo()
   {
      return accountNumber;
   }
   float acntBalance()
   {
      return balance;
   }

   static int noAccounts()
   {
      return count;
   }

   //transaction functions
   void deposit(float amount)
   {
      balance += amount;
   }
   virtual void withdrawal(float amount) = 0;

   //display function for displaying self on 'cout'
   void display()
   {
      cout << "Account " << accountNumber
           << " = "      << balance
           << "\n";
   }

   //make the following functions pure virtual
   Account *next()
   {
      return pNext;
   }
```

```
   protected:
     static int  count;              //number of accounts
     unsigned    accountNumber;
     float       balance;

     //pNext is still in Account but pFirst       //Note 2
     //has now been relegated to the subclasses
     Account     *pNext;
};
int Account::count = 0;

Account::Account(unsigned accNo, float initialBalance)
{
   accountNumber = accNo;
   balance = initialBalance;
   count++;
}

//addToList - by accepting a reference to pFirst
//            as an argument, addToList( ) can be called
//            from either Checking or Savings
void Account::addToList(Account * &pFirst)
{
   //this comes out of the constructor for Account
   if (pFirst == 0)
   {
      pFirst = this;       //empty list; make it first
   }
   else {                  //list not empty; look for last...
                           //...entry in the list
      for (Account *pA = pFirst; pA->pNext; pA = pA->pNext)
      {
      }
      pA->pNext = this;    //tack us onto end
   }
   pNext = 0;              //we're always last
}

//Checking - this class contains properties unique to
//           checking accounts.  Not much left is there?
class Checking : public Account
{
  public:
   //here the constructor defined inline
   Checking(unsigned accNo, float initialBalance = 0.0F) :
       Account(accNo, initialBalance)
   {
     addToList(Checking::pFirst);                   //Note 3
   }

   //overload pure virtual functions
   virtual void withdrawal(float amount);

   //return first object in Checking account list
   static Account* first( )                        //Note 4
   {
      return (Account*)Checking::pFirst;
   }
```

continued

```
   protected:
      static Account* pFirst;
};
Account *Checking::pFirst = 0;

void Checking::withdrawal(float amount)
{
   if (balance < amount )
   {
      cout << "Insufficient funds: balance " << balance
           << ", check "                      << amount
           << "\n";
   }
   else
   {
      balance -= amount;

      //if balance falls too low, charge service fee
      if (balance < 500.00F)
      {
         balance -= 0.20F;
      }
   }
}


//Savings - same story as Checking except that it also
//          has a unique data member
class Savings : public Account
{
  public:
   //here the constructor is defined as a separate
   //function just to show you the difference
   Savings(unsigned accNo, float initialBalance = 0.0F) :
      Account(accNo, initialBalance)
   {
      noWithdrawals = 0;
      addToList(Savings::pFirst);
   }

   //transaction functions
   virtual void withdrawal(float amount);
   static Account* first()
   {
      return (Account*)Savings::pFirst;
   }


  protected:
   int        noWithdrawals;
   static Account *pFirst;
};
Account* Savings::pFirst = 0;

void Savings::withdrawal(float amount)
{
   if (balance < amount)
```

```
    {
        cout << "Insufficient funds: balance " << balance
             << ", withdrawal "                 << amount
             << "\n";
    }
    else
    {
        if (++noWithdrawals > 1)
        {
            balance -= 5.00F;
        }
        balance -= amount;
    }
}

//prototype declarations
unsigned getAccntNo( );
void process(Account &account);
void outOfMemory( );
int main( );

//main - accumulate the initial input and output totals
int main( )
{
    /*loop until someone enters an 'X' or 'x'*/
    Account *pA;
    char      accountType;      //S or C

    unsigned keepLooping = 1;
    while (keepLooping)
    {
        cout << "Enter S for Savings, "
                "C for Checking, X for exit\n";
        cin  >> accountType;

        switch (accountType)
        {
            case 'c':
            case 'C':
                pA = new Checking(getAccntNo( ));
                if (pA == 0)
                {
                    outOfMemory( );
                }
                process(*pA);
                break;

            case 's':
            case 'S':
                pA = new Savings(getAccntNo( ));
                if (pA == 0)
                {
                    outOfMemory( );
                }
                process(*pA);
                break;
```

continued

```
          case 'x':
          case 'X':
              keepLooping = 0;
              break;

          default:
              cout << "I didn't get that.\n";
      }
  }

  //now present totals                          //Note 5
  float subTotal = 0.0F;
  float total = 0.0F;
  cout << "Account totals:\n";

  //we are now forced to display the lists separately
  for (pA = Checking::first( ); pA; pA = pA->next( ))
  {
      pA->display( );
      subTotal += pA->acntBalance( );
  }
  cout << "Total of all checking accounts = " << subTotal << "\n";
  total += subTotal;

  //repeat the process for savings
  subTotal = 0.0F;
  for (pA = Savings::first( ); pA; pA = pA->next( ))
  {
      pA->display( );
      subTotal += pA->acntBalance( );
  }
  cout << "Total of all savings accounts = " << subTotal << "\n";
  total += subTotal;

  cout << "Total worth of all accounts  = " << total << "\n";
  return 0;
}

//getAccntNo - return the account number entered
unsigned getAccntNo( )
{
  unsigned accntNo;
  cout << "Enter account number:";
  cin  >> accntNo;
  return accntNo;
}

//process(Account) - input the data for an account*/
void process(Account &account)
{
  cout << "Enter positive number for deposit,\n"
          "negative for withdrawal, 0 to terminate";

  float transaction;
  do
  {
      cout << ":";
      cin  >> transaction;
```

```
        //deposit
        if (transaction > 0)
        {
            account.deposit(transaction);
        }

        //withdrawal
        if (transaction < 0) {
            account.withdrawal(-transaction);
        }
    } while (transaction != 0);
}

//outOfMemory - generate out-of-memory message and quit
void outOfMemory( )
{
    cout << "Out of memory\n";
    abort( );
}
```

The goal is to split the linked list of *Account* objects into two linked lists, one of *Checking* objects and another of *Savings* objects. To do so, the static data member *pFirst* has been moved out of the class *Account* (*Note 2*) and into the classes *Checking* and *Savings* (*Note 4*). Giving each subclass its own *pFirst* pointer allows them to maintain their own separate linked lists. This change means that the member function *first()* must be moved into the subclasses as well. (The pointer *pNext* does not need to be moved because both types of accounts include pointers to the next member of their respective lists.)

Because *pFirst* is no longer a member of *Account*, the constructor for *Account* cannot refer it. Looked at another way, the constructor for *Account* cannot add the object to one of the lists because it does not know which list to add it to: the object is not yet either a *Savings* account object or a *Checking* account object.

The job of adding the object to the linked list must be moved into the constructor for *Savings* and *Checking* (*Note 3*). The work of adding an object to the list is the same for both classes, so there is not a problem with these classes calling a common function and passing the proper *pFirst* pointer upon which to operate (*Note 1*). (The argument to *addToList()* is a reference to a pointer so that the function can change the value of the pointer passed to it.)

The remainder of the program is the same as in BUDGET5 until the end of *main()*, where the program displays the lists of accounts. Rather than one loop as before, the program must now loop twice: the first time starting with the object returned from *Checking::first()* (that is, the first checking account) and a second time starting with the object returned by *Savings::first()* (that is, the first savings account) (*Note 5*).

The output from this program appears as follows:

```
Enter S for Savings, C for Checking, X for exit
S
Enter account number:1234
Enter positive number for deposit,
negative for withdrawal, 0 to terminate:100
:0
Enter S for Savings, C for Checking, X for exit
C
Enter account number:2345
Enter positive number for deposit,
negative for withdrawal, 0 to terminate:200
:0
Enter S for Savings, C for Checking, X for exit
S
Enter account number:3456
Enter positive number for deposit,
negative for withdrawal, 0 to terminate:300
:0
Enter S for Savings, C for Checking, X for exit
Enter account number:
C
Enter positive number for deposit,
negative for withdrawal, 0 to terminate:400
:0
Enter S for Savings, C for Checking, X for exit
X
Account totals:
Account 2345 = 200
Account 4567 = 400
Total of all checking accounts = 600
Account 1234 = 100
Account 3456 = 300
Total of all savings accounts = 400
Total worth of all accounts   = 1000
```

A second approach is to leave the objects mixed in the same linked list and divide them during the display process. This requires the addition of a run-time function (as explained in Chapter 20), called *runtimeType()* here. The return from *runtimeType()* is used to discriminate the objects. The class additions were shown in Chapter 20, so only the relevant section of *main()* appears here:

```
//now present totals
float cTotal = 0.0;
float sTotal = 0.0;
cout << "Account totals:\n";
for (pA = Account::first(); pA; pA = pA->next())
{
    pA->display();
    //keep checking and saving account totals separate
    switch(pA->runtimeType())
    {
        case Account::CHECKING:
            cTotal += pA->acntBalance();
```

```
        break;
    case Account::SAVINGS:
        sTotal += pA->acntBalance( );
        break;
    default:
        cout << "Unknown account type encountered\n";
    }
}
cout << "Checking account total = " << cTotal << "\n";
cout << "Savings  account total = " << sTotal << "\n";
cout << "Total worth            = " << (cTotal+sTotal) << "\n";
```

The *switch* statement keeps the checking and savings account totals in separate piles.

Neither approach is completely extensible because both must make explicit reference to the particular subclasses of *Account*. However, the first approach is the more flexible of the two.

This is one of those great questions because there is no wrong answer. My answer follows, but yours is probably just as right (or more so) even if it differs from mine. The concrete classes are in boldface. The abstract classes are not.

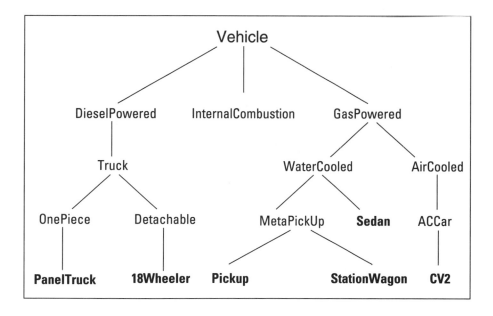

I started by dividing vehicles into gasoline and diesel-powered varieties. The two types of trucks provided were both diesel (I assumed), but they differed in that one has a detachable trailer and the other does not. The gasoline vehicles were divided along the lines of water cooled and air cooled. Water-cooled vehicles were divided into regular cars and cowboy Cadillacs (pickups). Many station wagons are more similar to pickups than sedans, so I threw them into the pickup category.

It's good practice to consciously build these types of class hierarchies. So, the next time you're lying back in the tub or caught in traffic, imagine adding other types of vehicles in this framework.

Part VI
Advanced Strokes: Optional Features

The 5th Wave   By Rich Tennant

"MISS LAMONT, WILL YOU GET ME TECHNICAL SUPPORT AT STRIPOC INTERACTIVE PLEASE?"

In This Part...

As I stated in the Introduction, it is not the goal in this book to turn you into a C++ language lawyer. I would be much happier if you came away with a solid understanding of the fundamentals of C++ and object-oriented programming. If you have carefully read and mastered the concepts presented so far, you should have that understanding by now.

The pages before this cover the essential features you need to know to produce a well-written, object-oriented C++ program. However, C++ is a big language (it has a serious case of feature-itis, if you ask me) and there are many features that we have not yet discussed. In Part VI, I present a summary of the additional features that I find most useful, along with my opinion as to when — and when not — to use them.

Chapter 21
Multiple Inheritance

• •

In This Chapter

▶ Introduction to multiple inheritance

▶ Avoiding ambiguities with multiple inheritance

▶ Avoiding ambiguities with virtual inheritance

▶ The ordering rules for multiple constructors

▶ Problems with multiple inheritance

• •

*1*n the class hierarchies we have discussed so far, each class has inherited from a single parent. This is the way things usually are in the real world. Some classes, however, represent the blending of two classes into one.

An example of such a class is the sleeper sofa. As the name implies, it is a sofa and also a bed (although not a very comfortable bed). Thus, the sleeper sofa should be allowed to inherit bed-like properties. To address this situation, C++ allows a derived class to inherit from more than one base class. This is called *multiple inheritance*.

How Does Multiple Inheritance Work?

To see how multiple inheritance works, let's expand on the sleeper sofa example. Figure 21-1 shows the inheritance graph for class *SleeperSofa*. Notice how this class inherits from class *Sofa* and from class *Bed*. In this way, it inherits the properties of both.

The code to implement class *SleeperSofa* looks like the following:

```
class Bed
{
  public:
    Bed();
    void sleep();
    int weight;
};
```

continued

```
class Sofa
{
  public:
    Sofa();
    void watchTV();
    int weight;
};

//SleeperSofa - is both a Bed and a Sofa
class SleeperSofa : public Bed, public Sofa
{
  public:
    SleeperSofa();
    void foldOut();
};

int main()
{
    SleeperSofa ss;
    //you can watch TV on a sleeper sofa...
    ss.watchTV();          //Sofa::watchTV()
    //...and then you can fold it out...
    ss.foldOut();              //SleeperSofa::foldOut()
    //...and sleep on it (sort of)
    ss.sleep();            //Bed::sleep()
    return 0;
}
```

Here the class *SleeperSofa* inherits from both *Bed* and *Sofa*. This is apparent from the appearance of both classes in the class declaration. *SleeperSofa* inherits all the members of both base classes. Thus, both of the calls *ss.sleep()* and *ss.watchTV()* are legal. You can use a *SleeperSofa* as a *Bed* or a *Sofa*. Plus the class *SleeperSofa* can have members of its own, such as *foldOut()*. Is this a great country or what?

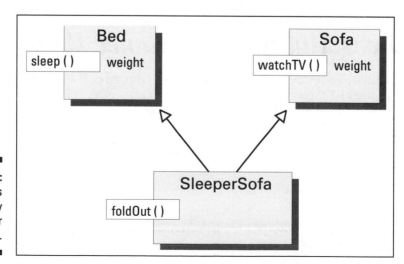

Figure 21-1:
Class
hierarchy
of a sleeper
sofa.

Inheritance Ambiguities

Although multiple inheritance is a powerful feature, it introduces several possible problems. One is apparent in the preceding example. Notice that both *Bed* and *Sofa* contain a member *weight*. This is logical because both have a measurable weight. The question is, "Which weight does *SleeperSofa* inherit?"

The answer is "both." *SleeperSofa* inherits a member *Bed::weight* and a separate member *Sofa::weight*. Because they have the same name, unqualified references to *weight* are now ambiguous. This is demonstrated in the following snippet:

```
#include <iostream.h>
void fn() {
   SleeperSofa ss;
   cout << "weight = "
        << ss.weight      //illegal - which weight?
        << "\n";
}
```

The program must now indicate one of the two weights by specifying the desired base class. The following code snippet is correct:

```
#include <iostream.h>
void fn()
{
   SleeperSofa ss;
   cout << "sofa weight = "
        << ss.Sofa::weight    //specify which weight
        << "\n";
}
```

Although this solution corrects the problem, specifying the base class in the application function isn't desirable because it forces class information to leak outside the class into application code. In this case, *fn()* has to know that *SleeperSofa* inherits from *Sofa*. These types of so-called *name collisions* were not possible with single inheritance but are a constant danger with multiple inheritance.

Virtual Inheritance

In the case of *SleeperSofa*, the name collision on *weight* was more than a mere accident. A *SleeperSofa* doesn't have a bed weight separate from its sofa weight. The collision occurred because this class hierarchy does not completely describe the real world. Specifically, the classes have not been completely factored.

Thinking about it a little more, it becomes clear that both beds and sofas are special cases of a more fundamental concept: furniture. (I suppose we could get even more fundamental and use something like object_with_mass, but furniture is fundamental enough.) Weight is a property of all furniture. This relationship is shown in Figure 21-2.

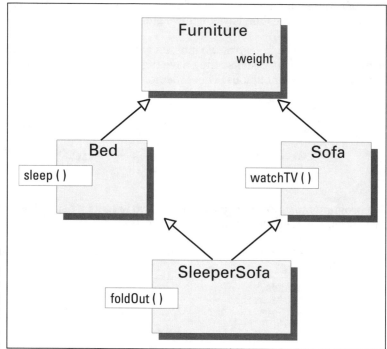

Factoring out the class *Furniture* should relieve the name collision. With much relief and great anticipation of success, I generated the following C++ class hierarchy:

```
#include <iostream.h>

//Furniture - more fundamental concept; this class
//            has "weight" as a property
class Furniture
{
  public:
    Furniture();
    int weight;
};

class Bed : public Furniture
{
  public:
    Bed();
    sleep();
};
```

```
class Sofa : public Furniture
{
  public:
    Sofa();
    void watchTV();
};
class SleeperSofa : public Bed, public Sofa
{
  public:
    SleeperSofa();
    void foldOut;
};

void fn()
{
    SleeperSofa ss;
    cout << "weight = "
         << ss.weight     //problem solved; right?
         << "\n";
}
```

Imagine my dismay when I find that this doesn't help at all — *weight* is still ambiguous. (I wish my weight were as ambiguous!) "Okay," I say (not really understanding why *weight* is still ambiguous), "I'll try casting *ss* to *Furniture*."

```
#include <iostream.h>
void fn()
{
    SleeperSofa ss;
    Furniture *pF;
    pF = (Furniture*)&ss; //use a Furniture pointer...
    cout << "weight = "   //...to get at the weight
         << pF->weight
         << "\n";
};
```

This doesn't work either. Now I get some strange message that the cast of *SleeperSofa** to *Furniture** is ambiguous. What's going on?

The explanation is straightforward. *SleeperSofa* doesn't inherit from *Furniture* directly. Both *Bed* and *Sofa* inherit from *Furniture* and then *SleeperSofa* inherits from them. In memory, a *SleeperSofa* looks like Figure 21-3.

We can see that a *SleeperSofa* consists of a complete *Bed* followed by a complete *Sofa* followed by some *SleeperSofa* unique stuff. Each of these subobjects in *SleeperSofa* has its own *Furniture* part, because each inherits from *Furniture*. Thus, a *SleeperSofa* contains two *Furniture* objects!

I haven't created the hierarchy shown in Figure 21-2 after all. The inheritance hierarchy I have actually created is the one shown in Figure 21-4.

But this is nonsense. *SleeperSofa* needs only one copy of *Furniture*. We want *SleeperSofa* to inherit only one copy of *Furniture*, and we want *Bed* and *Sofa* to share that one copy. C++ calls this *virtual inheritance* because it uses the *virtual* keyword.

I hate this overloading of the term *virtual* because *virtual inheritance* has nothing to do with virtual functions. ■

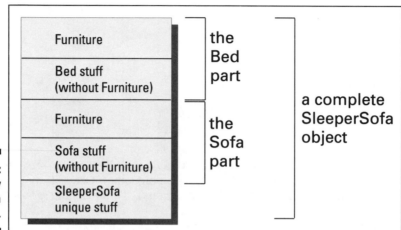

Figure 21-3:
Memory
layout of a
SleeperSofa.

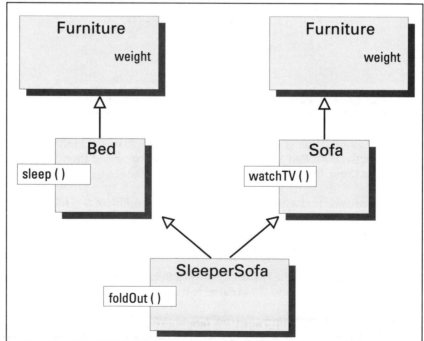

Figure 21-4:
Actual result
of our first
attempt.

Armed with this new knowledge, I return to class *SleeperSofa* and implement it as follows:

```
#include <iostream.h>
class Furniture
{
  public:
    Furniture() {}
    int weight;
};
class Bed : virtual public Furniture
{
  public:
    Bed() {}
    void sleep();
};
class Sofa : virtual public Furniture
{
  public:
    Sofa() {}
    void watchTV();
};
class SleeperSofa : public Bed, public Sofa
{
  public:
    SleeperSofa() : Sofa(), Bed() {}
    void foldOut();
};

void fn()
{
    SleeperSofa ss;
    cout << "weight = "
         << ss.weight
         << "\n";
}
```

Notice the addition of the keyword *virtual* in the inheritance of *Furniture* in *Bed* and *Sofa*. This says, "Give me a copy of *Furniture* unless you already have one somehow, in which case I'll just use that one." A *SleeperSofa* ends up looking like Figure 21-5 in memory.

Here we can see that a *SleeperSofa* inherits *Furniture*, then *Bed* minus the *Furniture* part, followed by *Sofa* minus the *Furniture* part. Bringing up the rear are the members unique to *SleeperSofa*. (Note that this may not be the order of the elements in memory, but that's not important for our purposes.)

Now the reference in *fn()* to *weight* is not ambiguous because a *SleeperSofa* contains only one copy of *Furniture*. By inheriting *Furniture* virtually, we get the desired inheritance relationship as expressed in Figure 21-2.

If virtual inheritance solves this problem so nicely, why isn't it the norm? There are two reasons. First, virtually inherited base classes are handled internally

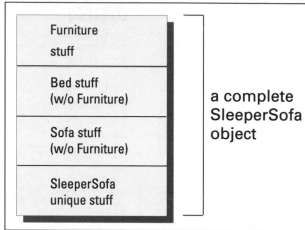

Figure 21-5:
Memory
layout of
SleeperSofa
with virtual
inheritance.

much differently than normally inherited base classes, and these differences
involve extra overhead. Second, sometimes you want two copies of the base
class (although this is unusual).

As an example of the latter, consider a *TeacherAssistant* who is both a *Student*
and a *Teacher*, both of which are subclasses of *Academician*. If the university
gives its teaching assistants two IDs — a student ID and a separate teacher ID
— class *TeacherAssistant* will need to contain two copies of class *Academician*.

Constructing the Objects of Multiple Inheritance

The rules for constructing objects need to be expanded to handle multiple
inheritance. The constructors are invoked in the following order:

- ✔ The constructor for any virtual base classes in the order in which they are
  inherited

- ✔ The constructor for any nonvirtual base classes in the order in which they
  are inherited

- ✔ The constructor for any member objects called out on the constructor line
  in the order in which they appear

- ✔ The constructor for the class itself

Notice that base classes are constructed in the order in which they are inherited and not in the order in which they appear on the constructor line.

In Conclusion, a Contrary Opinion

I should point out that not all object-oriented practitioners think multiple inheritance is a good idea. In addition, many object oriented languages don't support multiple inheritance.

Multiple inheritance is not an easy thing for the language to implement. This is mostly the compiler's problem (or the compiler writer's problem). But multiple inheritance adds overhead to the code when compared to single inheritance, and this overhead can become the programmer's problem.

More importantly, multiple inheritance opens the door to additional errors. First, there are the ambiguities mentioned in the section "Inheritance Ambiguities." Second, in the presence of multiple inheritance, casting a pointer from a subclass to a base class often involves changing the value of the pointer in sophisticated and mysterious ways. We'll leave the details to the language lawyers and compiler writers; however, I want to point out that this can result in unexpected results. For example:

```
#include <iostream.h>
class Base1 {int mem;};
class Base2 {int mem;};
class SubClass : public Base1, public Base2 {};

void fn(SubClass *pSC)
{
    Base1 *pB1 = (Base1*)pSC;
    Base2 *pB2 = (Base2*)pSC;
    if ((void*)pB1 == (void*)pB2)
    {
        cout << "Members numerically equal\n";
    }
}
int main()
{
    SubClass sc;
    fn(&sc);
    return 0;
}
```

pB1 and *pB2* are not numerically equal even though they came from the same original value, *pSC*, and the message *Members numerically equal* doesn't appear. (Actually, if *fn()* is passed a zero, the message does appear; for any nonzero address, the message doesn't appear. See how strange it gets?)

I suggest that you avoid using multiple inheritance until you are comfortable with C++. Single inheritance provides enough expressive power to get used to. Later, you can study the manuals until you're sure that you understand exactly what's going on when you multiply inherit. One exception is the use of commercial libraries such as Microsoft's Foundation Classes and Borland's Object-Window Library, which use multiple inheritance quite a bit. These classes have been checked out and are safe.

Don't get me wrong. I'm not out and out against multiple inheritance. The fact that Borland, Microsoft, and others use multiple inheritance effectively in their class libraries proves it can be done. If multiple inheritance weren't worth the trouble, they wouldn't use it. However, multiple inheritance is a feature that you might want to hold off on using until you're ready.

Chapter 22
Access Control Specifiers

● ●

In This Chapter

▶ Introduction to private members

▶ A further comparison of *class* and *struct*

▶ Non-public inheritance

▶ Guidelines for using *private* and *protected*

● ●

*T*he capability to hide members of the class from outside functions is an important part of object-oriented programming. So far, however, this access control has been presented as a binary situation: either you were in the club or you weren't, either you knew the secret handshake or you didn't. C++ provides a little more control than that. In this chapter, we discuss the other aspects of access control.

Really Exclusive Club: Private Members

In addition to *protected* and *public*, C++ defines another access control specifier called *private*. Members declared *private* are like *protected* members except they are not accessible from inherited classes.

When we started to look at data hiding back in Part III, I pointed out that letting a class hide its members from the prying op-codes of outside functions was a good thing. We didn't know anything about inheritance at that time, so there was only one class. Therefore, I didn't need to define exactly how far the boundary of the class should extend. So, is a subclass contained in the class, and does it therefore have access to the members of the class?

As long as we had only *protected* to hide our valuables, we assumed that subclass functions were inside the boundary: a subclass can access the protected members of a base class. The access control specifier *private* allows us to treat subclass functions as outside that boundary. Class members declared *private* are not accessible to any subclasses of that class.

When should I use private and when can I stay with protected?

The arguments for and against declaring members *private* go something like this: You don't have to look outside the current class to find all the functions that can manipulate a *private* member. That's good.

On the other hand, forcing subclass functions to access these members through access functions can greatly increase the number of access functions you need. That's bad. But, you say, using that argument, why not just make all members public and dispense with access functions entirely?

When we build a class, we should keep its logic separate from that of the surrounding program as much as possible. That's one of the reasons for data hiding.

Building a class is analogous to the way a carpenter builds a house on a block. Each house has certain well-defined connections to the block, such as electricity, water, sewer, and — the most critical of all — cable.

A subclass is not built as a standalone structure. Often, the subclass relies heavily on the class from which it inherits. Such a subclass is more like an extra room attached to an existing structure rather than a standalone house. You might like the extra room to be generic, but in practice this is rarely possible. The implementation of the subclass becomes bound to the details of the base class. In this situation, the advantages of data hiding are minimized.

Thus, it boils down to a matter of judgment. If your subclass is of the independent variety, the extra work of private inheritance is rewarded by increased decoupling. If your subclass is more of the "add-on room" variety, the result of private inheritance is just increased complexity.

How do I use private?

The keyword *private* looks and acts just like *protected* and *public*. This is demonstrated in the following *Example* class, which has *private, protected,* and *public* members:

```
class Example
{
  public:
   int accessibleToAll;
  protected:
   int accessibleToSubclasses;
  private:
   int onlyAccessibleToThisClass;
};
```

The order of the storage classes is not important. You can put your public members first and your private members last or the other way around. In addition, you can switch between one storage class and another as often as you like.

Secret Wills, or Non-Public Inheritance

Back when I first introduced inheritance, I noted that if there is *public* inheritance, there are probably other modes as well. (It's like my friend says, "If there's artificial intelligence, there's just got to be artificial stupidity.") In fact, there is *protected* inheritance and *private* inheritance. The differences are highlighted in Table 22-1.

class versus *struct*

You may be interested to know that a *class* starts out in *private* mode. Thus, I could have coded the *Example* class as follows:

```
class Example
{
    int onlyAccessibleToThisClass;
  public:
    int accessibleToAll;
  protected:
    int accessibleToSubclasses;
};
```

The only difference between keyword *class* and keyword *struct* in C++ is that *struct* starts out in *public* mode. (It does this to retain compatibility with C.) Therefore, I also could have coded the *Example* class as

```
struct Example
{
    int accessibleToAll;
  protected:
    int accessibleToSubclasses;
```

```
  private:
    int onlyAccessibleToThisClass;
};
```

C++ allows the programmer to mix and match the words *class* and *struct*, referring to the same class sometimes as a *class* and sometimes as a *struct*. Don't do it, however. The reader of your code will wonder what you're doing and you won't have a good explanation.

The general rule is to use *struct* if the structure is C compatible, that is, if it has

✔ No non-public members

✔ No member functions

✔ No base classes (doesn't inherit from anything)

Otherwise, use *class*. In addition, don't rely on the default access mode of *class*. Always specify; it's clearer that way.

Table 22-1: Access Mode versus Inheritance Type

Inheritance type	*Public*	Access mode *Protected*	*Private*
public	public	protected	private
protected	protected	protected	private
private	private	private	private

In a publicly inherited class, each of the members of the base class retain their same access modes in the subclass. Hence, as shown in Table 22-1, public maps to public, protected to protected, and private to private. (This is what we've seen until now.) In a protectedly inherited class, however, public members become protected in the inherited class; in the table, public maps to protected. Protected and private members are unchanged in the derived class. In a privately inherited class, everything becomes private.

Implementing private or protected inheritance is simply a matter of using the keyword *private* or *protected* where the keyword *public* appeared previously. The following code snippet compares private, protected, and public inheritance:

```
class Base
{
  public:
    int m1;
  protected:
    int m2;
  private:
    int m3;
};

class PrivateClass   : private   Base
{
    void test()
    {
      m1 = 1;
      m2 = 2;
      m3 = 3;                //not accessible
    }
};

class DerivedFromPri : public    PrivateClass
{
    void test()
    {
      m1 = 1;                //not accessible
      m2 = 2;                //not accessible
      m3 = 3;                //not accessible
    }
};
```

```
class ProtectedClass : protected Base
{
   void test()
   {
       m1 = 1;
       m2 = 2;
       m3 = 3;                    //not accessible
   }
};

class DerivedFromPro : public    ProtectedClass
{
   void test()
   {
       m1 = 1;
       m2 = 2;
       m3 = 3;                    //not accessible
   }
};

class PublicClass    : public    Base
{
   void test()
   {
       m1 = 1;
       m2 = 2;
       m3 = 3;                    //not accessible
   }
};

class DerivedFromPub : public    PublicClass
{
   void test()
   {
       m1 = 1;
       m2 = 2;
       m3 = 3;                    //not accessible
   }
};

void test()
{
   PrivateClass priObj;
   priObj.m1 = 1;            //not accessible
   priObj.m2 = 2;            //not accessible
   priObj.m3 = 3;            //not accessible

   ProtectedClass proObj;
   proObj.m1 = 1;            //not accessible
   proObj.m2 = 2;            //not accessible
   proObj.m3 = 3;            //not accessible

   PublicClass pubObj;
   pubObj.m1 = 1;
   pubObj.m2 = 2;            //not accessible
   pubObj.m3 = 3;            //not accessible
}
```

The class *Base* contains three members, *m1*, *m2* and *m3*, declared public, protected, and private, respectively. In addition, *Base* serves as a base class for the three classes *PrivateClass*, *ProtectedClass*, and *PublicClass* which are derived using private, protected, and public inheritance, respectively.

Being private, *m3* is accessible only to *Base* and not to any of the classes derived from it nor to non-member functions. This is demonstrated by the fact that references to *m3* are flagged with an error in all of the *test()* functions. *m2* and *m3* are both accessible to classes derived directly from *Base*. Thus, the references to these members from *PrivateClass::test()*, *ProtectedClass::test()*, and *PublicClass::test()* are allowed.

The class *PrivateClass* is inherited privately from *Base*. This means *m1* and *m2* are now privately accessible to the members of *PrivateClass* and, therefore, not accessible to classes derived directly from *PrivateClass*, such as *DerivedFromPri*.

The class *ProtectedClass* is protectedly inherited from *Base*, which compels both *m1* and *m2* to be protected. Both members are still accessible to both *ProtectedClass::test()* and *DerivedFromPro::test()*. However, the normally public *m1* is no longer accessible from the non-member *test()* when referenced through a *ProtectedClass* object.

The class *PublicClass* is publicly inherited from *Base*. All three members retain the same accessibility in *PublicClass* that they had in *Base*.

The default for inheritance is private. Again, it's not a good idea to rely on the default. Your code will be easier to read if you always specify the inheritance type. ■

When is a subclass not?

It is important to note that a privately or protectedly derived class is not a subclass. This is because the non-publicly derived class cannot do all the things that the base class can. Therefore, a non-publicly derived object cannot be used as a replacement for a base class object. Consider the following:

```
class Duck
{
  public:
    void quack();
};
class Mallard : public Duck {};
class LooneyToon: private Duck {};

void fn(Duck &duck)
{
    duck.quack();
```

```
    }
int main()
{
    Mallard daisy;
    LooneyToon daffy;
    fn(daisy);       //this is allowed...
    fn(daffy);       //...but this is not
    return 0;
}
```

The function *fn()* expects an object of type *Duck*, but the call *fn(daisy)* is actually passing an object of class *Mallard*. Why is that justified? An object of class *Mallard* IS_A *Duck* because it has all the members of a *Duck*. That is, anything you can ask a *Duck* to do, you can ask a *Mallard* to do.

If we now look at *daffy*, we see that what is true for *daisy* isn't quite true for *daffy*. We cannot pass *daffy* off as a *Duck* because the general public doesn't have access to its ducky functions. In this case, *fn()* can't get *daffy* to *quack()*. That is, *daffy.quack()* is not allowed, not because *daffy* does not have a member function *quack()*, but because that function is not publicly accessible.

If it don't quack like a duck, it ain't a duck. ■

Conclusion

When should you declare members *protected* and when should you declare them *private*? My preference is to limit data members as much as possible to *private*; however, I do give subclasses access to some key data members by making them *protected*. In addition, I rarely declare member functions *private*. I seldom, if ever, use anything but *public* inheritance.

If you find this entire chapter confusing, don't worry. Stick to *public* and *protected* members and *public* inheritance. You generally won't miss the others. ■

Chapter 23

Overloading Operators

● ●

In This Chapter

▶ Overview of overloading operators in C++

▶ Discussion of operator format versus function format

▶ Implementing operators as a member function versus as a non-member function

▶ The return value from an overloaded operator

▶ A special case: the cast operator

● ●

C++ allows the programmer to define the operators for user-defined types. This is called *operator overloading*. In this chapter we cover the generic case of operator overloading.

Normally, operator overloading is optional and usually not attempted by beginning C++ programmers. A lot of experienced C++ programmers don't think operator overloading is such a great idea either. Therefore, you can skip this chapter and return to it later when you feel curious. However, there are three operators that you will need to learn how to overload. So that you don't inadvertently skip them as well, they have been granted their own chapters, which immediately follow this one.

The following scenes depict graphic representations of software kludgery. If you begin to feel light-headed as you read this chapter, put the book down and rest. If symptoms persist, proceed immediately to the next chapter.

Operator overloading can introduce errors that are very difficult to find. Be sure you know how it works before you attempt to use it. ■

Why Do I Need to Overload Operators?

C++ considers user-defined types to be just as valid as intrinsic types, such as *int* and *char*. Because the operators are defined for the intrinsic types, why not allow them to be defined for user-defined types?

This is a weak argument, but I admit that operator overloading has its uses. Consider a class *USDollar*, for instance, which we will use to represent greenbacks. We will then define what the different operators mean when applied to the class.

Some of the operators make no sense at all when applied to dollars. For example, what would it mean to invert a *USDollar*? Turn it upside down? On the other hand, some operators definitely are applicable. For example, it makes sense to add a *USDollar* to or subtract a *USDollar* from a *USDollar*, the result being a *USDollar*. It also makes sense to multiply or divide a *USDollar* by a *double*. It probably does not make sense to multiply a *USDollar* by a *USDollar*.

Operator overloading can improve readability. Consider the following, first without overloaded operators:

```
//expense - calculate the amount of money paid
//          (including both principle and simple interest)
USDollar expense(USDollar principle, double rate)
{
   //calculate the interest expense
   USDollar intrest = principle.interest(rate);
   //now add this to the principle and return the result
   return principle.add(intrest);
}
```

With overloaded operators, the same function looks like the following:

```
//expense - calculate the amount of money paid
//          (including both principle and simple interest)
USDollar expense(USDollar principle, double rate)
{
   USDollar interest = principle * rate;
   return principle + interest;
}
```

Before we investigate how to overload an operator, we need to understand the relationship between an operator and a function.

How Does an Operator Function and a Function Operate?

An operator is nothing more than a built-in function with a peculiar syntax. One could imagine a language devoid of operators, with the operator functions contained in the standard library. A simple addition might look something like the following:

```
int a, b;
add(a, b);
```

To store the results of that addition into some third variable, the resulting expression would look a little more complicated:

```
int a, b, c;
store(c, add(a, b));
```

This isn't so far-fetched. Some languages, such as LISP, look like this.

The only problem with this format is that even a modestly complex expression can get difficult to read. For example the formula for the length of the hypotenuse ($c = $ sqrt($a^2 + b^2$)) expressed in functional format is less than clear:

```
double hypo, legA, legB;
store(hypo, sqrt(add(mult(legA, legA), mult(legB, legB))));
```

This same expression is easier to read in operator format:

```
double hypo, legA, legB;
hypo = sqrt(legA * legA + legB * legB);
```

(Maybe operator format seems easier to us only because it's what we as C programmers are used to. Maybe the functional format is clearer to the dedicated LISP programmer. Maybe we should try to be more open-minded and understanding of our fellow programmer. Maybe . . . Naaaah!)

What Does This Have to Do with Overloading Operators?

C++ gives each operator a functional name. The functional name of an operator is the operator symbol preceded by the keyword *operator* and followed by the appropriate argument types. For example, the + operator that adds an *int* to an *int* generating an *int* is called *int operator+(int, int)*.

The programmer can overload all operators, except ., ::, * (dereference), and &, by overloading their functional name. ■

The programmer cannot invent new operators. Nor can the precedence or format of the operators be changed. In addition, the operators cannot be redefined when applied to intrinsic types. Only existing operators can be overloaded for newly defined types.

How Does Operator Overloading Work?

Let's see operator overloading in action. The following shows class *USDollar* with an addition operator and an increment operator defined:

```
class USDollar
{
   friend USDollar operator+(USDollar&, USDollar&);
   friend USDollar& operator++(USDollar&);
  public:
   USDollar(unsigned int d, unsigned int c);
  protected:
   unsigned int dollars;
   unsigned int cents;
};

USDollar::USDollar(unsigned int d, unsigned int c)

{
   dollars = d;
   cents = c;
   while (cents >= 100) {
      dollars++;
      cents -= 100;
   }
}

//operator+ - add s1 to s2 and return the result
//            in a new object
USDollar operator+(USDollar& s1, USDollar& s2)
{
   unsigned int cents   = s1.cents   + s2.cents;
   unsigned int dollars = s1.dollars + s2.dollars;
   USDollar d(dollars, cents);
   return d;
}

//operator++ - increment the specified argument;
//             change the value of the provided object
USDollar& operator++(USDollar& s)
{
   s.cents++;
   if (s.cents >= 100)
   {
      s.cents -= 100;
      s.dollars++;
   }
   return s;
}

int main()
{
   USDollar d1(1, 60);
   USDollar d2(2, 50);
```

```
    USDollar d3(0, 0);
    d3 = d1 + d2;    //straightforward in use
    ++d3;
    return 0;
}
```

The class *USDollar* is defined as having an integer number of dollars and an integer number of cents less than 100. The constructor enforces the latter rule by reducing the number of cents by 100 at a time and increasing the number of dollars appropriately.

Here *operator+()* and *operator++()* have been implemented as conventional non-member functions. As such, they must be declared as friends to be granted access to the protected members.

Because *operator+()* is a binary operator (that is, it has two arguments), we see two arguments to the function (*s1* and *s2*). The *operator+()* takes *s1* and adds it to *s2*. The result of the expression is returned as a *USDollar* object from the function.

Notice that nothing forces *operator+(USDollar&, USDollar&)* to perform addition. You could have *operator+()* do anything you like; however, doing anything else besides addition is a REALLY BAD IDEA. People are accustomed to their operators performing in certain ways. They don't like their operators dancing about willy-nilly performing other operations. ■

The unary operators, such as *operator++()*, take a single argument. *operator++()* increments the *cents* field. If it goes over 100, it increments the dollar field and zeros out the cents.

Originally there was no way to overload the prefix operator *++x* separately from the postfix version *x++*. Enough programmers complained that the rule was made that *operator++(ClassName)* refers to the prefix operator and *operator++(ClassName, int)* refers to the postfix operator. A zero is always passed as the second argument. The same rule applies to *operator--()*.

There is little reason to use *operator++(ClassName, int)* for postfix. I find it extremely inelegant, but they didn't ask me. ■

If you provide only one *operator++()* or *operator--()*, it is normally used for both the prefix and postfix versions. The standard for C++ says that a compiler doesn't have to do this, but most do. ■

In use, the operators appear very natural. What could be simpler than *d3 = d1 + d2* and *++d3*?

A More Detailed Look

Why does *operator+()* return by value, but *operator++()* return by reference? This is not an accident, but a very important difference.

The addition of two objects changes neither object. That is, *a* + *b* changes neither *a* nor *b*. Thus, *operator+()* must generate a temporary object into which it can store the result of the addition. This is why *operator+()* constructs an object and returns this object by value to the caller.

Specifically, the following would not work:

```
//this doesn't work
USDollar& operator+(USDollar& s1, USDollar& s2)
{
    unsigned int cents = s1.cents + s2.cents;
    unsigned int dollars = s1.dollars + s2.dollars;
    USDollar result(dollars, cents);
    return result;
}
```

Although this compiles without a squeak of complaint, it generates flaky results. The problem is that the returned reference refers to an object, *result*, whose scope is local to the function. Thus, *result* is out of scope by the time it can be used by the calling function.

Why not allocate a block of memory from the heap, as follows?

```
//this sort of works
USDollar& operator+(USDollar& s1, USDollar& s2)
{
    unsigned int cents = s1.cents + s2.cents;
    unsigned int dollars = s1.dollars + s2.dollars;
    return *new USDollar(dollars, cents);
}
```

This would be fine except there is no mechanism to return the allocated block of memory to the heap. This type of error is called a *memory leak* and is often very hard to track down. Although this operator works, it slowly drains memory from the heap each time an addition is performed.

Returning by value forces the compiler to generate a temporary of its own on the caller's stack. The object generated in the function is then copied into the object as part of the return from *operator+()*.

How long does the temporary returned from *operator+()* hang around? Originally this was vague, but the standards people got together and decided that such a temporary remains valid until the "extended expression" is complete.

The *extended expression* is everything up to the semicolon. For example, consider the following snippet:

```
SomeClass f();
LotsAClass g();
void fn()
{
    int i;
    i = f() + (2 * g());
}
```

The temporary object returned by *f()* remains in existence while *g()* is invoked and while the multiplication is performed. This object becomes invalid at the semicolon. ■

Unlike *operator+()*, *operator++()* does modify its argument. Thus, there is no need to create a temporary or to return by value. The argument provided can be returned to the caller. In fact, the following function, which returns by value, has a subtle bug:

```
//this isn't 100% reliable either
USDollar operator++(USDollar& s)
{
    s.cents++;
    if (s.cents >= 100)
    {
        s.cents -= 100;
        s.dollars++;
    }
    return s;
}
```

By returning *s* by value, the function forces the compiler to generate a copy of the object. Most of the time, this is okay. But what happens with an expression like *++(++a)*? We would expect *a* to be incremented by 2. With the preceding definition, however, *a* is incremented by 1 and then a copy of *a* — not *a* itself — is incremented a second time.

The general rule is: If the operator changes the value of its argument, return the argument by reference; if the operator does not change the value of either argument, create a new object to hold the results and return that object by value. The input arguments can always be referential. ■

Operators as Member Functions

An operator, in addition to being implemented as a non-member function, can be a nonstatic member function. Implemented in this way, our example *USDollar* class appears as follows:

```
class USDollar
{
  public:
   USDollar(unsigned int d, unsigned int c);
   USDollar& operator++();
   USDollar  operator+(USDollar& s);
  protected:
   unsigned int dollars;
   unsigned int cents;
};


USDollar::USDollar(unsigned int d, unsigned int c)
{
   dollars = d;
   cents = c;
   while (cents >= 100)
   {
      dollars++;
      cents -= 100;
   }
}


//operator+ - add s1 to s2 and return the result
//            in a new object
USDollar USDollar::operator+(USDollar& s2)
{
   unsigned int c = cents   + s2.cents;
   unsigned int d = dollars + s2.dollars;
   USDollar t(d, c);
   return t;
}


//operator++ - increment the specified argument;
//             change the value of the provided object
USDollar& USDollar::operator++()
{
   cents++;
   if (cents >= 100)
   {
      cents -= 100;
      dollars++;
   }
   return *this;
}


int main()
{
   USDollar d1(1, 60);
   USDollar d2(2, 50);
   USDollar d3(0, 0);
   d3 = d1 + d2;          //very straightforward in use
   !!d3;
   return 0;
}
```

The non-member function *operator+(USDollar, USDollar)* has been rewritten as the nonstatic member function *USDollar::operator+(USDollar)*. At first glance, it appears that the member version has one fewer argument than the non-member version. If you think back, however, you'll remember that *this* is the hidden first argument to all nonstatic member functions.

This difference is most obvious in *USDollar::operator+()* itself. In the following, I show the non-member and member versions for comparison:

```
//operator+ - the non-member version
USDollar operator+(USDollar& s1, USDollar& s2)
{
    unsigned int cents   = s1.cents   + s2.cents;
    unsigned int dollars = s1.dollars + s2.dollars;
    USDollar d(dollars, cents);
    return d;
}
//operator+ - the member version
USDollar USDollar::operator+(USDollar& s2)
{
    unsigned int c = cents   + s2.cents;
    unsigned int d = dollars + s2.dollars;
    USDollar t(d, c);
    return t;
}
```

We can see that the functions are nearly identical. However, where the non-member version adds *s1* and *s2*, the member version adds the "current object" — the one pointed at by *this* — to *s2*.

The member version of an operator always has one less argument than the non-member version — the lefthand argument is implicit. ∎

Yet Another Overloading Irritation

Just because you have overloaded *operator*(double, USDollar&)*, that doesn't mean you have *operator*(USDollar&, double)* covered. Since these two operators have different arguments, they have to be overloaded separately. This doesn't have to be as big a drag as it would at first appear to be.

First, there is nothing which keeps one operator from referring to the other. In the case of *operator*()* we would probably do something like the following:

```
USDollar operator*(double f, USDollar& s)
{
    //...implementation of function here...
}
inline USDollar operator*(USDollar& s, double f)
```

continued

```
{
    //use the previous definition
    return f * s;
}
```

The second version merely calls the first version with the order of the operators reversed. Making it inline even avoids any extra overhead.

A second approach is to provide a conversion path to an existing operator. Suppose, for example, that we provided a constructor to convert a *double* into a *USDollar.*

```
class USDollar
{
    friend USDollar operator+(USDollar& s1, USDollar& s2);
  public:
    USDollar(int d, int c);
    USDollar(double value)
    {
        dollars = (int)value;
        cents = (int)((value - dollars) * 100 + 0.5);
    }
    //...as before...
}

void fn(USDollar& s)
{
    //all of the following use operator+(USDollar&, USDollar&)
    s = USDollar(1.5) + s;  //explicit conversion...
    s = 1.5 + s;       //...implicit conversion...
    s = s + 1.5;       //...in either order
    s = s + 1;         //even this works by converting the int...
                       //...into a double and then continuing...
                       //...as above
}
```

Now we need to define neither *operator+(double, USDollar&)* nor *operator+ (USDollar&, double)*. We can convert the *double* into a *USDollar* and use the *operator+(USDollar&, USDollar&)* already defined.

This conversion can be explicit, as shown in the first addition. It can also be left implicit, in which case C++ performs the conversion automatically.

Providing such conversion paths can save considerable effort by reducing the number of different operators the programmer must define.

Allowing C++ to make these conversions, however, can be dangerous. If there are multiple possible conversion paths, mysterious compiler errors can arise.

Suppose, for example, that a constructor *USDollar(int)* existed. Then *s = s + 1* would no longer be allowed, since the compiler would not know whether to convert 1 into a *double* and then into a *USDollar* using *USDollar(double)* or convert it directly into a *USDollar* using *USDollar(int)*. ■

Should you or shouldn't you?

When should the programmer implement an operator as a member and when as a non-member? The following operators must be implemented as member functions:

=   Assignment

()   Function call

[]   Subscript

->   Class membership

Other than the operators listed, there isn't much difference between implementing an operator as a member or as a non-member with the following exception: an operator like the following could not be implemented as a member function.

```
USDollar operator*(double factor, USDollar& s);
void fn(USDollar& principle)
{
    USDollar interestExpense = interest * principle
    //...
}
```

In order to be a member function, it would have to be a member of class *double*. We as mere mortals cannot add operators to the intrinsic classes. Thus, operators like the preceding must be non-member functions.

If you have access to the class internals, make the overloaded operator a member of the class. This is particularly true if the operator modifies the object upon which it operates.

Cast Operator

The cast operator can be overloaded as well. In practice, it looks like the following:

```
class USDollar
{
  public:
    USDollar(double value = 0.0);
    //the following function acts as a cast operator
    operator double()
```

continued

```
     {
         return dollars + cents / 100.0;
     }
   protected:
     unsigned int dollars;
     unsigned int cents;
};
USDollar::USDollar(double value)
{
   dollars = (int)value;
   cents = (int)((value - dollars) * 100 + 0.5);
}
int main()
{
   USDollar d1(2.0), d2(1.5), d3;
   //invoke cast operator explicitly...
   d3 = USDollar((double)d1 + (double)d2);
   //...or implicitly
   d3 = d1 + d2;
   return 0;
}
```

A cast operator is the word *operator* followed by the desired type. The member function *USDollar::operator double()* provides a mechanism for converting an object of class *USDollar* into a *double*. For reasons that are beyond me, cast operators have no return type. (The argument is, "You don't need it because you can tell the return type from the name." I prefer a bit of consistency.)

As the preceding example shows, conversions using the cast operator can be invoked either explicitly or implicitly. Let's look at the implicit case carefully.

In trying to make sense of the expression *d3 = d1 + d2* in the earlier code snippet, C++ first looked for member function *USDollar::operator+(USDollar)*. When that wasn't found, it looked for the non-member version of the same thing, *operator+(USDollar, USDollar)*. Lacking that as well, it started looking for an *operator+()* that it could use by converting one or the other arguments into a different type. Finally it found a match: If it converted both *d1* and *d2* to *double*s, it could use the intrinsic *operator+(double, double)*. Of course, it then has to convert the resulting *double* back to *USDollar* using the constructor.

This demonstrates both the advantage and disadvantage of providing a cast operator. Providing a conversion path from *USDollar* to *double* relieves programmers of the need to provide their own set of operators. *USDollar* can just piggy-back on the operators defined for *double*.

On the other hand, it also removes the ability of programmers to control which operators are defined. By providing a conversion path to *double*, *USDollar* gets all of *double*'s operators whether they make sense or not. In addition, going through the extra conversions may not be the most efficient process in the world. For example, the simple addition just noted involves three type conversions with all of the attendant function calls, multiplications, divisions, and so on.

Be careful not to provide two conversion paths to the same type. For example, the follow is asking for trouble:

```
class A
{
  public:
    A(B& b);
};
class B
{
  public:
    operator A();
};
```

If asked to convert an object of class *B* into an object of class *A*, the compiler will not know whether to use *B*'s cast operator *B:operatorA()* or *A*'s constructor *A::A(B&)*, both of which start out with a *B* and end up making an *A* out of it.

Perhaps the result of the two conversion paths would be the same, but the compiler doesn't know that. It must know which conversion path you really intended. If it can't determine this unambiguously, the compiler throws up its electronic hands and spits out an error. ■

Conclusion

Overloading a new class with the proper operators can lead to some simple and elegant application code. In most cases, however, operator overloading is definitely not necessary. In the following chapters, we examine when operator overloading is critical.

Chapter 24

The Assignment Operator

In This Chapter

▶ Introduction to the assignment operator

▶ Why and when the assignment operator is necessary

▶ Similarities between the assignment operator and its first cousin, the copy constructor

*W*hether or not you start out overloading all operators, you will need to learn to overload the assignment operator fairly early. The assignment operator can be overloaded for any user-defined class. By following the pattern provided in this chapter, you should be able to avoid difficulty when overloading this operator.

Why Is Overloading the Assignment Operator So Critical?

C defines only one operator that can be applied to structure types: the assignment operator. In C, the following is legal and results in a bitwise copy from *source* to *destination*:

```
void fn()
{
    struct MyStruct source, destination;
    destination = source;
}
```

To retain compatibility with C, C++ provides a default definition for *operator=()* for all user-defined classes. This default definition performs a member-by-member copy, like the default copy constructor. However, this default definition can be overloaded by an *operator=()* written specifically for the specified class.

The assignment operator is much like the copy constructor. In use the two look almost identical:

```
void fn(MyClass &mc)
{
   MyClass newMC = mc;    //this is the copy constructor
   newMC = mc;            //this is the assignment operator
}
```

The difference is that when the copy constructor was invoked on *newMC*, the object *newMC* did not already exist. When the assignment operator was invoked on *newMC*, it was already a *MyClass* object in good standing.

The copy constructor is used when a new object is being created. The assignment operator is used if the lefthand object already exists.

Like the copy constructor, an assignment operator should be provided whenever a shallow copy is not appropriate. (See the copy constructor in Chapter 15 for a further discussion of the fascinating topic of shallow versus deep copies.) ∎

How Do I Overload the Assignment Operator?

Overloading the assignment operator is similar to overloading any other operator. For example, an assignment operator has been provided as an inline member function for the following class *Name*. (Remember, the assignment operator must be a member function of the class.)

```
#include <stdlib.h>
#include <string.h>
#include <ctype.h>
class Name
{
  public:
   Name()
   {
      pName = (char*)0;
   }
   Name(char *pN)
   {
      copyName(pN);
   }
   Name(Name& s)
   {
      copyName(s.pName);
   }
   ~Name()
   {
      deleteName();
   }
   //assignment operator
   Name& operator=(Name& s)
```

```
    {
        //delete existing stuff...
        deleteName();
        //...before replacing with new stuff
        copyName(s.pName);
        //return reference to existing object
        return *this;
    }
  protected:
    void copyName(char *pN);
    void deleteName();
    char *pName;
};
//copyName() - allocate heap memory to store name
void Name::copyName(char *pN)
{
    pName = (char*)malloc(strlen(pN) + 1);
    if (pName)
    {
        strcpy(pName, pN);
    }
}
//deleteName() - return heap memory
void Name::deleteName()
{
    if (pName)
    {
        delete pName;
        pName = 0;
    }
}

int main()
{
    Name s("Claudette");
    Name t("temporary");
    t = s;              //this invokes the assignment operator
    return 0;
}
```

The class *Name* retains a person's name in memory, which it allocates from the heap in the constructor. The constructors and destructor for class *Name* are similar to those presented in Parts III and IV.

The assignment operator appears with the name *operator=()*. Notice how the assignment operator looks like a destructor followed by a copy constructor. This is typical. Consider the assignment in the example. The object *t* already has a name associated with it (*temporary*). In the assignment *t = s* the memory that the original name occupies must be returned to the heap by calling *deleteName()* before new memory can be allocated into which to store the new name by calling *copyName()*.

The copy constructor did not need to call *deleteName()* because the object didn't already exist. Therefore, memory had not already been assigned to the object when the constructor was invoked.

In general, an assignment operator has two parts. The first part resembles a destructor in that it deletes the assets that the object already owns. The second part resembles a copy constructor in that it allocates new assets. ■

Notice two details. First, the return type of *operator=()* is *Name&*. This matches the semantics of C. I could have made the return type *void*. However, if I did, the following would not work:

```
void otherFn(Name&);
void fn(Name& oldN)
{
    Name newN;
    otherFn(newN = oldN);
}
```

The results of the assignment *newN = oldN* would be *void*, the return type of *operator=()*, which does not match the prototype of *otherFn()*. Declaring *operator=()* to return a reference to the "current" object and returning **this* retains the C semantics that we have all come to know and love.

The second detail to notice is that *operator=()* was written as a member function. Unlike other operators, the assignment operator cannot be overloaded with a non-member function.

The assignment operator must be a nonstatic member function. The special assignment operators, such as += and *=, have no special restrictions and can be non-member functions. ■

Conclusion

Providing your class with an assignment operator can add considerable flexibility to the application code. However, if this is too much for you or if you can't make copies of your object, overloading the assignment operator with a protected or private function will keep anyone from accidentally making an unauthorized shallow copy. For example:

```
class Name
{
  //...just like before...
  protected:
   //assignment operator
   Name& operator=(Name& s)
   {
       return *this;
   }
};
```

With this definition, assignments like the following are precluded:

```
void fn(Name &n)
{
    Name newN;
    newN = n;        //generates a compiler error -
                     //function has no access to op=()
}
```

This copy-protection for classes may save you the trouble of overloading the assignment operator.

Chapter 25

Stream I/O

● ●

In This Chapter

▶ Rediscovering stream I/O as an overloaded operator

▶ Using stream file I/O

▶ Using stream buffer I/O

▶ Writing your own inserters and extractors

▶ Behind the scenes with manipulators

● ●

I presented a first look at stream I/O in Part II. What I couldn't say then was that stream I/O is not a new keyword or an exotic new syntax but just the right and left shift operators overloaded to perform input and output, respectively.

In this chapter, I explain stream I/O in more detail. (You're old enough to know the truth now.) I must warn you that stream I/O is too large a topic to be covered completely in a single chapter — entire books are devoted to this one topic. I can get you started, though, so that you can perform the main operations.

How Does Stream I/O Work?

Stream I/O is based on the include file *iostream.h*. This file includes prototypes for several *operator>>()* and *operator<<()* functions. The code for these functions is included in the standard library, which your C++ program links with. Some of these prototypes look like the following:

```
//for input we have:
istream& operator>>(istream& source, char *pDest);
istream& operator>>(istream& source, int  &dest);
istream& operator>>(istream& source, char &dest);
//...and so forth...
//for output we have:
ostream& operator<<(ostream& dest, char *pSource);
ostream& operator<<(ostream& dest, int   source);
ostream& operator<<(ostream& dest, char  source);
//...and so it goes...
```

Buzzword time: When overloaded to perform I/O, *operator>>()* is called the extractor and *operator<<()* is called the inserter. ■

Let's look in detail at what happens when I write the following:

```
#include <iostream.h>
void fn()
{
    cout << "My name is Randy\n";
}
```

First, C++ determines that the lefthand argument is of type *ostream* and the righthand argument is of type *char**. Armed with this knowledge, it finds the prototype *operator<<(ostream&, char*)* in *iostream.h*. C++ generates a call to this function, the *char** inserter, passing the function the string *"My name is Randy\n"* and the object *cout* as the two arguments. That is, it makes the call *operator<<(cout, "My name is Randy\n")*. The *char** inserter function, which is part of the standard C++ library, performs the requested output.

How did the compiler know that *cout* is of class *ostream*? This and a few other global objects are also declared in *iostream.h*. A list is shown in Table 25-1. These objects are constructed automatically at program startup, before *main()* gets control.

This is analogous to the way *stdin* and *stdout* are opened by the C startup code. ■

Table 25-1: Standard Stream I/O Objects

Object	Class	Purpose
cin	istream	Standard input
cout	ostream	Standard output
cerr	ostream	Standard error output
clog	ostream	Standard printer output

And just what is an *ostream* anyway? An *ostream* object contains the members necessary to keep track of output. In a similar vein, *istream* describes an input stream.

The C equivalent is *struct FILE*, which is defined in *stdio.h*. The function *fopen()* opens a file for input and output. *fopen()* returns a pointer to a *FILE* object into which it has stored the information necessary for subsequent I/O operations. This object is returned in calls to the *fx()* functions, such as *fprintf()*, *fscanf()*, and *fgets()*. ■

Also defined as part of the stream I/O library are a number of subclasses of *ostream* and *istream*. These subclasses are used for input and output to files and internal buffers.

The fstream Subclasses

The subclasses *ofstream*, *ifstream*, and *fstream* are defined in the include file *fstream.h* to perform stream input and output to a disk file in much the way the *fx()* functions (*fprintf()*, *fscanf()*, *fopen()*, *fclose()*, and others) perform file I/O in C. These three classes share a number of member functions that are used to control input and output, many of them inherited from *istream* and *ostream*. A complete list is provided with your compiler documentation, but let me get you started.

Class *ostream*, which is used to perform file output, has several constructors, the most useful of which is

```
ofstream::ofstream(char *pFileName,
            int mode = ios::out,
            int prot = filebuff::openprot);
```

The first argument is a pointer to the name of the file to open. The second and third arguments specify how the file will be opened. The legal values for *mode* are listed in Table 25-2 and those for *prot* in Table 25-3. These values are bit fields that are ORed together (the classes *ios* and *filebuff* are both parent classes of *ostream*).

Table 25-2: Values for *mode* in the *ofstream* Constructor

Flag	Meaning
ios::ate	Append to the end of the file, if it exists
ios::in	Open file for input (implied for *istream*)
ios::out	Open file for output (implied for *ostream*)
ios::trunc	Truncate file if it exists (default)
ios::nocreate	If file doesn't already exist, return error
ios::noreplace	If file does exist, return error
ios::binary	Open file in binary mode (alternative is text mode)

Table 25-3: Values for *prot* in the *ofstream* Constructor

Flag	*Meaning*
filebuf::openprot	Compatibility sharing mode
filebuf::sh_none	Exclusive; no sharing
filebuf::sh_read	Read sharing allowed
filebuf::sh_write	Write sharing allowed

For example, the following program opens the file *MYNAME* and then writes some important and absolutely true information into that file:

```
#include <fstream.h>
void fn()
{
   //open the text file MYNAME for writing - truncate
   //whatever's there now
   ofstream myn("MYNAME");
   myn << "Randy Davis is suave and handsome\n"
       << "and definitely not balding prematurely\n";
}
```

The constructor *ofstream::ofstream(char*)* expects only a file name and provides defaults for the other file modes. If the file *MYNAME* already exists, it is truncated; otherwise, *MYNAME* is created. In addition, the file is opened in compatibility sharing mode.

A second constructor *ofstream::ofstream(char*, int)* allows the programmer to specify other file I/O modes. For example, if I wanted to open the file in binary mode and append to the end of the file if the file already exists, I would create the *ostream* object as follows. (In binary mode, newlines are not converted to carriage returns and line feeds on output nor converted back to newlines on input.)

```
void fn()
{
   //open the binary file BINFILE for writing; if it
   //exists, append to end of whatever's already there
   ofstream bfile("BINFILE", ios::binary | ios::ate);
   //...continue on as before...
}
```

The member function *bad()* returns 1 if the file object has an error. To check whether the file was opened properly in the earlier example, I would have coded the following:

```
#include <fstream.h>
void fn()
{
    ofstream myn("MYNAME");
    if (myn.bad())          //if the open didn't work...
    {
        cerr << "Error opening file MYNAME\n";
        return;             //...output error and quit
    }
    myn << "Randy Davis is suave and handsome\n"
        << "and definitely not balding prematurely\n";
}
```

All attempts to output to an *ofstream* object that has an error have no effect until the error has been cleared by calling the member function *clear()*. ■

The destructor for class *ofstream* automatically closes the file. In the preceding example, the file was closed when the function exited.

Class *ifstream* works much the same way for input, as the following example demonstrates:

```
#include <fstream.h>
void fn()
{
    //open file for reading; don't create the file
    //if it isn't there

    ifstream bankStatement("STATEMNT", ios::nocreate);
    if (bankStatement.bad())
    {
        cerr << "Couldn't find bank statement\n";
        return;
    }
    while (!bankStatement.eof())
    {
        bankStatement >> accountNumber >> amount;
        //...process this withdrawal
    }
}
```

The function opens the file *STATEMNT* by constructing the object *bankStatement*. If the file does not exist, it is not created. (We assume that the file has information for us, so it wouldn't make much sense to create a new, empty file.) If the object is bad (for example, if the object was not created), the function outputs an error message and exits. Otherwise, the function loops, reading the *accountNumber* and withdrawal *amount* until the file is empty (end-of-file is true).

An attempt to read an *ifstream* object that has the error flag set, indicating a previous error, returns immediately without reading anything. ■

The class *fstream* is like an *ifstream* and an *ofstream* combined (in fact, it inherits from both). An object of class *fstream* can be created for input or output or both.

The strstream Subclasses

The classes *istrstream*, *ostrstream*, and *strstream* are defined in the include file *strstrea.h*. (The file name appears to be truncated because MS-DOS allows no more than 8 characters for a file name.) These classes allow the operations defined for files by the *fstream* classes to be applied to character strings in memory. This is much like the *sx()* functions in C, *sprintf()* and *sscanf()*.

For example, the following code snippet parses the data in a character string using stream input:

```
#include <strstrea.h>
char* parseString(char *pString)
{
    //associate an istrstream object with the input
    //character string
    istrstream inp(pString, 0);

    //now input from that object
    int accountNumber
    float balance;
    inp >> accountNumber >> balance;

    //allocate a buffer and associate an
    //ostrstream object with it
    char *pBuffer = new char[128];
    ostrstream out(pBuffer, 128);

    //output to that object
    out << "account number = " << accountNumber
        << ", balance = $" << balance;
    return pBuffer;
}
```

For example, *pString* might point to the following string:

```
"1234 100.0"
```

The object *inp* is associated with that string by the constructor for *istrstream*. The second argument to the constructor is the length of the string. In this example, the argument is 0, which means "read until you get to the terminating NULL."

On the output side, the object *out* is associated with the buffer pointed to by *pBuffer*. Here again, the second argument to the constructor is the length of the buffer. A third argument, which corresponds to the mode, defaults to *ios::out*.

You can set this argument to *ios::ate*, however, if you want the output to append to the end of whatever is already in the buffer rather than overwrite it.

The buffer returned in the preceding code snippet given the example input would contain the string

```
"account number = 1234, balance = $100.00"
```

Manipulators

So far, we have seen how to use stream I/O to output numbers and character strings using default formats. Usually the defaults are fine, but sometimes they don't cut it.

For example, I for one was less than tickled when the total from the example BUDGET program came back *249.600006* instead of *249.6* (or, better yet, *249.60*). There must be a way to bend the defaults to our desires. True to form, C++ provides not one way but two ways to control the format of output.

First, the format can be controlled by invoking a series of member functions on the stream object. For example, the number of significant digits to display is set using the function *precision()* as follows:

```
#include <iostream.h>
void fn(float interest, float dollarAmount)
{
   cout << "Dollar amount = ";
   cout.precision(2);
   cout << dollarAmount;
   cout.precision(4);
   cout << interest
        << "\n";
}
```

In this example, the function *fn()* sets the precision to 2 immediately before outputting the value *dollarAmount*. This gives us a number such as *249.60*, the nice type of result we want. It then sets the precision to 4 before outputting the interest.

A second approach is through what are called manipulators. (Sounds like someone behind the scenes of the New York Stock Exchange, doesn't it? Well, manipulators are every bit as sneaky.) *Manipulators* are objects defined in the include file *iomanip.h* to have the same effect as the member function calls. (You must include *iomanip.h* to have access to the manipulators.) The only advantage to manipulators is that the program can insert them directly into the stream rather than resort to a separate function call.

If we rewrite the preceding example to use manipulators, the program appears as follows:

```
#include <iostream.h>
#include <iomanip.h>
void fn(float interest, float dollarAmount)
{
    cout << "Dollar amount = "
         << setprecision(2) << dollarAmount
         << setprecision(4) << interest
         << "\n";
}
```

The most common manipulators and their corresponding meanings are given in Table 25-4.

Table 25-4: Common Manipulators and Stream Format Control Functions

Manipulator	Member function	Description
dec	flags(10)	Set radix to 10
hex	flags(16)	Set radix to 16
oct	flags(8)	Set radix to 8
setfill(c)	fill(c)	Set the fill character to c
setprecision(c)	precision(c)	Set display precision to c
setw(n)	width(n)	Set width of field to n characters *

* This returns to its default value after the next field is output.

Watch out for the width parameter (*width()* function and *setw()* manipulator). Most parameters retain their value until they are specifically reset by a subsequent call, but the width parameter does not. The width parameter is reset to its default value as soon as the next output is performed. For example, you might expect the following to produce two 8-character integers:

```
#include <iostream.h>
#include <iomanip.h>
void fn()
{
    cout << setw(8)      //width is 8...
         << 10           //...for the 10, but...
         << 20           //...default for the 20
         << "\n";
}
```

What you get, however, is an 8-character integer followed by a 2-character integer. To get two 8-character output fields, the following is necessary:

```
#include <iostream.h>
#include <iomanip.h>
void fn()
{
   cout << setw(8)      //set the width...
        << 10
        << setw(8)      //...now reset it
        << 20
        << "\n";
}
```

Thus, if you have several objects to output and the default width is not good enough, you must include a *setw()* call for each object. ∎

Which way is better, manipulators or member function calls? Member functions provide a bit more control because there are more of them. In addition, the member functions always return the previous setting so you know how to restore it (if you want). Finally, a query version of each member function exists to allow you to just ask what the current setting is without changing it. This is shown in the following example:

```
#include <iostream.h>
void fn(float value)
{
   int previousPrecision;

   //...doing stuff here...

   //you can ask what the current precision is:
   previousPrecision = cout.precision();

   //or you can save the old value when you change it
   previousPrecision = cout.precision(2);
   cout << value;

   //now restore the precision to previous value
   cout.precision(previousPrecision);
   //...do more neat stuff...
}
```

Even with all these features, the manipulators are the more common, probably because they look neat. Use whatever you prefer, but be prepared to see both in other people's code.

Custom Inserters

The fact that C++ overloads the left shift operator to perform output is really exciting because you are free to overload the same operator to perform output on classes you define. (Okay, *really exciting* is a bit extreme. I suppose finding out that you just won the lottery would be really exciting. This falls more in the category of syntactically satisfying.)

This is the much-vaunted extensibility of stream I/O that I have alluded to but avoided explaining until now. Consider, for example, our *USDollar* class introduced in Chapter 23, extended with a *display()* member function:

```
#include <iostream.h>
#include <iomanip.h>
class USDollar
{
  public:
   USDollar(double v = 0.0)
   {
      dollars = v;
      cents = int((v - dollars) * 100.0 + 0.5);
   }
   operator double()
   {
      return dollars + cents / 100.0;
   }
   void display(ostream& out)
   {
      out << '$' << dollars << '.'
         //set fill to 0's for cents
         << setfill('0') << setw(2) << cents
         //now put it back to spaces
         << setfill(' ');
   }

  protected:
   unsigned int dollars;
   unsigned int cents;
};

//operator<< - overload the inserter for our class
ostream& operator<< (ostream& o, USDollar& d)
{
   d.display(o);
   return o;
}

int main()
{
   USDollar usd(1.50);
   cout << "Initially usd = " << usd << "\n";
   usd = 2.0 * usd;
   cout << "then usd = " << usd << "\n";
   return 0;
}
```

The *display()* function starts by displaying $, the dollar amount, and the obligatory decimal point. Notice that output is to whatever *ostream* object it is passed and not necessarily just to *cout*. This allows the same function to be used on *fstream* and *strstream* objects, both of which are subclasses of *ostream*.

When it comes time to display the cents amount, *display()* sets the width to 2 positions and the leading character to 0. This ensures that numbers smaller than 10 display properly.

Notice how class *USDollar*, rather than access the *display()* function directly, also defines an *operator<<(ostream&, USDollar&)*. The programmer can now output *USDollar* objects with the same ease and grace of the intrinsic types, as the example *main()* function demonstrates.

The output from this program is as follows:

```
Initially usd = $1.50
then usd = $3.00
```

You may wonder why the *operator<<()* returns the *ostream* object passed to it. This allows the operator to be chained with other inserters in a single expression. Because *operator<<()* binds from left to right, the following expression

```
void fn(USDollar& usd, float i)
{
    cout << "Amount " << usd << ", interest = " << i;
}
```

is interpreted as

```
void fn(USDollar& usd, float i)
{
    (((cout << "Amount ") << usd) << ", interest = ") << i;
}
```

The first insertion outputs the string *"Amount"* to *cout*. The result of this expression is the object *cout*, which is then passed to *operator<<(ostream&, USDollar&)*. It is important that this operator return its *ostream* object so that the object can be passed to the next inserter in turn.

Had we declared the return type of the insertion operator *void*, a perfectly valid usage such as the preceding example would generate a compiler error because you can't insert a string into a *void*. The following error is worse because it's more difficult to find:

```
ostream& operator<<(ostream& os, USDollar& usd)
{
    usd.display(os);
    return cout;
}
```

Notice that this function returns not the *ostream* object it was given but the *ostream* object *cout*. This is easy to do because *cout* is far and away the most commonly referenced *ostream* object. (*cout* has already been voted into the *ostream* Hall of Fame.)

This problem doesn't become visible until the following comes along:

```
void storeAccounts(int account,
                   USDollar balance,
                   char *pName)
{
   ofstream outFile("ACCOUNTS", ios::ate);
   outFile << account << balance << pName;
}
```

The *int account* outputs to *outFile* through the function *operator<<(ostream&, int&)*, which returns *outFile*. Then *USDollar* outputs to *outFile* through *operator<<(ostream&, USDollar&)*, which incorrectly returns *cout*, not *outFile*. Now *pName* outputs to *cout* instead of to the file as intended.

Smart Inserters

We would often like to make the inserter smart. That is, we would like to say *cout << baseClassObject* and let C++ choose the proper subclass inserter in the same way that it chooses the proper virtual member function. Because the inserter is not a member function, we cannot declare it virtual directly. This is not a problem for the clever C++ programmer, as the following example demonstrates:

```
#include <iostream.h>
#include <iomanip.h>
class Currency
{
  public:
   Currency(double v = 0.0)
   {
      unit = v;
      cent = int((v - unit) * 100.0 + 0.5);
   }
   virtual void display(ostream& out) = 0;

  protected:
   unsigned int unit;
   unsigned int cent;
};

class USDollar : public Currency
{
  public:
   USDollar(double v = 0.0) : Currency(v)
   {
   }
   //display $123.00
   virtual void display(ostream& out)
   {
      out << '$' << unit << '.'
```

```
                << setfill('0') << setw(2) << cent
                << setfill(' ');
      }
    };

    class DMark : public Currency
    {
      public:
        DMark(double v = 0.0) : Currency(v)
        {
        }
        //display 123.00DM
        virtual void display(ostream& out)
        {
            out << unit << '.'
                //set fill to 0's for cents
                << setfill('0') << setw(2) << cent
                //now put it back to spaces
                << setfill(' ')
                << " DM";
        }
    };

    ostream& operator<< (ostream& o, Currency& c)
    {
        c.display(o);
        return o;
    }

    void fn(Currency& c)
    {
        //the following output is polymorphic because
        //operator(ostream&, Currency&) is through a virtual
        //member function
        cout << "Deposit was " << c
             << "\n";
    }
    int main()
    {
        //create a dollar and output it using the
        //proper format for a dollar
        USDollar usd(1.50);
        fn(usd);

        //now create a DMark and output it using its own format
        DMark d(3.00);
        fn(d);
        return 0;
    }
```

The class *Currency* has two subclasses, *USDollar* and *DMark*. In *Currency* the *display()* function is declared pure virtual. In each of the two subclasses, this function is overloaded with a *display()* function to output the object in the proper format for that type. The call to *display()* in *operator<<()* is now a virtual call. Thus, when *operator<<()* is passed *USDollar*, it outputs the object like a dollar. When passed *DMark*, it outputs the object as a deutsche mark.

Thus, although *operator<<()* is not virtual, because it invokes a virtual function the result is virtual perfection:

```
Deposit was $1.50
Deposit was 3.00 DM
```

This is another reason why I prefer to perform the work of output in a member function and let the non-member operator refer to that function.

But why the shift operators?

I have already explained the desirability of stream I/O (mostly it's type safe and extensible). However, you might ask, "Why use the shift operators? Why not use another operator? Why not use another mechanism?"

It didn't have to be the shift operators. The developers of C++ could have agreed on some standard function name such as *output()* to perform output and simply overloaded that function name for all the intrinsic types. Compound output would have looked something like the following:

```
void displayName(char *pName, int age)
{
    output(cout, "The name passed was ");
    output(cout, pName);
    output(cout, "; his age is ");
    output(cout, age);
    output(cout, "\n");
}
```

The left shift operator was chosen instead for several reasons. First, it's a binary operator. This means we can make the *ostream* object the lefthand argument and the output object the righthand argument. Second, left shift is a very low priority operator. Thus, expressions like the following work as expected:

```
#include <iostream.h>
void fn(int a, int b) {
    cout << "a + b" << a + b << "\n";
//operator+ has higher precedence than operator<<
//so this expression is interpreted as
// cout << "a + b" << (a + b) << "\n";
//and not interpreted as
// (cout << "a + b" << a) + (b << "\n");
}
```

Third, the left shift operator binds from left to right. This is what allows us to string output statements together. For example, the previous function is interpreted as follows:

```
#include <iostream.h>
void fn(int a, int b) {
    ((cout << "a + b") << a + b) << "\n";
}
```

But having said all this, the real reason is probably just that it looks really neat. The double less than, <<, looks like something is moving out of the code, and the double greater than, >>, looks like something is coming in. And, hey, why not?

Conclusion

As mentioned, stream I/O is too complicated to cover in a single chapter of any book, but I hope this chapter has been enough of an introduction to get you started. You can refer to your compiler documentation for a complete listing of the various member functions you can call. In addition, the relevant include files, such as *iostream.h* and *iomanip.h*, contain prototypes with explanatory comments for all the functions.

The next chapter presents a topic that is not part of C++ but important enough to be a required part of any programmer's repertoire: signature fields.

Chapter 26

Object Validation
and Signature Fields

● ●

In This Chapter

▶ Validating your objects

▶ The results of invalid objects

▶ Turning validation off and on

● ●

*O*bject validation is not actually a feature of C++, but I think it should be in every C++ programmer's toolbox. Therefore, I decided to include it in this book.

Programmers, especially beginning programmers, complain a lot about pointers. One problem they have is figuring out whether to use one asterisk or two asterisks and whether that ampersand is really necessary. Even after you get the compiler to accept your input, you're not out of the woods. Making sure your pointers point to the right things is just as important.

Problems with pointers never correct themselves. For example, suppose you have a linked list with a broken link. That is, one of the pointers in the linked list points not to the next member in the list but off into space. As your program comes puffing along through this linked list, it will eventually encounter this diversion. With no way of knowing its mistake, the program will vector off into uncharted memory like a train that has jumped the track. The chances that it will find the way back home are just about as good as the chances of a derailed train hopping back onto the track.

In addition, pointer problems often don't become apparent until the program has progressed some distance from the source of the problem. The broken link in our example may exist for some time before the program encounters it and crashes. This makes finding pointer problems extremely difficult.

Of course, the best approach is to not make any pointer mistakes. Write only perfect programs and you don't have to worry about pointer problems. Barring that, the next best approach is to identify pointer problems as close to the source as possible so that the problem can be identified and corrected.

Invoking Member Functions with Invalid Pointers

Let's consider the consequences of invoking a member function with an invalid object address. Many programmers misunderstand when I say "invoke a member function with an invalid object address." I get responses like, "But that's what strong typing is for! If I call function *fn(MyClass*)* with something other than a pointer to *MyClass*, the compiler is supposed to generate a compiler error!" Not so. Strong typing catches problems like the following:

```
void fn2(MyClass*);
void fn()
{
    SomeOtherClass soc;
    fn2(&soc);        //the argument type is wrong
}
```

Here the object is valid. That is, it's a valid *SomeOtherClass* object, but it's not the type of object *fn2()* is expecting.

The type of problem I'm looking for is shown in the following:

```
void fn2(MyClass*);
void fn()
{
    MyClass *pMC;
    fn2(pMC);             //the argument type is correct
}
```

Here *pMC* is declared to be a pointer to a *MyClass* object, which is what *fn2()* expects. But *pMC* doesn't, in fact, point to a *MyClass* object because it hasn't been initialized yet. Like all uninitialized auto variables, it contains garbage, white noise, nada. This is the type of problem to which I refer here. (This example is obvious, but pointer problems arise in myriad and subtle ways.)

So What Are the Consequences?

Let's consider the following example function:

```
class MyClass
{
```

```
   public:
     static  void staticFn();   //case 1
             void normalFn();   //case 2
    ,virtual void virtualFn();  //case 3
};

void fn(MyClass *pMC)
{
   pMC->staticFn();
   pMC->normalFn();
   pMC->virtualFn();
}
```

If *pMC* doesn't contain a valid address upon entry into the function *fn()*, what is the effect of each of the three function calls?

Case 1 Static functions don't receive the address of the object; only the type of the object is used to determine the class. Therefore, invoking a static member function with an invalid object address has no deleterious effect.

Case 2 Normal functions receive the address of the current object as the hidden first argument, the *this* pointer. When invoked with a bad object address, the *this* pointer is invalid. If the function tries to save anything into the current object, it writes into uncharted memory. Whatever the function tries to read from the object is garbage. Therefore, invoking a normal function with an invalid object address causes erratic results and may result in memory being overwritten.

Case 3 Virtual functions use information hidden in the object to find the function to call. (Those morbidly curious about the details should read the Appendix.) If the object is invalid, the call is immediately fatal.

Table 26-1 summarizes these results.

Table 26-1: Results of Calling a Member Function with a Bad Object

Function type	Result
Static	No problem
Normal	Unpredictable and maybe fatal results
Virtual	Immediately fatal

You can recognize the results of invoking a virtual member function with an invalid address in the debugger. An attempt to single step into the call hangs the computer or terminates the computer immediately, without ever arriving at the function. ■

So What Do We Do About Invalid Pointers?

Careful C++ programmers should outfit their classes with extra bulwarking to detect when the object is invalid, as would be the case when using an invalid pointer. For example, the programmer can define a non-static data member to contain a signature field unique to the class. This field is initialized in the constructors and cleared in the destructor. By checking this field, the programmer can determine at other times whether the object is valid.

The following shows the class *USDollar* outfitted with a signature field:

```cpp
#include <iostream.h>
#include <iomanip.h>
class USDollar
{
  public:
   USDollar(double v = 0.0)
   {
      dollars = v;
      cents = int((v - dollars) * 100.0 + 0.5);
      signature = 0x1234;    //it's a valid object now
   }
  ~USDollar()
   {
      if (isLegal("destructor"))
      {
         signature = 0;      //it's no longer a valid object
      }
   }
   operator double()
   {
      if (isLegal("double"))
      {
         return dollars + cents / 100.0;
      }
      else
      {
         return 0.0;
      }
   }
   void display(ostream& out)
   {
      if (isLegal("display"))
      {
         out << '$' << dollars << '.'
             << setfill('0') << setw(2) << cents
             << setfill(' ');
      }
   }
   int isLegal(char *pFunc);
  protected:
   unsigned int signature;
   unsigned int dollars;
   unsigned int cents;
```

```
};
//isLegal - check the signature field. If it doesn't
//           check out, generate error and return indicator
int USDollar::isLegal(char *pFunc)
{
    if (signature != 0x1234)
    {
        cerr << "\nInvalid USDollar object address passed to "
             << pFunc
             << "\n";
        return 0;
    }
    return 1;
}
ostream& operator<< (ostream& o, USDollar& d)
{
    d.display(o);
    return o;
}

void printSalesTax(USDollar &amount)
{
    cout << "Tax on "
         << amount
         << " = "
         << USDollar(0.0825 * amount)
         << "\n";
}
int main()
{
    cout << "First case\n";
    USDollar usd(1.50);
    printSalesTax(usd);
    cout << "\n";
    cout << "Second case\n";
    USDollar *pUSD;
    printSalesTax(*pUSD);
    return 0;
}
```

The signature field is set in the constructor and cleared in the destructor. Each class presumably gets a unique signature value. Instead of checking the signature field directly, a member function *isLegal()* is used to compare *signature* with the expected *0x1234*. If there is not a match, *isLegal()* outputs a warning message and returns an indication to the caller.

I added a call to *isLegal()* to the beginning of each member function. If the signature does not check out, each function returns without storing anything in the faulty object and thereby doing unknown harm. (The warning message from *isLegal()* alerts the programmer to the problem.)

The little program provided shows how *isLegal()* works. The first dollar amount, *usd*, is declared properly. The addition of *isLegal()* has no visible effect on the output.

The pointer *pUSD*, however, has not been declared properly. The programmer has forgotten to initialize it. Thus *pUSD* doesn't point to anything in particular.

When *printSalesTax()* attempts to use this invalid object, the error messages start to fly, making the problem immediately obvious:

```
First case
Tax on $1.50 = $0.12
Second case
Invalid USDollar object address passed to double
Tax on
Invalid USDollar object address passed to display
 = $0.00
```

When these error messages begin to appear, the programmer knows to set a breakpoint on the output statement in *isLegal()* and rerun the program. As soon as the breakpoint is encountered, the programmer can then backtrack to
determine how things managed to get so screwed up.

What Else Can isLegal () Do?

Although the test function *isLegal()* is not limited to checking the signature field, this is the single most important check it can make. You can add any other checks you like as well.

For a class *Student*, you might want to check that the social security number is 9 digits, that the name is present and legal, that the age is not less than 0 or more than 150, and on and on and on. The more checks you can add, the more likely you are to catch bugs during debug before they slip unnoticed into the field.

You may be worried about the overhead introduced by *isLegal()*, especially because it is called at the beginning of every member function. "I can't afford that," you say. "My programs have to be lean and efficient."

This is a classic case of having your cake and eating it too. After you have completed debugging the program, replace the definition of *isLegal()* with an inline "do nothing" version as follows:

```
class USDollar
{
   //...everything the same as before...
   int isLegal(char *pF)
   {
      return 1;
   }
   //...carry on...
};
```

Calling this function generates no overhead. You will want to keep a copy of the original definition of *isLegal()*, however, so you can reinstall it if an unexpected bug pops up.

 A really shrewd optimizer (which is what you'll want to be using if you're generating the final version anyway) might even notice that the error paths of the calling functions have been rendered unreachable by an *isLegal()* that always returns 1, and remove the "dead code."

Borland C++ 4.0 and Microsoft Visual C++ are really shrewd optimizers. Turbo C++ is not. ■

Conclusion

Object validation is a voluntary technique. To many, it may seem like too much work. But I assure you that object validation saves much more time than it costs. Pointer problems are often difficult and time-consuming to track down. Avoiding such problems or catching them early is worth the few extra checks.

Part VII
The Part of Tens

SYSTEM PURGE

In This Part...

What ...*For Dummies* book would be complete without a "Part of Tens"? In Chapter 27, we cover ten ways to avoid adding bugs to your C++ programs. (Most of these suggestions work for C programs too at no extra charge.) In Chapter 28, we look at almost ten features that are not covered in this book. Finally, Chapter 29 lists the ten most important compiler options (plus a few more) from the ocean of possibilities.

Chapter 27

Ten Ways to Avoid Adding Bugs to Your Program

- -

In This Chapter

▶ Enable all warnings and error messages

▶ Use STRICT compilation

▶ Insist on clean compiles

▶ Adopt a clear and consistent coding style

▶ Limit the visibility

▶ Use a signature field

▶ Comment your code while you write it

▶ Single step every path at least once

▶ Don't overload operators

▶ Avoid multiple inheritance

- -

Enable All Warnings and Error Messages

The syntax of C++ allows for a lot of error checking. When the compiler encounters a construct that it cannot decipher, it has no choice but to generate an error message. Although the compiler attempts to synch back up with the next statement, it does not attempt to generate an executable program.

During all its digging around in your source code, a good C++ compiler also looks for suspicious looking syntactical constructs, such as the following code snippet:

```
#include "student.h"
#include "class.h"
Student* addNewStudent(Class class, char *pName, SSNumber ss)
{
```

continued

```
     if (pS = new Student(pName, ss))
     {
         class.addStudent(pS);
     }
     return pS;
}
```

Here, we see that the program first creates a new *Student* object that it then adds to the *Class* object provided (presumably *addStudent()* is a member function of *Class*). The *if* statement in the function makes sure that the address returned from *new* is not zero. (Remember that *new* returns a zero if there is not enough heap memory to satisfy the request.) However, the good people at Borland, Microsoft, and other places also know that it is common to mistake an assignment (*operator=*) with a comparison (*operator==*). This makes the *if* statement here suspicious — maybe the programmer meant to write *if (pS == new)*.

Fortunately, the default when the compiler is installed is to enable most types of checks for suspicious constructs (although the default for Visual C++ is to not flag this particular error). This error checking can find problems during compilation that you would otherwise have to find on your own with the debugger. Unfortunately, not all such warnings are enabled, but I have noticed a trend for more of these errors to be enabled by default.

Disabling warning and error messages is a bit like unplugging the red lights on your car dashboard because they bother you. Ignoring the problem will not make it go away. If your compiler has a Syntax Check from Hell mode, enable it. Both Microsoft and Borland have an Enable All Messages option — set it. You will save time in the end.

Use STRICT Compilation

In addition to enabling all warnings, some compilers (most notably compilers that support Microsoft Windows programming) also support a mode called strict compilation. For historical reasons, the *defines* in *Windows .H* files have loose type compliance requirements. These rules were later tightened. To keep old code from immediately "breaking," however, the tighter typing regulations are enforced only if the symbol *STRICT* is defined.

Therefore, defining the symbol *STRICT* before including Windows-based include files results in much tighter type checking. In practice, it looks like the following:

```
#define STRICT
#include <windows.h>
//...program continues...
```

Windows programming is way beyond the scope of this book, but you might want to keep the *STRICT* keyword in mind if you start looking into C++ for Windows.

Insist on Clean Compiles

Don't start debugging your code until you remove or at least understand all the warnings generated during compilation. It does no good to enable all the warning messages if you then ignore them. If you don't understand the warning, look it up. What you don't know will hurt you.

If you understand the problem but can't correct it, disable the warning for that function. For example, functions in Windows applications often must declare a large number of arguments that they might not use, as in the following example:

```
int someFunction(int message, unsigned param, long lParam)
{
    //...function really needs only message and param;
    //it doesn't use lParam...
    return 1;
}
```

The compiler will normally flag this as suspicious because *lParam* is declared but never used. Removing the name of the unused variable removes the "argument not used" warning, as the following example demonstrates:

```
int someFunction(int message, unsigned param, long)
{
    //function still uses message and param but there's...
    //...no more warning message
    return 1;
}
```

By removing the name *lParam* from the function declaration, we are informing the compiler that we do not intend to reference that variable.

Adopt a Clear and Consistent Coding Style

Coding in a clear and consistent style not only enhances the readability of the program, but also results in fewer coding mistakes. Remember, the less brain power you have to spend deciphering the C++ syntax, the more you have left over for thinking about the logic of the program at hand. A good coding style should enable you to do the following with ease:

- Differentiate class names, object names, and function names
- Know something about the object based on its name
- Differentiate preprocessor symbols from C++ symbols; that is, #*defined* objects should stand out
- Identify blocks of C++ code at the same level (this is the result of consistent indentation)

In addition, you need to establish a standard module header that provides information about the functions or classes in the module, the author (presumably that's you), the date, the version of the compiler you are using, and a modification history. Here's the header that I prefer; you can adopt your own:

```
//      Class MyClass
//      S. R. Davis
//      Modification History:
//         Date    Initials    Change
//         xxx     SRD         Initial release
//
//      Abstract:
//      The MyClass class is an example class in a modern
//      classless society. Ostensibly, MyClass should be
//      undifferentiable from YourClass, for to do otherwise
//      would be to admit differences between peoples, which
//      ....and so it goes....
//
//      Hardware Dependencies:
//         80286 or above with numeric coprocessor
//
//      Software Dependencies:
//         SteamDriven C++, Version 1.0 running under
//         CRUDE (Cd-Rom User Development Environment)
```

Finally, all programmers involved in a single project should use the same style. Trying to decipher a program with a patchwork of different coding styles is confusing.

Limit the Visibility

Limiting the visibility of class internals to the outside world is a cornerstone of object-oriented programming. The class is responsible for its own internals; the application is responsible for using the class to solve the problem at hand.

Specifically, limited visibility means that data members should not be accessible outside the class, that is, they should be marked as private or protected. In addition, member functions that application software does not need to know about should also be protected.

A related rule is that public member functions should trust application code as little as possible. Any argument passed to a public member function should be treated as though it might cause bugs, until it has been proven safe. A function such as the following is an accident waiting to happen:

```
class Array
{
  public:
```

```
Array(int s)
{
    size = 0;
    pData = new int[size];
    if (pData)
    {
        size = s;
    }
}

~Array()
{
    delete pData;
    size = 0;
    pData = 0;
}

//either return or set the array data

int data(int index)
{
    return pData[index];
}

int data(int index, int newValue)
{
    int oldValue = pData[index];
    pData[index] = newValue;
    return oldValue;
}

protected:
    int size;
    int *pData;
};
```

The function *data(int)* allows the application software to read data out of *Array*.
This function is too trusting; it assumes that the index provided is within the
data range. What if the index is not? On a non-memory-protected system, such
as DOS, a random piece of data will probably be grabbed. On a memory-
protected system, a memory protection fault might be generated. The function
data(int, int) is even worse because it overwrites an unknown location.

What's needed is a check to make sure the index is in range. In the following,
only the *data(int)* function is shown for brevity:

```
int data(unsigned int index)
{
    if (index >= size)
    {
        cout << "Array index out of range (" << index << ")\n";
        return 0;
    }
    return pData[index];
}
```

Now an out-of-range index will be caught by the check. (Making *index* unsigned precludes the necessity of adding a check for negative *index* values.)

Use a Signature Field

In the preceding example, we were able to add a check to the function to make sure that the index was within the legal range for the given *Array* object. But what if the *Array* object itself was invalid? One of the few ways we can determine whether the object itself is valid is to add a type of ID field, which I refer to as a *signature field* in this book.

The addition of a signature field allows the member function one further level of testing. A signature field can be coupled with an *isLegal()* type function to confirm that the object being passed into the public member function is, in fact, in good health. (I would love to cover this topic again, but it was already covered so well in Chapter 26.)

Comment Your Code While You Write It

I think you can avoid errors if you comment your code while you write it rather than wait until everything works and then go back and add comments. I can understand not taking the time to write voluminous headers and function descriptions until later, but there's always time to add short comments while writing the code.

Short comments should be enlightening. If they're not, they aren't worth much and we should be doing something else instead. You need all the enlightening you can get while you're trying to make your program work. When you pick up a piece of code that you wrote a few days ago, comments that are short, descriptive, and to the point can make a dramatic contribution to helping you figure out exactly what it was you were trying to do.

In addition, consistent code indentation and naming conventions also make the code easier to understand. It's all very nice when the code is easy to read after you're finished with it, but it's just as important that the code be easy to read while you're writing it. That's when you need the help.

Single Step Every Path at Least Once

As a programmer, it's important for you to understand what your program is doing. Nothing gives you a better feel for what's going on under the hood than single stepping the program with a good debugger. (The debuggers included in the IDE of interactive compilers will work just fine.)

Beyond that, as you write a program, you'll sometimes need raw material to figure out some bizarre behavior. Nothing gives you that material better than single stepping new functions as they come into service.

Finally, when a function is finished and ready to be added to the program, every logical path needs to be traveled at least once. Bugs are much easier to find when the function is examined by itself rather than after it's been thrown into the pot with the rest of the functions and your attention has gone on to new programming challenges.

Don't Overload Operators

Other than using the two stream I/O operators *operator<<()* and *operator>>()* and the assignment operator *operator=()*, you should probably hold off overloading operators until you feel comfortable with C++. Although a good set of overloaded operators can increase the utility and readability of a new class, overloading operators other than the three just listed is almost never necessary. You can get the same effect by defining and using the proper public member functions instead.

After you've been C-plus-plusing for a few months, feel free to return and start overloading operators to your heart's content.

Avoid Multiple Inheritance

Multiple inheritance, like operator overloading, adds another level of complexity that you don't need to deal with when you're just starting out. Fortunately, most real-world relationships can be described with single inheritance. (Some claim that multiple inheritance is not necessary at all — I'm not one of them.)

Feel free to use multiply inherited classes from commercial libraries, such as the Borland OWL or the Microsoft and Symantec MFC classes. These companies have spent a considerable amount of time setting up their classes, and they know what they're doing.

After you feel comfortable with your level of understanding of C++, experiment with setting up some multiple inheritance hierarchies. In that way, you'll be ready when the unusual situation that requires multiple inheritance to describe it accurately does arise.

Chapter 28

Almost Ten C++ Features
Not Covered in This Book

● ●

In This Chapter

▶ Templates

▶ Exceptions

▶ Run-time type identification (RTTI)

▶ Name spaces

▶ Overloading *new* and *delete*

▶ Class string

▶ Pointer to member operators ->* and .*

▶ Intel 16-bit pointers

● ●

*1*n this chapter, I present some features that were not discussed in detail in
this book. Some features, such as RTTI, have not been adopted into the C++
standard yet, although it's all but certain that they will be. Others, such as exceptions, are supported by only one or two compilers so far. Presenting them is
pointless unless you happen to own one of those compilers. None of these features is required to produce good, well-written, object-oriented C++ programs.

So why mention them now? You should know that these features exist so that
as you feel comfortable with the basics of C++ you can return to the previously
indecipherable documentation that came with your compiler. The knowledge
you will have gleaned from this book plus your experience will allow you to
slice through your compiler's documentation with razor sharp insight.

Templates

Templates allow the programmer to define a pattern for a function or a class.
Another programmer can then come along and instance that template with a

given type or types. For example, you might create a template class called *LinkedList<T>* where the type of the objects being linked, *T*, is not specified until later. The applications programmer can then instance the template class with his or her own class, say *USDollar*, creating a class *LinkedList<USDollar>* that represents a linked list of dollars. Another programmer can instance the same template with a different class, say *Student*, generating a different class *LinkedList<Student>* that represents a linked list of students.

Templates are used mostly by library designers who are writing generic code to be used in many different applications.

Exceptions

Exceptions allow a program to handle in a straightforward fashion problems that arise during execution. To understand exceptions, let me first show you the problem. The following presents several functions in outline:

```
void fn1()
{
    fn2();
}
void fn2()
{
    MyClass mc2;
    fn3()
}
void fn3()
{
    MyClass mc3;
    //...perform computation...
}
```

We can see that *fn1()* performs some computing and then calls *f2()*, which in turn calls *fn3()*. (This calling sequence could be considerably deeper, involving many functions, but let's consider three functions here.) Now suppose that while performing some computation, *fn3()* realizes that things are goofed up. For example, *fn3()* might have divided by zero or found an invalid object signature. In most languages, the proper way to handle this situation is to return an error indication to the calling function. The problem is that the function must also return an error to the function that called it, and so on until the program finally gets back to the point where it can clean up and "start over."

This constant checking of error returns is such a problem that C provides another mechanism, known as the *setjmp* and *longjmp* function pair. The *setjmp* function saves the information required to allow the *longjmp* to return to that point in the program. Thus, using this approach, the program saves its state early. If the program detects a critical error later, it *longjmp*s back to this point, where the program can simply start over.

The *longjmp* approach is fine for C, but with C++ there's a problem: When a function returns, it must destruct any objects it has created so that the assets are returned properly. This process is called *unwinding the stack*. If the program *longjmps* from one function to another function much higher in the calling sequence, it does not allow the functions in the middle to unwind the stack properly. In our previous example, if *f3()* *longjmps* back up to *f1()*, the stacks for *f2()* and *f3()* are not unwound. Any objects created by these functions on the stack are not destructed.

Exceptions allow the program to exit gracefully from many levels deep in function calls and have all the necessary destructors invoked automatically. In our example, *fn3()* would *throw* an exception that *fn1()* would *catch*. (*throw* and *catch* are terms associated with exceptions.) C++ unwinds the stack automatically, destructing any intermediate objects as necessary. Handling exceptions properly is important when writing industrial-grade programs.

Run-Time Type Identification

Run-time type identification, or RTTI, is a little trick that allows the application to determine the run-time type of an object. (The run-time type is different than the declared type. See the discussion on virtual functions in Chapter 20 if you don't know the difference.) You shouldn't learn this feature until you've been coding in C++ for a long time; otherwise you might use it too often. RTTI is necessary only on rare occasions, and overuse of RTTI defeats the extensibility of inheritance.

Name Spaces

Library writers have the problem that there is always the possibility that a function name defined in their library will be the same as a function name chosen by an application programmer, causing a "name collision." Name spaces solve this problem by allowing library writers to define a different "name space" for each library.

These segregated name spaces are kept from the general name space in the same way that the phone company might set up separate phone books for a metropolitan area: one big phone book for the city, with separate smaller phone books for the 'burbs. A Jill Smith in the suburbs is not confused with a Jill Smith in the city because the names have been segregated. If you call information and ask for the number of Jill Smith, with no further specification, you get the one in the city. If you want the number for Jill Smith in the suburbs, you have to specify the name of the town.

Unless you intend to write commercial C++ libraries, you probably don't care much about name spaces.

Overloading new and delete

new and *delete* are considered operators and are overloadable in the same way as other operators. This allows programmers to define their own heap management. However, if it's not a good idea to overload operators, it's definitely not a good idea to overload *new* and *delete*.

Class String

Due to the limitations of C-type ASCIIZ strings, C++ has added a standard *String* class. This class overloads operators to perform common string operations such as assignment and concatenation. *String* objects behave a lot more like strings in Pascal. Class *String* is nice but definitely not necessary. Look up *String* in the compiler documentation if you want to use it.

Pointer to Member Operators ->* and .*

Just as it is possible to define pointers to normal functions, it is possible to define pointers to member functions. However, the normal syntax for invoking functions with a pointer won't work for a member function because in this syntax there is no way to pass the object that the member function expects. Thus, a new operator is required for calling pointers to member functions. Beginning programmers seldom use pointers to functions and use pointers to member functions even less.

Intel 16-Bit Pointers

Near pointers, far pointers, and Intel 16-bit pointer arithmetic are other topics not covered in these pages. First, such pointers are handled in C++ in the same way that they're handled in C. If you know how to work with Intel pointers in C, you already know how to work with them in C++. Second, it will soon go away anyway. UNIX, OS/2, Windows NT, Win32s, and all versions of Windows after 3.1 already use 32-bit pointers. If you are using an operating system that uses 16-bit pointers and you don't want to mess with them, just select the small model (for your small DOS programs) or the large model (for everything else).

Remember the following:

- ✔ You can't declare a single array larger than 64K. This doesn't come up all that often anyway, unless you're a physics type.

- ✔ Don't assign pointers to integers or vice versa. (I've worked on several architectures in which pointers and integers were not the same size.)

Chapter 29

The Ten Most Important Compiler Switches (Plus Two More)

In This Chapter

▶ Outline inline functions

▶ Define preprocessor symbols

▶ Include debug information in *.obj*s

▶ Check for stack overflow

▶ Memory model

▶ Type of floating-point support

▶ Compiler optimizations

▶ Enable exceptions/RTTI

▶ Data alignment

▶ Processor support

▶ Standard stack frame

▶ Precompiled headers

*M*odern compilers offer a bewildering assortment of compiler switches. What is all this stuff? Is it important whether I have deep virtual base classes or will a shallow one do? Should my vtble pointer follow member pointers, as the option says, or go its own way?

For the most part, these options are better left in their original state, as they come from the factory. If you do decide to dingle with any of them, be sure that all the functions you link together have all options set the same way.

You may want to use a few options occasionally. This chapter lists the ten most wanted compiler options. (Okay, there are really twelve, but they're all important.) The most important are at the top of the list and the least important are at the bottom. Options that aren't on the list are probably not worth worrying about.

Outline Inline Functions

Inline functions are difficult to debug because most debuggers treat them as a single expression, no matter how many expressions they contain. Thus, the programmer cannot single step an inline function.

To handle this problem, most compilers define an outline option to automatically outline all inline functions. Set this option during debugging when you need to single step your inline functions. Then reset this flag when your inline functions are working.

This flag can be set and cleared on a module-by-module basis. Programs built with the outline flag set will execute slower because the program does not get the benefits of inline functions.

Define Preprocessor Symbols

All C and C++ compilers allow preprocessor symbols to be defined through compiler options. This can be for including and removing code sections without editing the source file.

For example, suppose I wrote a class with an extensive *isLegal()* member function (as described in Chapter 26) to check objects to make sure they are kosher. Calling this function involves considerable overhead, so I may not want to leave it in the delivered product. However, I'll want to use the function again someday when I modify the program, so I don't want to delete the function either.

An easy solution is the following:

```
class Example
{
  public:
    int isLegal()
    {
#ifdef PRODUCTION
      return 1; //for production version, just return "okay"
#else
      //...continue on with checks as before...
#endif
    }
    //...remainder of class definition
};
```

Here we can see that if the preprocessor symbol *PRODUCTION* is defined, all calls to *isLegal()* return 1 immediately. (In addition, because *isLegal()* is declared inline, there is no overhead.) Thus, *PRODUCTION* is normally left undefined. Right before the final testing, however, adding the preprocessor definition *PRODUCTION* as a compiler option strips all error checking overhead without modifying the source files. Slick.

The same trick works for #*if*s that have been included to handle compiler or operating system differences. Often this is unnecessary, however, because compilers automatically define their own preprocessor directives to indicate such things.

Include Debug Information in .objs

Debuggers, whether standalone or built into the compiler, require information about the program being tested in order to know where to set breakpoints and how to examine variables. When the include debug information flag is set, the compiler includes this symbol information into .*obj* (object) files for the debugger to use.

Setting this flag greatly increases the size of the .*obj* file and the resulting executable file. Normally during the debugging phase, you will want to always include debug information in .*obj* files. If the objects become so large that the compiler has trouble building the program in available memory, you can reduce the overall size of the program by setting this flag only in modules currently being tested. Note, however, that you won't be able to set breakpoints in objects compiled without this switch.

When you have finished debugging, this debug information is unnecessary. Rebuild the entire program with the include debug information flag cleared to reduce the size of the executable file. This switch has no effect on program performance.

Check for Stack Overflow

Each program is allocated a certain amount of stack when it begins execution. Because it is very difficult to determine how much stack a program might need, it is always possible that the program will use more stack than was allocated to it, resulting in a *stack overflow*.

Setting the check for stack overflow flag causes the compiler to include code at the beginning of each function to make sure that a stack overflow does not occur. Although this code does slow down the execution of the program, during the debugging phase it is well worth it because stack overflows can be difficult to recreate and diagnose.

After debugging is complete, you can rebuild the entire program with the check for stack overflow flag cleared. Setting this flag increases the size of the executable file only slightly and decreases the performance.

Memory Model

The term *memory model* refers to the default size of a pointer in the program. The architecture of the Intel processor allows both 16-bit pointers and 32-bit pointers. The memory model refers to whether the default pointer size is 16 or 32 bits.

Setting the memory model for your DOS program to small will make it execute slightly faster (maybe 10 to 20 percent faster). The cost is that your program will not be able to access more than 64K of data and 64K of code. This is enough for most small programs and utilities.

If you need more storage than this, setting the memory model to large gives you 32-bit code and data pointers. This allows you access to 640K of code and data combined. (You might think that 32 bits would get you more, but this is not so due to the way that the Intel pointers work.) Even then, no single array can exceed 64K.

If you can live with the other limitations but you want an array larger than 64K, try the huge memory model. (If you understand memory models, you can also declare the single array to be huge and retain the same memory model.) The huge memory model raises the single array limitation but at considerable cost in execution performance.

Finally, if you're programming for Windows 3.1 or earlier, you'll need to select the large or huge model. If you're programming for Win32s, Windows NT, UNIX, OS/2, or later versions of Windows, you can select 32-bit pointers. This utilizes the true 32-bit pointers of the 80386 and later processors, which means that you can access all available memory. However, your programs will not execute on 80286 or earlier processors.

Type of Floating-Point Support

The type of floating-point support you select can greatly affect the size of your program and the types of machines that can execute it. To understand the options, you must first understand how floating-point numbers (*float*s and *double*s) are handled in a PC.

The Intel processors have no native instructions for performing math on floating-point numbers. However, all such processors since the 8086 include support for a second processor, called a numeric coprocessor (NP), that can be used to perform such operations. Sometimes the NP is a separate chip. On some later chips, such as the 80486DX and Pentium, the NP is a separate part of the existing chip.

The numeric coprocessor acts like a good work dog. It waits quietly for something to do. When the main processor comes up on a floating-point operation, it passes the *float* or *double* along with the operation to the numeric coprocessor and tells it to "sick 'em." The NP comes back lickety-split with an answer and starts waiting again.

If your computer does not have a numeric coprocessor, it must perform all floating-point operations. Because the computer doesn't have any native instructions to do this, the compiler vendors must include libraries of routines to perform such operations. These libraries are much slower than the NP, however. In computational-intensive applications, a computer without a numeric coprocessor can be ten or more times slower than one with the coprocessor.

The floating-point switches allow you to control the type of floating-point support included in your application. The options generally break down as follows:

- *No floating-point support.* If your program does not declare any *float*s or *double*s, select this option. The floating-point libraries will not be included in your executable program.

- *Emulation always.* This option includes the library of routines that emulate the NP. In addition, this option says "don't use the NP even if it's present." Programs built with this option execute at the same (slow) speed on all machines, whether or not they have a numeric coprocessor.

- *Test for NP.* This option includes the emulation library. When the program starts, it first tests for the presence of a numeric coprocessor. If one is present, all subsequent calls to the emulation library use the NP instead. This is the default for most compilers because programs built with this option execute on all machines but utilize the NP, if present.

- *NP instructions inline.* Instead of inserting calls to the floating-point library, this option includes NP instructions directly in the program. This option generates the fastest executable file because it avoids the overhead of making calls to the emulation routines. In addition, the emulation library is not linked into the program, resulting in a smaller program. The only disadvantage is that a program created with this option will not execute on a machine that does not have a numeric coprocessor.

Compiler Optimizations

Modern compilers can do many things to make the resulting compiler execute faster. For example, the compiler can move instructions or unwind loops to improve efficiency.

Some of these optimizations can make a significant improvement in the execution speed of the resulting program. Many, however, can confuse the debugger or make the program appear to do strange things when executed under the debugger. Thus, during debugging it's a good idea to turn off most optimizations.

One optimization that you might want to leave on even during debugging is the avoid redundant reloads optimization, in which the compiler attempts to keep commonly used variables cached in a register like a *register* variable. This optimization does not generally affect debugging but it might affect the way the program executes.

When you have finished debugging, you can enable all options and rebuild the entire program. Compilation with optimizations enabled may take considerably longer than with them disabled.

Enabling optimization for speed improves the performance of the program, perhaps resulting in a larger executable file. Enabling optimization for size reduces the size of the file, perhaps resulting in decreased performance.

Enable Exceptions/RTTI

Exceptions and RTTI (run-time type identification) are two features that were mentioned in Chapter 28 but not presented in detail in this book. Most features in C++ were designed to not add overhead if they are not used. Exceptions and RTTI, however, are unusual in that enabling them adds overhead to the program even if you do not use them. For example, the compiler must put extra code at the beginning and end of each function to save information that would be necessary if the current function calls a function that raised an exception.

If none of the C++ code being developed and none of the libraries being used raise exceptions, this overhead is not necessary. Disabling exceptions reduces the size of the executable file and improves the performance, perhaps by as much as 10 percent, but the resulting program cannot field any exceptions that might arise. The overhead of RTTI is somewhat less than that introduced for exceptions support.

Data Alignment

Data alignment refers to how variables are aligned in memory. Consider the following code snippet:

```
void fn()
{
   char c;
   long l;
   //...and so it goes...
}
```

Let's assume that the character *c* is allocated on an even address, say location 0x100 for simplicity. Now the question is where should the variable *l* be allocated?

It could be given the next free address, 0x101. This is called *byte alignment*. The problem with byte alignment is that it is easier for some processors to read and write a double word long if it is stored on a natural address. (A *natural address* for a two-byte object is an even address, a natural address for a four-byte object is an address evenly divisible by four, and so on.)

Thus, if the compiler were to store *l* at address 0x102 or, even better, 0x104, accesses to *l* would be faster on some processors. Storing *l* at 0x102 is called *word alignment*, and storing *l* at 0x104 is called *double word alignment*. (The 8088 processor does not benefit from either, the 8086 and 80286 benefit from word alignment but not double word alignment, and the 80386 and above benefit from both single and double word alignment.)

Because not all processors benefit from word and double word alignment, many compilers make it optional. Selecting byte alignment removes any wasted space, but results in slightly reduced performance depending on the processor. I suggest that you leave double word alignment enabled and try to arrange your declarations to avoid any wasted space. If you cannot and if your data structures are really big, see if selecting byte alignment helps.

Processor Support

Setting the minimum processor supported flag tells the compiler the minimum CPU requirements for the program. Selecting a later processor, such as the 80386 or 80486, allows the compiler to utilize more sophisticated instructions that earlier processors, such as the 8086 or 80286, may not have.

The optimum setting for this flag is probably 80386. Few 80286-based machines (and even fewer 8086 or 8088 machines) are still in service. Selecting 80486 or

Pentium doesn't add much (if anything) because these processors add few addition-al instructions over the 80386. (They mostly execute the existing instructions faster.)

If you set this switch to 80386, the resulting program will not execute on an 80286- or 8086-based machine. Setting this switch improves the performance of the program, although usually not by very much. Notice that setting this switch does not cause the compiler to generate the full 32-bit addresses supported by the 80386 and its successors. This switch has no perceptible effect on executable program size and can be set on a module-by-module basis (although there's no reason to do so).

Standard Stack Frame

When control first passes to a function, it sets up a stack frame. The *stack frame* (without getting into the gory details) is where local auto variables are kept. The stack frame must be taken down when the program returns from the function.

Setting up and taking down stack frames takes time, and this time is unnecessary if the function has no local auto variables. In this case, clearing the standard stack frame option allows the compiler to not set up a standard stack frame.

Debuggers have a hard time dealing with functions that do not have a standard stack frame set up. During debugging, it is best to force all functions to have a standard stack frame, whether they need it or not. After debugging is completed, you may want to rebuild with the standard stack frame option disabled.

Precompiled Headers

The precompiled headers switch allows the compiler to write the results of compiling the *.H* include files to a separate file. The next time you compile that module, or any other module that includes the same *.H* files, the compiler reads this saved information rather than recompile the same files. Often the standard C++ include files are considerably larger than the application code, so enabling precompiled headers can increase compilation speed considerably.

To get the maximum benefit from precompiled headers, try to include the same *.H* files in the same order in each module. Enabling precompiled headers should have no effect on the executable file produced. When precompiled headers are turned on, they should automatically sense a change to a header file and cause the precompiled headers to rebuild. If you suspect otherwise, you may turn precompiled headers off.

Appendix

How Do Virtual Functions Work, Anyway?

• •

*I*n this appendix, I want to take the time to explain in general terms how polymorphism works. I assume that you have read Parts III, IV, and V, and that you understand classes, inheritance, and all that stuff.

When I present virtual functions to students, many quietly accept that the compiler can tell which function to call based on the run-time type of the object. How the compiler does this is not too important. After all, the compiler does a lot of things, so why worry about this one piece of magic? If you are this type of student, you might want to skip this appendix.

Other students just can't rest until they understand what the machine code is doing when the C++ program calls a virtual function. How does it *know* which function to call? Knowing the mechanism behind this particular piece of magic makes it easier for these students to understand and use polymorphism.

I can't explain exactly how your compiler handles polymorphism (the details differ from compiler to compiler), but it isn't necessary, thank goodness. A general description of the solution used by all compilers is sufficient.

Sex, Lies, and v_tables

When you create a class that has virtual functions, the compiler automatically adds an extra member that it doesn't tell you about. Let's assume that this member is at offset 0 in the class, although it could be almost anywhere. When an object of this class is constructed, the class constructor automatically stores a pointer to this hidden member. This pointer points to a structure known for historical reasons as the v_table (pronounced "vee table"). The v_table contains a list of pointers to all the virtual functions defined in the class.

Suppose we have the following class hierarchy:

```
class Base
{
  public:
    virtual void f1();
    virtual void f2();
            void nonVirtualFn();
    int d1;
};

class SC : public Base
{
  public:
    virtual void f3();
    virtual void f1();
    int d2;
}

Base base;
SC subclass1;          //declare two subclass elements
SC subclass2;
```

Given this, memory looks like that shown in Figure A-1. Here we can see that the object *base* has two members: the data member *d1* that we declared and the hidden v_table pointer. This pointer points to *Base::v_table*, whose elements point to the two virtual functions declared in *Base*, that is, *Base::f1()* and *Base::f2()*. Any nonvirtual functions such as *Base::nonVirtualFn()* do not appear in the v_table.

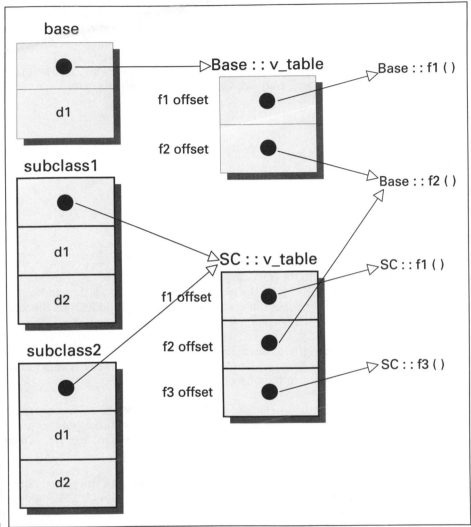

Figure A-1:
A v_table
configuration
of two
classes with
virtual
functions.

Similarly, the subclass *SC* starts out looking like *Base* except that its v_table pointer points to *SC::v_table*. In addition, any data members unique to *SC*, such as *d2*, are tacked onto the end of the class. Two objects of class *SC* have been declared to highlight the fact that while both objects must have their own v_table pointers, all objects of the same class share the same v_table.

Let's examine *SC::v_table* in detail. First notice that the offsets of the virtual functions are identical to those found in *Base::v_table*. Any virtual functions unique to *SC* are tacked onto the end of the v_table.

Also notice where the individual elements point. Because *SC* inherits *Base::f2()*, the pointer at f2 offset points to *Base::f2()*. However, *f1()* is overloaded in *SC*, so the pointer at f1 offset points not at *Base::f1()* but *SC::f1()*.

Armed with this knowledge, let's examine the following code snippet to see how it all works. Specifically, let's tear apart the two calls in *fn()*.

```
void fn(Base &b)
{
    b.f1();
    b.f2();
}

void main()
{
    fn(base);
    fn(subclass1);
}
```

The code generated by the first call — *b.f1()* in *fn()* — generates machine instructions to do the following. For the call *b.f1()*, the program starts with the structure pointed at by the object's v_table pointer. It then indexes into this v_table by the proper offset for the function *f1()* and fetches the function address it finds there. The program then calls that function.

The first time *fn()* is called, the object passed to it is *base*. Thus, when we follow the instructions, we find that *base*'s v_table pointer points to *Base::v_table*, and the function at the offset for *f1()* is *Base::f1()*.

The second time *fn()* is called, the object is *subclass1*. When we replay the same instructions, we find that the *subclass1* v_table pointer points to *SubClass1::v_table,* and the function at offset f1 is *SubClass::f1()*. Calling that address sends us to a different function.

The call *b.f2()* generates the same instructions with the phrase "offset for the function *f2()*" substituted for "offset for the function *f1()*." Replay the call *b.f2()*, once for a *Base* object and again for an *SC* object until you are convinced that the program ends up in the same function *Base::f2()* for both the object *base* and the object *subclass1*.

If this explanation is a bit too wordy for you, perhaps the following comparison with C will suffice: *b.f()* is identical to *(*b.v_table[f_offset])()*.

Conclusion

From this discussion, we can see why calling a virtual function with an invalid object is fatal. If the object's address is invalid, the v_table member offset does not contain the address of a v_table. When the program tries to find a function address there, it ends up performing the computer equivalent of falling off the edge of the world.

This also shows why calling virtual functions involves a small amount of extra time overhead and why the objects themselves have a small amount of memory overhead.

The v_table shown works only for single inheritance. Multiple inheritance v_tables are considerably more complicated and are beyond the scope of this book. The performance overhead is greater as well. (Many compilers allow you to turn off support for multiple inheritance to avoid this extra overhead.) However, I hope that the explanation here has convinced you that polymorphism is not magic and that the overhead is reasonable, despite what you might have heard.

Glossary

abstraction The concept of simplifying a real-world concept into its essential elements. Abstraction allows software classes to represent what would otherwise be hopelessly complicated real-world concepts.

analysis phase The phase of development during which the problem is analyzed to determine its essential elements.

callback function A function invoked by the operating system when a specific event occurs.

class member Another term for static member.

classification The grouping of similar objects. For example, warm-blooded, live-bearing, suckling animals are grouped together into the classification mammals.

code segment The part of a program containing executable instructions.

coding phase The phase during which the results of the design phase are turned into code.

constructor A special member function invoked automatically when an object is created.

copy constructor A constructor whose argument is a reference to an object of the same class. For example, the copy constructor for class *Z* is declared *Z::Z(Z&)*.

data segment The block of memory where C and C++ keep global and static variables. See *code segment* and *stack segment*.

deep copy A copy made by replicating the object plus any assets owned by the object, including objects pointed at by data members of the object being copied.

default constructor The constructor that has a *void* argument list.

design phase The phase of development during which the solution to the problem is formulated. The input to this phase is the result of the analysis phase.

disambiguation The process of deciding which overloaded function a call refers to by comparing the use to the prototypes of the overloaded functions.

early binding The normal, non-polymorphic calling method. All calls in C are bound early.

expression A sequence of subexpressions and operators. A C or C++ expression always has a type and a value.

extensibility The capability to add new features to a class without modifying existing code that uses that class.

friend A function or class that is not a member of the class but is granted access to the private and protected members of the class.

function declaration The description of a function giving its name, the name of the class with which the function is associated (if any), the number and type of any arguments, and the type of any value returned by the function.

function prototype declaration A function declaration that contains no code.

function signature Another name for the full function name (including argument types and return type).

global variable A variable declared outside a function and therefore accessible to all functions.

heap Memory allocated to the program through calls to *malloc( )*. Such memory must be returned to the heap through calls to *free( )*.

inheritance The capability of a class in C++ to assume the properties of an existing class.

inline function A function expanded at the point it is called, much like a macro definition.

instance member Another term for a normal, non-static member.

instance of a class A declared object of the specified type. For example, in the *int i* declaration, *i* is an instance of class *int*.

late binding The process by which polymorphism is accomplished in C++. This process is described in the Appendix.

local variable A variable declared in a function and therefore accessible to only that function.

member function A function defined as part of a class in the same way a data member is defined.

method Another term for member function.

paradigm A way of thinking; an approach to programming. Used in the context of the object-oriented paradigm or the functional programming paradigm. (Pronounced "pair-a-dime," as in 20 cents.)

object-oriented programming Programming that is based on the principles of data hiding, abstraction, inheritance, and polymorphism.

operator overloading Defining a meaning for intrinsic operators when applied to a user-defined class.

outline function A conventional function that is expanded at the point it is declared. Any subsequent references to the function generate a call to the point in memory where the function is expanded. See *inline function*.

overloading Giving two different functions the same name. Such functions must be differentiable by the number or types of their arguments.

pointer variable A variable that contains an address.

polymorphism The capability to decide which overloaded member function to invoke on the basis of the real-time type of the object, not the declared type of the object.

private A class member accessible only to other members of the same class.

protected A class member accessible to other members of the same class and members of any subclass. Protected members are not accessible publicly.

public A class member accessible outside the class.

pure virtual function A virtual member function that has no implementation.

reference variable A variable that serves as an alias to another variable.

shallow copy A binary, bit-for-bit copy.

short-circuit evaluation A technique by which the righthand subexpression of a binary expression is not evaluated if its value would not effect the value of the overall expression. This occurs with two operators, && and ||. For example, in the expression *a && b*, if the lefthand argument evaluates to 0 (false), there is no need to evaluate the righthand argument because the result will still be 0.

signature field A non-static data member that is given a particular value. This value can be checked in the member functions to determine whether *this* points to a valid object. This is a highly effective debugging technique.

stack segment The part of a program in memory that contains the non-static, local variables.

static data member A data member not associated with the individual instances of the class. For each class, there is one instance of each static data member, irrespective of how many objects of that class are created.

static member function A member function that has no *this* pointer.

stream I/O C++ input/output based on overloading *operator<<* and *operator>>*. The prototypes for these functions are in the include file *iostream.h*.

this The pointer to the current object. *this* is an implicit, hidden, first argument to all non-static member functions. *this* is always of type "pointer to the current class."

variable type Specifies the size and internal structure of the variable. The built-in, or intrinsic, variable types are *int*, *char*, *float*, and *double*.

virtual class A class that contains one or more pure virtual functions. Such a class cannot be instanced with an object.

v_table A table that contains the addresses of the virtual functions of a class. Each class that has one or more virtual member functions must have a v_table. (See the Appendix for an explanation of the v_table, if you're morbidly curious.)

Index

• Symbol •

<<, 87, 90
#define, 39, 61, 75, 93, 371
... (ellipses), 14, 73
#include, 61
; (semicolon), 329
/ (slash), 57-58
[ ] (square brackets), 199, 200
~ (tilde), 147

• A •

abstract classes, 267-282
  definition of, 274
  passing, 277-278
abstraction, 107-109, 128
  definition of, 397
  factoring and, 272
access control specifiers, 315-321
adapters, color, 277
addCourse( ), 117-118, 120, 129
addStudent( ), 370
alignment, data, 389
ambiguity, 185, 216, 305, 307
analysis phase, definition of, 151, 397
angle( ), 133
anonymous programming, 213-215
ANSI (American National Standards Institute), 2, 5, 9, 10, 215
ANSI C (Standard C), 40, 73, 69, 246

const and, 63
polymorphism and, 262
as a preferred programming language, 9
virtual member functions and, 278
arguments
  constructive, 177-195
  default, declaring functions with, 83-86
arrays
  allocating, 199-201
  indexing, 27-28
  initialization of, 63
  pointers and, 27-28
  structures and, 33-34, 36
assignGrades( ), 138
assignment style, 190
auto, 11, 12

• B •

bad( ), 346
Base::fn( ), 258
Base::staticFn( ), 263
BASIC, 54
b.fn( ), 258, 262
binding, definition of, 255, 397, 398. See also polymorphism
blocks, definition of, 60
Booch, Grady, 157-158
brackets, square, 199, 200
BUDGET1.C, 39-46
BUDGET2.CPP, 93-98, 283
BUDGET3.CPP, 159-166, 235, 283
BUDGET4.CPP, 229-236
BUDGET5.CPP, 283-289

bug(s). See also debugging; error(s)
  comments and, 374
  declaring variables and, 60
  enabling all error messages and, 368-369
  enabling all warnings and, 368-369
  good coding style and, 371-372
  insisting on clean compiles and, 371
  limiting visibility and, 372-374
  multiple inheritance and, 375
  operator overloading and, 375
  protected members and, 131
  signature fields and, 374
  single stepping paths and, 374-375
  STRICT compilation and, 370
  ten ways to avoid adding, 369-375
byte alignment, 389

• C •

calcDistanceFromSun( ), 62
calcTuition( ), 254, 256
callback function, definition of, 31, 397
CASE, 155
changeArgument( ), 66, 67
char, 11, 10, 200, 324

char*, 25, 90, 179, 215, 217, 344
cin, 89, 344
class (keyword), 117, 317
classes, 4
  abstract, 267-282
  attributing properties to, 155-157
  factoring, 267-282
  finding, 151-176
  naming, 155
  object-oriented design and, 151-152
  objects and, comparison of, 139-141
  relationship between, describing, 154-157
  storage, 11-13
  transforming structures into, 115-118
  type conversion and, 213-218
classification, 107, 109-111, 397
  functional, 110, 111
  object-oriented, 110
  reasons for, 110-111
clear( ), 347
code. *See also* coding
  blocks of, definition of, 60
  legacy, 73
  segments, definition of, 397
coding. *See also* code
  phase, definition of, 151, 397
  style, avoiding bugs and, 371-372
color adapters, 277
comments, 374
  new style, 57-58, 93
  old style, 57-58
compatibility, operator overloading and, 337

compiler switches, 383-390
  checking for stack overflow and, 385-386
  compiler optimizations and, 388
  data alignment and, 389
  defining preprocessor symbols and, 384-385
  exceptions and, 388
  floating-point support and, 386-387
  memory model and, 386
  outlining inline functions and, 384
  precompiled headers and, 390
  processor support and, 389-390
  stack frames and, 390
const, 60-63, 64, 93, 189
constructor, 139-149, 191-192, 200. *See also* copy constructor
  allocating arrays and, 199
  appearance of, when outlined, 179-180
  argumentative, 177-195
  automatic, 205-207
  base class, 249-250
  constructing class members with, 185-190, 194-195
  crashing, 192
  default, 182-185, 187, 205, 249, 397
  definition of, 141, 143, 397
  errors and, 183, 184, 209
  global objects and, 191-194
  in BUDGET4.CPP, 236
  inheritance and, 249
  initialization and, 142, 146, 177, 178
  malloc( ) and, 197-198

multiple, 312
object validation and, 362-363
order of construction and, 190-195
overloading, 181-183, 332
performing type conversion with, 213, 215-218
reasons for, 141-142
static data members and, 221, 223, 224
stream I/O and, 345-346, 347
virtual member functions and, 264
written as outline functions, 143
conversion
  paths, to existing operators, 332, 334-335
  type, 213-218
copy constructor, 203-214, 337-340
  deep copy and, 208-211
  definition of, 397
  nameless objects and, 213-214
  shallow copy and, 208-211
  temporary objects and, 211-212
copyName( ), 339
cout, 344, 353, 354
CPU (central processing unit), 40, 71, 389-390
crashes, the constructor and, 192
CRC (Class-Responsibility-Collaboration) Methods, 155-157

Dahl, O. J., 54
data alignment, 389

data(int), 373
data(int,int), 373
data segments
  definition of, 397
  global variables in, 12
date( ), 79
debugging. *See also* bug(s);
    error(s)
  compiler switches and,
    384, 385, 388
  constructors and, 144,
    187, 192-193
  inline functions and, 78,
    384
  insisting on clean com-
    piles and, 371
  object validation and, 361
  polymorphism and, 256,
    258
  standard stack frames
    and, 390
  static data members and,
    220
declaration, definition of,
    69
deep copy, definition of,
    397
default constructor,
    182-185, 187, 205, 249,
    397
#define, 39, 61, 75, 93, 371
definition, description of,
    69-70
delete, 197-201, 229, 380
deleteName( ), 339
deposit( ), 116, 159, 165
design phase, definition of,
    151-152, 397
destructor, 141, 146-148
  appearance of, when
    outlined, 179-180
  in BUDGET4.CPP, 236
  the copy constructor and,
    208-209, 211

inheritance and, 250
object validation and,
    362-363
operator overloading and,
    340
order of construction
    and, 191, 195
reasons for, 146-147
static data members and,
    224
stream I/O and, 347
virtual member functions
    and, 264-265
Dijkstra, E. W., 54
disambiguation, definition
    of, 125, 397
display( ), 159, 165, 352-353,
    355
DOS, 64, 373, 381, 386
double, 10, 16, 386-387
double word alignment,
    389

• E •

early binding, definition of,
    255, 397
efficiency, 112-113
ellipses, 14, 73
emulation, 387
enum, 282
error(s). *See also* bug(s);
    debugging
  abstract classes and, 274
  coding, avoiding needless,
    40
  compile time, 83
  constructors and, 183,
    184, 209
  defining preprocessor
    symbols and, 385
  exceptions and, 379
  function prototypes and,
    70-71

inheritance and, 274, 313,
    320
link, 274
macros and, 75-76
object validation and,
    360, 364, 365
operator overloading and,
    323, 328, 329, 332, 340
passing by value and, 98
polymorphism and, 262
protected members and,
    130
side effect, definition of,
    46
stream I/O and, 88, 89, 90,
    346, 347, 353, 375
example3( ), 72-73
exceptions, 378-379, 388
Execute, 192
expressions
  definition of, 14, 397
  extended, 329
  introduction to, 14-21
  sub-, definition of, 14
extensibility, 112, 261, 352
  definition of, 397
extern, 11, 82

• F •

f( ), 18, 21, 82, 329
factoring, class, 267-282
  definition of, 272
fclose( ), 345
fgets( ), 344
file extensions
  C, 40
  CPP, 72, 120
  CXX, 72
  EXE, 74, 192
  H, 14, 72, 76, 120, 370, 390
  HXX, 72
  OBJ, 83
findName( ), 226

finishWithObject( ), 264
flexibility, 111, 112, 340
float, 10, 16, 36, 79, 185, 215, 262, 386-387
floating-point support, 386-387
fn ( ), 12, 25, 29, 38, 142, 144, 192, 204-205, 207, 211, 216, 221, 249, 254-255, 258, 262-263, 277-280, 282, 311, 321, 349, 360-361, 394
fn1( ), 37-38, 68, 378-379
fn2( ), 68, 360, 378-379
fn3( ), 378-379
foldOut( ), 306
fopen( ), 344, 345
forest( ), 140
Fortran, 54, 71
fprintf( ), 344, 345
free( ), 30, 197-199
friends, 135-138, 158
    definition of, 135-136, 397
fscanf( ), 89, 344, 345
fstream, 345-348, 352
fstream.h, 345
function(s). *See also* function prototypes; specific functions
    declaring, 13-14, 83-86, 397-398
    default arguments to, 83-86
    naming, 79, 82-83
    operators and, comparison of, 325
    overloading, 79-83, 85-86, 93
    passing pointers to, 28-30
    passing variables to, by reference, 67-68
    structures and, 37-38
    sufficiently different, concept of, 81-82

function prototypes, 69-94, 120
    declaring, 69-70, 72-74
    definition of, 13
    friends and, 136
    Miranda prototypes, 14
    rules for, 14
fx( ), 344, 345

• G •

g( ), 18, 19, 21, 329
global variables
    constructors and, 186
    declaring, 59-60
    definition of, 11, 398
    static data members and, 220
GOTO, 54
grade( ), 129
grade(float), 131
GraduateStudent:: calcTuition( ), 254
gs.calcTuition( ), 254

• H •

HAS_A relationship, 250-251, 268
headers, precompiled, 390
hidden items. *See* private items
Hoare, A., 54
hours( ), 129

• I •

if statements, 280, 370
ifstream, 347
#include, 61
inheritance, 130, 245-251. *See also* polymorphism
    abstract classes and, 267-282

class factoring and, 267-282
constructing base classes and, 249-250
definition of, 5, 245, 247, 398
HAS_A relationships and, 250-251, 268
IS_A relationships and, 247, 248, 254, 268, 279-280
multiple, 305-314, 375, 395
non-public, 317-321
overloading member functions and, 253-255
private, 317-320, 321
protected, 248, 317-320, 321
public, 317-320, 321
reasons for, 246-247
v_tables and, 395
virtual, 307-312
init( ), 93, 142, 159, 165
initChecking( ), 45
initialization, 221, 223
    of arrays, 63
    the constructor and, 142, 146, 177, 178
    of const variables, 62-63
    malloc( ) and, 198
    of reference variables, 67
    of structures, 34
    styles, 190
initialize( ), 136, 276-277
inline functions, 74-79, 384
    definition of, 398
inlining
    member functions, 119, 263
    virtual functions, 263
insert( ), 260
instance(s)
    definition of, 109, 398
    members, definition of, 398

int, 10, 14-16, 24-25, 30, 36, 65, 79, 186, 200, 215, 262, 324-325
int*, 25
iomanip.h, 349, 357
iostream.h, 89, 98, 343, 344
IR sensors, 157
IS_A relationship, 247, 248, 254, 268, 279-280
isLegal( ), 363, 364-365, 374, 384-385
istream, 344, 345-348
istream.h, 357
istrstream, 348-349

• K •

Kernighan, Brian, 9
keywords
  auto, 11, 12
  class, 117, 317
  const, 60-63
  delete, 197-201
  extern, 82
  friend, 135-138
  inline, 74-79
  new, 197-201
  operator, 325-326
  private, 130, 315-320, 321
  protected, 127-138, 315-320, 321
  public, 117, 127, 129-130, 248, 315-320, 321
  register, 13
  struct, 33, 115-117, 317
  union, 46
  virtual, 257-258, 310, 311
  void, 185

• L •

late binding, definition of, 255, 398. See also polymorphism

legacy code, 73
libraries
  emulation, 387
  floating-point support and, 387
  heap memory and, 30, 31
  inheritance and, 375
  name space for, 379-380
  standard, 325, 343, 344
  stream I/O, 344, 345
limits.h, 10
linked lists, 223-224, 378
  in BUDGET4.CPP, 236
  structures and, 36-37
links, broken, object validation and, 359
lists, linked. See linked lists
local variables, 12-13
  declaring, 59-60
  definition of, 12, 398
long, 30
long double, 10
long int, 10
loops
  in BUDGET4.CPP, 236
  inline functions and, 78
  for loops, 20, 58-60, 78, 98

• M •

macros
  #define, 75
  inline functions and, 75-76
  naming, 39
main( ), 46, 66, 67, 140
  accessing member functions and, 123
  in BUDGET3.CPP, 165
  in BUDGET5.CPP, 289
  the constructor and, 144, 146, 178-179, 188, 191, 192-193
  the destructor and, 149

finding classes and, 156-157
inheritance and, 249
nameless objects and, 215
overloading member functions and, 125
protected members and, 133, 135
static data members and, 221
stream I/O and, 344, 353
type conversion and, 216
malloc( ), 30, 38, 197-199, 200
manipulators, 349-341
  definition of, 349
MATH.CPP, 72
MATH.HPP, 72
max( ), 72, 78
maxi( ), 78
member functions. See also constructor; destructor; virtual member functions
  accessing, 121-124
  declaring, 117-119
  definition of, 398
  finding classes and, 158
  implementing operators as, 333
  invoked with invalid pointers, 360-364
  vs. manipulators, 351
  naming, 117-118
  overloading, 123-125, 253-255
  static, 224-227, 263, 361, 399
memory, 45
  absence of register variables from, 12
  alignment of variables in, 389

the constructor and, 146, 208-210
copying objects and, 37
delete and, 197-201, 229, 380
the destructor and, 146
free( ) and, 30, 197-199
heap, definition of, 398
leaks, 328
malloc( ) and, 30, 38, 197-199, 200
model, 386
new and, 197-212, 229, 236, 370, 380
object validation and, 361
operator overloading and, 328, 339
passing variables and, 68
structures and, 37, 38
virtual member functions and, 264
volatile variables and, 63
method, definition of, 117, 398. *See also* member functions
min( ), 72
Miranda prototypes, 14
MOD_A.CPP, 82
mode, values for, 345
multiply( ), 13-14
multiply.h, 13, 14

• N •

nameless objects, 213-218
name spaces, 379-380
naming
  classes, 155
  constants, 61
  declaration and, 69
  functions, 79, 82-83, 117-118
  macros, 39
  name mangling and, 82-84

operators, 325-326
pointers, 39
variables, 39-40
new, 197-212, 229, 236, 370, 380
nextStudent( ), 222
nFn( ), 227
number( ), 224-225
Numeric Coprocessor (NP), 387

• O •

object-based languages, definition of, 255
object-oriented analysis and design (OOA&D), 151-157
object-oriented programming (OOP), 55
  definition of, 398
  inheritance and, 245-246
  introduction to, 107-113
  polymorphism and, 255-257
  protected members and, 127-128
objects
  changing the type of, 213-218
  creating, 139-141
  definition of, 34
Open File window, 192
operator+( ), 327, 328, 329, 331, 332, 334
operator++( ), 327, 328, 329
operator*( ), 331-332
operator<<( ), 343-344, 353-356, 375
operator>>( ), 343-344, 375
operator=( ), 337, 339, 340
operator(s). *See also* operator overloading; specific operators

assignment, 15, 19-20, 34, 333, 337-341
binary, 327
bitwise, 17
Boolean, 18
cast, 333-335
class membership, 333
comma, 19-20
complete list of, 15-16
conversion paths to, 332, 334-335
decrement, 16
defined for structures, 34
format, vs. function format, 325-326
functions and, comparison of, 325
increment, 16
introduction to, 14-21
logical, 18
mathematical, 15, 16-17
as member functions, 329-331, 333
miscellaneous, 20
naming, 325-326
order of precedence for, 15-16, 20-21, 326
pointers and, 25-27, 35-36
shift, 351-352, 356
short-circuit evaluation and, 18, 19, 21
special considerations for, 20-21
subscript, 333
ternary, 19
unary, 327
operator overloading, 323-335, 380
assignment operators and, 333, 337-341
cast operators and, 333-335
copy-protection and, 340-241

default definitions and, 337
definition of, 398, 323
errors and, 323, 328, 329, 332, 340, 375
examples of, 326-329
operators as member functions and, 329-331, 333
reasons for, 324
return values and, 328-329
stream I/O and, 343-357
optimizations, compiler, 388
OS/2, 64
ostream, 344-348, 352, 353, 356
ostrstream, 348-349
otherFn( ), 340
outline functions, 76, 77
    definition of, 398
overloading. *See also* operator overloading
    the constructor, 181-183
    member functions, 123-125
overriding, operator precedence, 20-21

● P ●

paradigms, definition of, 398
parentheses, 20-21, 30, 190
PDL (Preliminary Design Language), 151, 152-153, 157
pFn, 30, 31, 74
pointers, 23-32, 74, 121
    arrays and, 27-28
    to C structures, 35-37
    const applied to, 63
    declaring, 23-25
    incrementing, 26-27

Intel 16-bit, 381
invalid, invoking member functions with, 360
to member operators, 380
memory model and, 386
naming, 39
object validation and, 359-361
operations on, 25-27, 35-36
passing, to functions, 28-30, 31
static data members and, 223, 224
stream I/O and, 344, 345
sufficiently different, concept of, 81-82
virtual member functions and, 264, 392
polymorphism, 255-265, 283, 391-392, 395
    abstract classes and, 277-278
    definition of, 255, 398
    examples of, 257-261
    reasons for, 255-257
precision ( ), 349
Preliminary Design Language (PDL), 151, 152-153, 157
preprocessor symbols, defining, 384-385
printf( ), 73, 98
    name mangling and, 82-83
    stream I/O and, 87-91
printSalesTax( ), 364
private items, 130, 315-320, 321
    definition of, 398
    operator overloading and, 340-341
problem domain, definition of, 151
process( ), 93, 98, 165, 289

processChecking( ), 45, 46, 98
processSavings( ), 46, 98
prot, values for, 346
protected items, 127-138, 315-320, 321
    the constructor and, 142
    definition of, 398
    inheritance and, 248, 249
    limiting visibility and, 372
    operator overloading and, 340-341
    reasons for, 127-135
    static data members and, 227
prototypes. *See* function prototypes
public items, 117, 127, 129-130, 248, 315-321
    bugs and, 372, 375
    definition of, 398
    limiting visibility and, 372
    operator overloading and, 375

● R ●

radius( ), 133
readability, 324, 371-372, 375
records, variant, 46
reference variables
    constructors and, 189
    definition of, 399
register, 11, 12, 13
registration( ), 137
remove( ), 260
reusing, software, 111
Ritchie, Dennis, 9
run-time identification (RTTI), 377, 379, 388
run-time types, 256, 258, 279-282, 391
runtimeType( ), 280

• S •

SC::nFn( ), 227
scanf( ), 87-88, 89, 98
scope, class, 282
semicolons, 329
set( ), 133, 134
setw( ), 350, 351
shallow copy, definition of, 399
short-circuit evaluation, definition of, 399
short int, 10
signature(s), 80, 81
  definition of, 398
  fields, 363-365, 374, 399
slash character, 57-58
software reuse, 111
someFunction( ), 256
someOtherFn( ), 14
space, white, definition of, 58
sprintf( ), 348
square( ), 75, 79, 80
ss.sleep( ), 306
ss.watchTV( ), 306
sscanf( ), 348
stack(s)
  frames, 390
  overflow, 385-386
  segments, definition of, 399
  unwinding, 379
Standard C (ANSI C), 40, 73, 69, 246
  const and, 63
  polymorphism and, 262
  as a preferred program-ming language, 9
  virtual member functions and, 278
static data members, 219-227
  access rules for, 221

definition of, 399
public, 221
reasons for, 219-220
referencing, 221-224, 227
static member functions, 224-227, 263, 361, 399
staticVar, 12
stdin, 89, 344
stdio.h, 98, 344
stdout, 89, 344
stream I/O, 3, 87-91, 93, 343-357
  custom inserters and, 351-354
  definition of, 399
  errors and, 88, 89, 90, 346, 347, 353, 375
  extensibility and, 88
  fstream subclasses and, 345-348
  introduction to, 89-90, 343-345
  manipulators and, 349-351
  shift operators and, 351-352, 356
  smart inserters and, 354-357
  standard stream I/O objects, list of, 344
  strstream subclasses and, 348-349
  the width parameter and, 350
STRICT, 370
strings, class, 380
strongly-typed language, 278
Stroustrup, Bjarne, 53, 57
strstream, 352
struct, 33-38, 54, 115-117, 317
structures
  the C structure, introduc-tion to, 33-38, 115

definition of, 33-34
functions and, 37-38
pointers to, 35-37
transformed into classes, 115-118
Student::addCourse( ), 117-118, 122-124
Student::calcTuition( ), 254
STUDENT.CPP, 120
Student::grade( ), 125
STUDENT.H, 120
STUDENT.HPP, 119
Student::Student( ), 143, 144, 182
SubClass::fn( ), 258
switch( ), 282
switches, compiler, 383-390
  checking for stack overflow and, 385-386
  compiler optimizations and, 388
  data alignment and, 389
  defining preprocessor symbols and, 384-385
  exceptions and, 388
  floating-point support and, 386-387
  memory model and, 386
  outlining inline functions and, 384
  precompiled headers and, 390
  processor support and, 389-390
  stack frames and, 390
switch statements, 280, 282
sx( ), 348
symbols
  ... (ellipses), 14, 73
  preprocessor, defining, 384-385
  ; (semicolon), 329
  / (slash), 57-58

[ ] (square brackets), 199, 200
~ (tilde), 147

● *T* ●

templates, 378
test( ), 258, 262, 320
tilde character, 147
Turbo Debugger, 192
turnOff( ), 260
turnOn( ), 260

● *U* ●

union, 46
UNIX, 9, 31, 72
upperCase, 25

● *V* ●

v_tables, 392-394, 399
validation, object, 359-365
variables. *See also* global variables; local variables
changing the value of, in a calling function, 29
constant, 60-63
declaring, 10-11, 58-61, 190
naming, 39
pointer, definition of, 23-24
reference, 65-68
types, definition of, 10-11, 399
volatile, 63-65
variant records, 46
VGA display, 277
video cards, color adapter, 277

virtual (keyword), 257-258, 310, 311
virtual member functions, 253-265, 391-395
abstract classes and, 274-279, 281-282
in BUDGET5.CPP, 283-289
identifying, 261-263
object validation and, 361
overloading, 253-255, 268, 277
pure, 274-279, 283-289, 355, 398
static member functions and, 263
stream I/O and, 354-355
v_tables and, 275, 392-394, 399
visibility, limited, 372-374
void, 14, 72-73, 145, 185, 340, 353

● *W* ●

white space, definition of, 58
width( ), 350
withdrawal( ), 159, 165, 268, 273-276, 278-279, 289
word alignment, 389
write( ), 276-277

● *X* ●

x.calcTuition( ), 254
xOffset( ), 133

● *Y* ●

yOffset( ), 133

TM

PROGRAMMING
BOOK SERIES

C++ For Dummies
Disk Offer

Tired of typing all that code? The programs presented in this book (including the solutions to the exercises) are available on a separate disk for $5.00 plus $2.50 shipping and handling. (I guess that makes it $7.50 U.S. all together.) To order, send your check payable to *SJ&K Software* to this address:

SJ&K Software
Route 5 Box 107K
Greenville, TX 75402

Texas residents add appropriate sales tax.

Indicate whether you need a 5¼ inch or 3½ inch floppy disk. If you don't give a preference, you'll receive a 3½ inch disk (formatted for 1.44 MB).

Note that the disk does *not* include a compiler (at that price, did you expect it to?) or anything else that was not printed in the book.

This offer is not associated with IDG Books.

 **YES!**
Please keep me informed about IDG's World of Computer Knowledge.
Send me the latest IDG Books catalog.

COMPUTER
BOOK SERIES
FROM IDG